# God, Marx,
# and the Future

# God,
# Marx,
# and the
# Future

*Dialogue with Roger Garaudy*

by
RUSSELL BRADNER NORRIS

FORTRESS PRESS            Philadelphia

Library of Congress Catalog Card Number 73-88357

ISBN-0-8006-0269-2


3981I73    Printed in the United States of America    1-269

To My Mother and Father

# Table of Contents

# *Preface*

No intellectual work is ever accomplished in a vacuum; every such effort represents the accumulation and convergence of a wide variety of factors: advice, inspiration, suggestions, and just plain hard work. This book is no exception. To begin with, the author's own background combines experience in both the sciences and theology, and so it seemed natural to search for some way of integrating, so to speak, theory and praxis. The Christian-Marxist dialogue, which is only in its most primitive stages here in America, offered such an opportunity. Nevertheless, the elements which were to coalesce into this book might have remained inchoate and unpublished were it not for certain timely advice and help from Dr. Roger Mehl and Dr. Gérard Siegwalt of the University of Strasbourg in France. It was Dr. Mehl's emphasis on the importance of transcendence that first led to an awareness of this problem. The selection of Roger Garaudy to represent the Marxist side of the dialogue came about because of a chance remark by Dr. Siegwalt. Finally, a theological predilection for eschatology, encouraged by Dr. Carl Braaten of the Lutheran School of Theology at Chicago, precipitated the present research into transcendence as a function of the future.

Hence it seems not only natural but necessary to express appreciation and gratitude to the many whose help and encouragement contributed to this book: Dr. Roger Mehl, whose advice and criticism formed the broad outlines of the present work; Dr. Gérard Siegwalt, who also provided additional counsel; Dr. Vilmos Vajta, for the cooperation and support of the Institute for Ecumenical Research in Strasbourg; Pastor Gustave Koch, director of the Protestant Seminary in Strasbourg, whose friendship was invaluable during my days at the *Stift*; Dr. Carl Braaten, who provided the inspiration for my research; Dr. Stewart Hermann, who painted such a glowing picture of his student days at Strasbourg that I was encouraged to go and see for myself; Dr. Rodolphe Peter, for his help with reference materials; my parents, who have given so very much that I could never sufficiently express my gratitude; the World Council of Churches, L'Eglise de la Confession d'Augsbourg d'Alsace et de Lorraine, and the Lutheran Church in America – Board of Theological Education, all of whom cooperated in making this book possible; Mlle. Alice Heyler, who with great patience and fidelity struggled through the first manuscript; and Miss Ann Puchalla, who typed the final draft.

> I thank my God in all my remembrance of you, always in every prayer of mine for you all making my prayer with joy, thankful for your partnership in the gospel from the first day until now.
>
> —Phil. 1:3–5

# ABBREVIATIONS

ATD   Roger Garaudy.  *From Anathema to Dialogue.* Translated by Luke O'Neill. New York: Herder & Herder, 1966.

DEM   Roger Garaudy.  *Dieu est mort.* Paris: Presses Universitaires de France, 1962.

GPG   Roger Garaudy.  *Garaudy par Garaudy.* Paris: Editions de la Table Ronde, 1970.

HCHM   Roger Garaudy.  *L'homme chrétien et l'homme marxiste.* Paris: La Palatine, 1964.

HM   Roger Garaudy.  *Humanisme marxiste.* Paris: Editions Sociales, 1967.

KM   Roger Garaudy.  *Karl Marx.* Translated by Nan Aptheker. New York: International Publishers, 1967.

MCES   Roger Garaudy.  *Marxistes et chrétiens: Entretiens de Salzbourg.* Translated by Michel Louis. Paris: Mame, 1968.

MEE   Roger Garaudy.  J. Hyppolite, J. P. Vigier, J. P. Sartre, *Marxisme et existentialisme.* Paris: Plon, 1962.

MR   Roger Garaudy.  *Marxisme et religion.* (Text of the conference organized at the Catholic University of Louvain, 7 April 1965, by the *Ad Lucem* society.) Bruxelles: Cercle d'éducation populaire, cahier 17, 1965.

MTC   Roger Garaudy.  *Marxism in the Twentieth Century.* Translated by René Hague. New York: Charles Scribner's Sons, 1970.

PH   Roger Garaudy.  *Perspectives de l'homme.* Paris: Presses Universitaires de France, 1966.

PMFS   Roger Garaudy.  *Pour un modèle francais de socialisme.* NRF. Paris: Gallimard, 1968.

QMM   Roger Garaudy.   *Qu'est-ce que la morale marxiste?* Paris: Editions Sociales, 1963.

RE    Roger Garaudy.   *Reconquête de l'espoir.* Paris: Editions Bernard Grasset, 1971.

RSR   Roger Garaudy.   *D'un réalisme sans rivages.* Paris: Plon, 1963.


Unless otherwise indicated, all translations throughout this book have been supplied by the author.

# Introduction

If it were possible to characterize historical periods by certain widespread attitudes, this last third of the twentieth century might aptly be termed an era of dialogue. Barriers between men previously thought impregnable are yielding to the persistent forces of change; channels of communication long sealed are reopening with startling results. It is therefore in the spirit of the times that this book appears in dialogical form. It proposes to bring together in creative tension two opposing world views, two standards of value, two philosophical perspectives. The first is represented by the avant-garde Marxist thinker, Roger Garaudy; the second, more properly characterized by a certain trend or movement in contemporary theology, concentrates on eschatology, hope, and the future. Christians and Marxists might, until recently, have seemed rather unlikely candidates for dialogue; throughout most of the hundred or so years since Marx their relationship has been more often than not blocked at the level of polemic and anathema. Recent events in both the sociopolitical sphere and in philosophy and theology have, however, conspired to bring together in conversation these two systems of thought so long separated by suspicion and misunderstanding.

In France, the roots of this dialogue extend back more than thirty years to the policy of *la main tendue* of the French Communist party in the 1930s. Maurice Thorez, former general secretary of the party, wrote in 1937:

> The promise of a redeemer brightens the first page of universal history, the Catholic says; the promise of a universal city, reconciled in labor and in love, sustains the efforts of the proletariat as it strives toward the happiness of all men. . . ."[1]

1

But it would be a mistake to see this "open-hand" policy as an isolated or singular event; rather, it reflects the convergence of a number of factors: social, political, philosophical, and even theological. Among these one ought certainly to include a growing sense of urgency stemming from the immanent possibility of the extinction of the human race through nuclear conflict. Recent decades have, in this regard, witnessed an increasing preoccupation with prediction and control of the future, culminating in the new disciplines variously grouped under the heading "futurology." Roger Garaudy himself singles out three world historical events as having provided the impetus for this new emphasis on the future: the incredible development of science and technology, the emergence of the Third World of newly decolonized nations, and the development of socialism as a viable system.[2]

There is no doubt that the dizzying rate of change in our nuclear age has been a driving force behind man's efforts to plan and control his future. As Walter Capps perceptively notes,

> Men sense that unless the future can be planned, unless human responsibility possesses a creative function with respect to that future, there may be no future at all for mankind. . . . Prediction is not enough. Rather, the future must be mediated. And mediation occurs only when those who are going to live in the future bear the capabilities of controlling and planning it. The future men have is, in some sense, the future men want. And the future men want they can intend to be.[3]

This idea—that men can and must decide what kind of future they wish to live in—is a fundamental assumption underlying the Christian-Marxist dialogue. The followers of Christ and the followers of Marx are coming to realize that there are not only certain advantages to working together toward a common future; there may not *be* a future unless they do!

Theology, like philosophy and science, has also developed a new interest in the future, in eschatology and the possibility of hope; this concern, however, interacts dialectically with the emergence of a new and dramatic phenomenon: what Roger Mehl has referred to as the "crisis of transcendence."[4] Few indeed are the historical eras in which the human psyche is so profoundly shaken that the very perception and apprehension of reality is significantly altered. The twentieth century is such an epoch, not merely in terms of technical progress or social upheaval, but in the fundamental change in man's intellectual orientation. This radical turning in the development of Western man is signaled by a wholly unprecedented occurrence: the loss of the awareness of transcendence, of what has traditionally, in most times and places, been called "God." "We must realize that the death of God is an historical event, that God has died in our cosmos, in our history, in our *Existenz*."[5] The enormity of such an event becomes clearer when we realize that throughout history every race, every people, every tribe and clan has understood itself in relation to *some* transcendent reality—a God or gods or simply some metaphysical absolute—which defended order and reason from the chaotic forces beneath the surface.[6] Men might ignore the gods, but never doubt their ultimate reality; only the village idiot espoused a genuine atheism.

The magnitude of the crisis has been astutely described by Roger Mehl:

> This crisis, certainly the most important ever known, not only to Western man, but to human consciousness, is silhouetted behind all the great philosophical and theological debates.[7]

Mehl locates the origins of the crisis in three great revolutions in human thought over the last century. The first of these is the desacralization of nature.[8] Prior to the advent of modern science, the human mind had engaged itself in a long struggle to pierce the veil of objective phenomena and reach the "true" reality there concealed. The search for this transcendent reality was dealt a heavy blow by the development of the empirical sciences, which effectively robbed the noumenal world of all real content. The second upheaval was purely philosophical, but its consequences were perhaps even more devastating. The Kantian critique eliminated once and for all the possibility of attaining absolute reality either by reason or by intuition. Finally, transcendence has been "debunked" by the increasing preoccupation of men with the immanent historical process, to the exclusion of any absolute or normative values "beyond" or "above" history.

The effect of these three intellectual revolutions has been to render the notion of transcendence untenable for the vast majority of men. This conclusion is reinforced by sociologist Peter Berger in terms of "plausibility structures," a concept developed by Karl Mannheim in the 1920s.[9] Essentially what this means is that the concept of reality actually credible to people depends in large part on the support this concept receives from the larger society. In a so-called primitive society where gods and demons are accepted as normal, the atheist finds himself the object of intense psychological and social pressure to conform his ideas to the group norm. The present situation is just the reverse: in a society where transcendence and the supernatural have become generally ignored, if not actually scorned, those who cling to the minority opinion find themselves under tremendous yet subtle pressure to surrender such "archaic" and "unscientific" beliefs. These pressures are so seductive and so irresistible that few individuals can withstand them for long.

Berger concludes that traditional techniques for dealing with and describing transcendence must be abandoned, and the human condition reexamined to discover new "signals of transcendence"—points at which man comes in contact *in his own existence* with a vision of reality greater than himself.[10] Thence arises the possibility of an anthropologically derived understanding of transcendence which moves by analogy from universal human experiences, such as hope, joy, love, moral outrage, etc., to the inference of their ultimate source and ground. By singling out "hope" as one of the most common "signals" of transcendence, Berger has put his finger on the intersection point of a great number of contemporary philosophical and theological initiatives. At the same time, we are forcibly reminded of the intent of our work, for this renewed interest in the possibilities of talking about transcendence is not confined to theologians, nor even to Christians; it is remarkable that man like Roger Garaudy, an historical materialist, can also affirm the need to search for a new understanding of transcendence.[11]

Yet, that Garaudy should join the voices urging a new approach to the problem is only just; after all, Marxism played a key role in the destruction of the more traditional concepts of transcendence. The social implausibility of transcendence is at least partially grounded in the Marxist desacralization and devalorization of history, i.e., the elimination of any absolute or transcendent values that might have been revealed in and through the movement of history.[12] Marx relativized history by locating the center of all values and norms in man, specifically in man's labor. The subtle infiltration of anthropocentrism into all areas of philosophy, ethics, and even theology since Marx is eloquent testimony to the attractive power of the anthropological presupposition. But at the same time that it undermined the foundations of traditional ideas about transcendence, Marxism—borrowing its eschatological imperative from Christianity—unwittingly planted the seeds for a new approach to the problem. Marx based his analysis of work on the idea of "project," on the possibility for man to project a desired end or goal which then acts as the "law" of his labor.[13] Projection then implies a direct relation to the future in which the goal of the labor will be realized. Thus, in an intriguing paradox, while stripping away every absolute value or reality that might constitute a path to transcendence in the traditional sense, Marx opened the door to a wholly new and unexpectedly promising approach to *transcendence as futurity*.

Of course, it would be naïve to assert that Marxism is the single unique source of the new emphasis on futurity. Rather, Marxism and Christianity both share in a larger and growing interest to be found in all areas of modern thought. To quote Walter Capps,

> Within theology and philosophy a stress on hope and on future is sufficient to reconstitute conceptual patterns. And that is no mean accomplishment. But the very interest in undertaking this reconstitutive task may simply reflect the much larger, general temper.[14]

This "general temper" of the times is to be detected in a variety of parallel developments in philosophy, science, theology, and biblical research. The key insight in these contemporary efforts has focused on the human need to orient oneself toward the future, the need for *hope*. It was Carl Braaten who, in a recent article, recalled the observation of Immanuel Kant that "the whole interest of reason, speculative as well as practical, is centered in the three following questions: (a) what can I know? (b) what ought I to do? (c) what may I hope?"[15] Kant's own problematic suggests that the first question, that of epistemology, requires a critique of *pure* reason. Similarly, the question of "oughtness," the ethical question, is the topic of attention in a critique of *practical* reason. Interestingly, the third question, that of hope, is referred to the critique of *judgment*, or aesthetic sensitivity. Kant's own format suggests that hope is accessible through an examination of aesthetic categories. By the same token, evidently, the possibility of hope is linked to and dependent on an access to the future.[16]

This third Kantian question, the one concerning hope, had been more or less ignored in theology and philosophy until fairly recently. The preoccupation of Neo-orthodoxy with revelation and ethics had the effect of precluding any real confrontation with the question of the future. It was the Marxist philosopher Ernst Bloch, in his *Prinzip Hoffnung*, who marked the first significant philosophical attempt to focus on the phenomenon of hope as a constitutive element in human existence. Bloch had great influence on Moltmann and other members of the so-called school of hope in German theology, so much so that the school is sometimes viewed as a derivative of Bloch's ideas. The close relationship is evident from a random selection of Bloch's own writings:

> Socialism and Christianity have many kinds of concordance, especially in the most important matters. It is good that it is so, both in order to give depth to the avowal of socialism as well as—and perhaps even more important—to give the avowal of Christianity a sign of genuineness, and in such a manner that a new era of Christianity will be indicated, one which will light the way as the light of hope: a new era in which the kingdom of the Son of Man will occur not merely as something "above." If the salvation in the Gospel is to become "flesh"—for us or for the men following—there must not be merely something above, but also something before us.[17]

In spite of such striking passages, it would be peremptory and naïve to describe the present theological emphasis on eschatology and the future as a simple derivative of Bloch's philosophy of hope. Its pedigree is more complicated than such a simplistic reduction would suggest.

Similarly, the theology of hope cannot be identified as an offshoot of the philosophy of Teilhard de Chardin, although both clearly share in the same general philosophical orientation.

> The synthesis of the God of the Above and the God of the Ahead: this is the only God whom we shall in the future be able to adore in spirit and in truth.[18]

Any theology of the future must adapt itself to the recent integration of evolutionary theory as a formative factor in theological reflection; however, that is not to establish a direct relationship between Teilhard and the theologians of hope. As Moltmann pointed out, Teilhard linked eschatology to nature; the theologians of hope have linked eschatology to history.[19]

Finally, the theology of hope is not simply an extension of process philosophy, although once again there is a certain parallelism. Process philosophy develops concepts which tend to see time and change as normative. It provides a mental framework within which all these theological and social developments can be held together. Walter Capps has observed that, in formal terms, all these movements seem to be saying the same thing: (a) that the model of reality must be conceived horizontally rather than vertically; (b) that time and change are regulative, not permanence and staticity; (c) that the future orientation of reality is evaluated on the basis of the realization of possibility.[20] But when all is said and done, it must be firmly reiterated: the theology of hope is not a process philosophy derivative, any more than it is the simple outgrowth of *any* one source of inspiration. It represents, rather, the convergence of a variety of related interests. The distinguishing mark of all of these is "the attempt to make transcendence meaningful not by isolating it . . . but by conditioning it by the reality of time."[21]

Thus, from a certain viewpoint the school of hope suggests a theological orientation which might remain functional even in a time of widespread secularization. One of the characteristics of secular man is his unwillingness to be forced into a frame of reference in which the direction of interests and values is essentially otherworldly. But a theology influenced by the school of hope responds to the needs of secular man without that kind of dependency. Therefore, such a theology survives the process of secularization and represents a way of articulating the Christian kerygma in terms of the prevailing thought-world.

We have briefly touched upon some of the more significant developments leading to the opening of a genuine dialogue between Christians and Marxists: (a) an interest in the future shared by modern men in all fields of endeavor; (b) the recent stress in biblical theology on the elements of eschatology and apocalyptic; (c) a tendency in certain forms of theology and philosophy to restrict metaphysical speculation through the use of linear-progressive models of reality.

Marxism has not been immune to these forces of change in recent years. It has, for instance, shared in a gradual maturation of utopian thinking common to all Hegelian-influenced schools of thought, e.g., the emergence in the Frankfort school of social thought of a certain critical skepticism regarding the inner limitations of all political utopias.[22] Garaudy himself exercises considerable restraint in his projections of the coming socialist future. This realism is coupled with a firm rejection of Stalinist dogmatism. Such concessions on the part of Garaudy mark significant contributions to the dialogue. They also point to certain fundamental convergences between Garaudy's humanist Marxism and the theology of hope.

Basically, this is because many of Garaudy's presuppositions are the same as those of the school of hope. Both, for example, accept the critique of Feuerbach, particularly in judging otherworldliness to be a block to human progress. Both sense that the "heaven syndrome" has tended to keep men poor by reconciling them to their earthly poverty. Both believe that restricting salvation to the hereafter implies the obviation of human hope. Each is sensitive to the plight of the underprivileged peoples of the world, and each believes that those peoples cannot be emancipated as long as they continue to depend on obsolete theologisms. Each rejects the "privatization" of the benefits of religion. Each associates salvation with the overcoming of *corporate* alienation, an alienation which is apparent in societal class conflicts. And each judges traditional patterns of Christian belief to be a contributing factor in alienation. Thus Garaudy can challenge his Christian partners in dialogue to shake off traditional theological formulations and join in the search for newer, more dynamic expressions of faith, expressions which will not hold back the creative spirit of man, but propel it forward.

> The demands made by communists on their Christian companions are in no way incompatible with their beliefs. Marxists expect from them only that their faith, released from class ideologies, permits them:
> —the recognition of the autonomy of human values in science and action,
> —the affirmation of the promethean ambition of a continuous creation of the world and of man by man,
> —the clear decision to accept the word and the reality of socialism as a possibility of the fulfillment of each and every man.[23]

At this point, however, a word of caution is in order. While Marxism and an eschatologically determined Christian faith have many points of congruency, profound differences remain. The critique of religion as alienation, as the "opium of the people," has not yet been dealt with. The question of ethical values and norms, the "ends versus the means," remains unanswered. The problem of freedom in a materialist philosophy, the role of human initiative in history, and the value of the individual person rise up to haunt the dialogue even before it begins. And, most significantly for our purposes, the notion of transcendence as futurity appears as a question mark overshadowing every other point of agreement. Is it possible for the Marxist to speak in a meaningful way of transcendence? Does the word mean the same thing when uttered by a Marxist vis-à-vis a Christian? How does this transcendent absolute relate to my individual existence, what is my reaction to it, and how does it affect my freedom? This book proposes to explore these pressing questions through a critical conversation with one particular Marxist—Roger Garaudy—and *his* interpretation of Marxism. Our perspective will be largely determined by the theology developed by Jürgen Moltmann, Karl Rahner, Wolfhart Pannenberg, Johann Baptist Metz, and Carl Braaten. Others may be called on as the need arises, but only insofar as they contribute to the central theological issue—a common concern of Marxists and Christians for the future of man and his world.

A word of explanation is in order on the choice of Roger Garaudy to represent the Marxist side of this dialogue. Garaudy personifies a rather special kind of Marxism. Roger Shinn asserts that "Garaudy's Communism is neither Stalinist nor Marxist. It is what some Communists derisively call revisionist."[24] Garaudy vindicates his interpretation by frequent appeals to the young Marx, but this hermeneutical preference for the *Philosophical Manuscripts of 1844, The German Ideology,* and *The Holy Family* does not necessarily discredit Garaudy's interpretation; Christians, too, exercise selectivity in reading the Scriptures. The upshot of this discriminating choice of texts is the discovery of the humanist and idealist Marx, the celebrant of freedom, creativity, and historical initiative. This observation is not to be taken as a condemnation of Garaudy's approach. There are undoubtedly a number of images of Marx to be reconstructed from the vast literature available; Garaudy has simply made a selection that offers great possibilities for Christian-Marxist rapprochement. This is undoubtedly the chief reason for choosing him to act as the Marxist partner in our dialogue.

Beyond this fundamental justification, Garaudy is an ideal subject since he has entered wholeheartedly into the debate by publishing a long list of books, papers, and articles dealing with problems related to the Christian-Marxist question. These are listed in the bibliography. Moreover, Garaudy represents in his own person the struggle between these two world views.[25]

Born in 1913 to an atheist, working-class family in Marseille, Garaudy converted to Protestantism at the age of fourteen. At the age of twenty, while remaining a Christian, he associated himself with the Marseille contingent of the French Communist party, at which time he began to study intensively the writings of Marx. The dialectical relationship of Christianity and Marxism in his life continued during his higher education. At the faculty of letters in Aix-en-Provence he followed the last lectures of Maurice Blondel. Later, in 1935–36, he was a student at Strasbourg where he remained in close contact with the theologians of the "Evangelical Circle." At the time, Karl Barth and Kierkegaard were the center of interest and discussion.

After finishing the first stages of his education, Garaudy entered into active party service. It was about this time that he first met Maurice Thorez, then general secretary of the party. The two remained close friends until the death of Thorez. When war broke out, Garaudy was sent to North Africa by the French government because of his record of "subversive" activities. After demobilization, he was arrested and spent nearly three years in prison camps as an "individual dangerous to national defense and public safety." While a prisoner, he conducted courses for deportees aided by but two books: the Bible and Hegel's *Science of Logic*! At the war's end, Garaudy remained for some time in Algeria working for the party, until his anti-colonial activities made it necessary for him to return to France. After the war, he was promoted to an official party post, and served as deputy to the National Assembly from 1959 to 1962. One of the founders of the Center for Marxist Research and Study, he acted as its director from 1960 to 1970. During this time he also organized the widely successful "Weeks of Marxist Thought."

In 1953 Garaudy defended his thesis under Gaston Bachelard at the Sorbonne, and received his Doctor of Letters degree; his dissertation, heavily dogmatic, was entitled "The Materialist Theory of Understanding." In 1962, when the banning of the Communist party forced him to resign his seat in the National Assembly, he devoted himself full time to academics, first as professor of philosophy at the University of Clermont-Ferrand, then at the University of Poitiers, where he continues today as professor of philosophy and aesthetics. This concern for the philosophical ramifications of art and creativity has remained a central focus of his life, leading to close friendships with artists such as Louis Aragon, Pablo Neruda, Diego Rivera, and Paul Eluard. His studies on Picasso, Kafka, St.-John Perse, and Fernand Léger represent significant contributions to the elaboration not only of a Marxist aesthetic, but a Marxist conception of the "whole man."

Throughout his life, Garaudy has retained an active interest in religion and the religious question, and the development of his thinking on the matter can be characterized by certain definite transitions. In 1948 he published a study on the Vatican, condensed in his book *The Church, Communism and Christians*. This early work is a masterpiece of traditional Marxist polemic. Almost entirely negative, it zeroes in on the power and wealth of the Roman Catholic church as evidence of its captivity to bourgeois capitalism and class ideology. But the Twentieth Party Congress in Moscow and the revelation of the "Stalinist perversion" worked a remarkable change in Garaudy. Turning his back on his "dogmatic" period (he refused to allow republication of his doctoral thesis), he began an investigation of the philosophical foundations of political revolution that led to a reappraisal of Christianity as a force for social change. *Marxist Humanism* and *Marxists Respond to Their Catholic Critics*, both published in 1957, show considerable growth over his earlier work.

But the shocks to Garaudy's intellectual development were not over. The second Vatican Council in the early sixties led to the two well-known books now translated into English as *From Anathema to Dialogue* and *Marxism in the Twentieth Century*. Here Christianity is praised as having contributed definite positive values in the human struggle, even to Marxism! This alone might prompt a more detailed examination of Garaudy's work; but it appears that he has not yet ceased rethinking his Marxist philosophy. The latest of Garaudy's books, *Reconquest of Hope*, moves beyond even his most advanced position in *From Anathema to Dialogue*. Love, sin, and even grace are integrated into the Marxist perspective and given a humanist interpretation!

As his thinking has matured, Garaudy has come to view two contributions of Christianity as basic to any Marxist humanism: subjectivity and transcendence. In *From Anathema to Dialogue*, he asserts frankly that Marxism can only hope to go beyond Christianity to the extent that

> . . . it bears within itself the extraordinary Christian heritage, which it must investigate still more. Living Marxism, which has proven its fruitfulness and its effectiveness in history, in political economy, in revolutionary struggle and in the building of socialism, owes it to itself in philosophy to work out a more profound theory of subjectivity, one which is not subjectivist, and a more profound theory of transcendence, one which is not alienated.[26]

This openness on the part of Garaudy to the possibility of a genuine exchange between Christians and Marxists is what makes possible the dialogical nature of this study.

Finally, a few remarks are necessary concerning the scope and limitations of our work. An exhaustive study of the Christian-Marxist question would require several volumes at the least, and each chapter in the present book could be developed at much greater length. Realizing that in trying to say everything one often ends up by saying nothing at all, we have imposed strict limits on our research. First of all, we have narrowed the Marxist side of the dialogue to but one man: Roger Garaudy. This is clearly a highly selective choice, since Garaudy represents a rather special kind of Marxism, one easily amenable to Christian interpretation.

On the other hand, perhaps the selection of theologians from several theological traditions may appear too vague or general. This would indeed be unfortunate, since no other approach seemed to respond adequately to Garaudy's far-ranging apologetic. In the end it appeared necessary to choose either a number of Marxists to respond to a single theologian, or a number of theologians to react to a specific Marxist; we have chosen the latter route.

Finally, we have narrowed the debate by limiting ourselves to the consideration of a single problem; that of transcendence as a function of the power and mystery of the future. Once again, it could justly be pointed out that this is a somewhat artificial choice of topic. Harvey Cox, for example, has suggested that in responding to Garaudy on a philosophical plane, Christians fall into the subtle trap of forgetting that Marxism is essentially defined by *praxis*, by practice, and not by ideas.[27] If this has happened in our study, it was by no means intentional. Indeed, the thrust throughout has been to emphasize that the Christian notion of God as the power of the absolute future is a more profound understanding of transcendence than Garaudy's, an understanding that drives Christians to concrete action in the present. Nevertheless, Cox's criticism is a valid one, and must be kept in mind in any genuine dialogue of Christians and Marxists.

## NOTES

1. ATD, p. 85.
2. Cf. ATD, p. 39.
3. Walter H. Capps, "The Hope Tendency," in *Crosscurrents,* vol. 18, no. 3 (summer 1968), p. 3. Cf. also Capps, ed. *The Future of Hope* (Philadelphia: Fortress Press, 1970).
4. Roger Mehl, "La Crise de la transcendance," in *Revue d'histoire et de philosophie religieuses,* vol. 49, no. 4 (1969).
5. Thomas J. J. Altizer and William Hamilton, *Radical Theology and the Death of God* (New York: Pelican, 1968), p. 26.
6. Mircea Eliade has written numerous studies on the importance of "sacred reality" in the lives of so-called primitive peoples. Cf. e.g., *The Sacred and the Profane,* trans. Willard R. Trask (New York: Harcourt Brace, 1959). See also Peter Berger, *The Social Reality of Religion* (London: Faber and Faber, 1969), for a detailed study of the function of religion in society. E.g., pp. 26–27: "Religion is the human enterprise by which a sacred cosmos is established. . . . The sacred cosmos emerges out of chaos and continues to confront the latter as its terrible contrary. This opposition of cosmos and chaos is frequently expressed in a variety of cosmogonic myths."
7. Mehl, "La Crise," p. 342.
8. Harvey Cox also mentions this development in *The Secular City* (New York: Macmillan, 1965), and even gives partial credit for the process of desacralization to the biblical account of creation. Cf. e.g., p. 23: "The Genesis account of Creation is really a form of 'atheistic propaganda.' It is designed to teach the Hebrews that the magical vision, by which Nature is seen as a semi-divine force, has no basis in fact."
9. Peter Berger, *A Rumor of Angels* (New York: Doubleday & Company, 1969), pp. 43 ff. See also Peter Berger, *Social Reality,* p. 45.
10. Berger, *A Rumor of Angels,* p. 65.
11. Cf. ATD, p. 112.
12. Roger Mehl, in a discussion of the modern notion of history, explains that "this history is not some sort of progressive incarnation of absolute and transcendent values, which would have an existence in themselves. No, values appear within history, generated and carried by it, just as recognized

by those two fraternal enemies, Marxism and existentialism. And if there is an *eschaton,* it can only be a recapitulation of history. Transcendence can no longer be anything but an alibi for those who desert the combat of history and surrender the creation of values." ("La Crise de la transcendance," pp. 346–347.)

13. Cf. *infra,* Chapter Three, the section entitled "Creativity and the Transcendence of Man," especially p. 80. Cf. also p. 67.

14. Capps, "The Hope Tendency," p. 4.

15. Carl Braaten, "Toward a Theology of Hope," in *Theology Today,* vol. 24, no. 2 (1967), p. 208.

16. According to Tillich, Kant's third critique was the only one to offer the possibility of breaking out of the prison of finitude. In attempting to bring together theoretical and practical reason, Kant showed that certain judgments *are* possible, e.g., "the judgment that in art there is an inner aim in every representation of meaning." Paul Tillich, *Perspectives on 19th and 20th Century Protestant Theology,* ed. Carl E. Braaten (New York: Harper & Row, 1967), p. 69.

17. Ernst Bloch, quoted by Capps, "The Hope Tendency," p. 27. Garaudy, it might be noted, seldom mentions Bloch, although he is apparently influenced by many of Bloch's ideas. This may signal more a political reticence than simple ignorance, since Bloch has for some time been identified as a "black sheep" within the Marxist fold.

18. ATD, p. 54.

19. Cf. Capps, "The Hope Tendency," p. 4.

20. Ibid., p. 6.

21. Ibid., p. 7.

22. Cf. Roland Siebert, "Political Theology," in the *Ecumenist* (Paulist Press), vol. 9, no. 5 (July/August 1971). E.g., p. 70: "The political theologians admit, with the social thinkers of the Frankfort School, the necessity of real and concrete utopias for the development of a new society of freedom and peace. . . . While the members of the Frankfort School regard utopian thinking as a bulwark of human dignity . . . some of them . . . have become aware of the dangers present in political utopias." Cf. also Robert Havemann, MCES, pp. 265–272, esp. p. 271: "Utopia and reality will never be in perfect agreement. But when a society claims already to be a proleptic realization of its utopia, it destroys all faith in its future."

23. PMFS, p. 377.

24. Cf. Roger Shinn, "Discussion: Communist-Christian Dialogue," in *Union Seminary Quarterly Review,* vol. 22, no. 3 (March 1967), p. 214.

25. The following brief biographical sketch is drawn from Serge Perottino, *Garaudy* (Paris: Editions Seghers, 1969), pp. 184–188.

26. ATD, p. 96.

27. Cf. Harvey Cox, "Discussion: Communist-Christian Dialogue," in *Union Seminary Quarterly Review,* vol. 22, no. 3 (March 1967), pp. 224 ff.

# ONE

# Alienation and Atheism

## ALIENATION

The philosophical departure point for Roger Garaudy, as for all Marxist thought, is man. But Garaudy clearly states that by the term *man* he does not mean some metaphysical construct, the traditional *humanum*. Rather he begins with man in the context of society; there he discovers that "this situation is one in which man is rent apart."[1] In other words, when we examine modern, social man we are struck by the fact that people are oppressed, enslaved, victims of poverty, war, and economic exploitation, in spite of our present technological ability to put an end to these evils. The young Marx concluded that man is in a state of estrangement from his true nature; he has been warped and mutilated by the very structure of capitalist society. He is, in effect, alienated.[2]

Alienation can be described in a variety of ways, but its effects on man are invariably negative. From a purely social perspective, it is the destruction of any possibility of a universal human culture: "alienation is the splitting of the 'we,' its mutilation."[3] But it is more: alienation deprives man of his specifically human dimension. The true nature of man is centered in the possibility of projecting future goals, in the possibility of choice. Economically, alienation makes choice a class privilege, thus stripping man of his humanity and making him into an object.

The effects of economic alienation are clearly evident in the altered relationship of man to nature. Domesticated nature is the product of human effort. Even before the finished products of, say, bread and steel, wheat and iron ore already represent the crystallized work of generations of human beings. But somehow this "inorganic body of man"[4] has become estranged from its creator. Nature, so full of humanity, has ceased to bear the personal imprint of the artist or artisan, and has become instead simply a medium of exchange. What Marx referred to in *Capital* as "dead work," the accumulated labor of centuries witnessing to the creative power of human beings—this "dead work" now appears as an alien force, turning on man to control or destroy him. Both nature and man are reduced to the rank of objects. In the words of St. Paul, "All of nature groans with pain." (Rom. 8:22) "In this world where everything is bought and sold, right up to the air and light refused to the slums, in this world made by man it appears that nothing remains but things."[5]

Thus man is alienated both from himself and from the works of his hands. A stranger to nature and his own self, he finds the world around him has become a world of objects. The human qualities of choice and freedom are suppressed and twisted by the machinations of an economy ruled by inflexible objective and objectifying relationships. Man, nature, and the creations of man—all are reduced to the status of merchandise on the open market. These are the effects of alienation.

Religion, Garaudy believes, is both cause and product of alienation. Estrangement springs from "the fact that man externalizes what is within him, what constitutes his essence."[6] On the basis of this definition, he describes religion in the fashion of Feuerbach as the projection of the true nature of man onto the image of an imaginary God. The resultant split of man into real and imaginary components is a form of alienation. On the other hand, religion alone is not the primary source of man's predicament. As Marx indicates in the Fourth Thesis on Feuerbach, religious projection is rooted in the fact that man is a stranger to himself: "The real world is torn by internal contradictions."[7] Marx thus locates the basis of religious alienation in the real world of history.[8]

## Hegel, Feuerbach, and Alienation

The philosophy of Hegel constitutes a primary source for the Marxist critique, and for that reason Garaudy has devoted an entire volume to the study of him.[9] Hegel posed a fundamental question, one that our age is still in the process of working out. Born at a break-point in history, he not only described, but lived and experienced the tearing apart of his world. Hegelian philosophy is therefore particularly well suited to an age similarly torn by historical convulsions, when personal and social goals no longer coincide, but conflict. Reaching maturity at the height of the French Revolution, influenced by such minds as Goethe, Fichte, and Schelling, Hegel found a correspondence between political revolution and philosophical development. There was no cause and effect relationship, but rather a common source: "the rending of society and the splitting of man."[10]

The agony experienced by Hegel marked the beginning of an era of world turmoil extending into our own century. Such an historical period is characterized by a rupture in man's conception of reality and, as a result, the "schizophrenic" splitting of the human psyche, a division or separation of interior and exterior existence. In such a divided world, "the individual cannot act with all his individuality as human totality, as total man."[11] In other words, our actions are no longer free, but controlled by external conditions and forces which distort and mutilate us. Neither man nor the work of his hands constitute ends in themselves; instead, they become means to ends imposed by others. Our lives are dominated by irresistible forces that strip us of our very humanity. All our works become alienated from us, whether institution, law, or belief. The only possible solution to this contradiction at the heart of our world, for Hegel, was through "conciliation" by means of art, religion, and philosophy. Each of these offered a way of attaining true freedom; that is, a way of making oneself "at home" in this world, of escaping the clash of external forces.

Hegel's solution to the problem of alienation is unsatisfactory to Garaudy because Hegel did not reveal the true source of this alienation. He did not see that in a capitalist system based on private ownership of the means of production, the worker participates in social labor only through the medium of the market in which are exchanged already alienated products of labor. However, Hegel did put forward the fundamental insight that, in every social system based on private property, the totality of social life, from religion to the state, appears to the individual as an exterior reality or force, alienated from his true existence.

Thus the greatness of Hegel lies in his having uncovered the basic contradictions in reality together with the laws of their development. His limitation, however, "was to have remained within alienation and, consequently, not to have been able to leave speculative ground in order to resolve the contradictions."[12] Hegel continued to be a prisoner of his idealist philosophy, asserts Garaudy, and always believed that the proper perception of reality would reconcile the fundamental rupture in human existence. Nevertheless, the fact that Hegel transposed the real world into a world of abstractions did not prevent him from discovering the dialectical nature of that real world. Garaudy insists that the method of Hegel can be disengaged from his system and, indeed, that this is precisely what Marx accomplished. Hegel himself wrote to a friend in 1814, "I remain convinced that the World Spirit gave our age its watchword: to go forward."[13] The only way to go beyond Hegel is to do precisely that, to go forward in the unflinching search for the internal dialectic of reality while refusing to stop at some intermediate and limited stage of historical development.

Finally, Hegel carried out a profound analysis of the laws of alienation, albeit in a purely speculative fashion. He demonstrated that men, acting within the context of their "species-life," externalize themselves "into institutions and objects which appear to the consciousness of the individual as foreign, transcendent, and alienated realities."[14] His error, however, was in believing the historical manifestation of alienation under the conditions of capitalism to be an eternal and unavoidable result of the objectification of labor. Thus Hegel confused alienation and objectification, a natural consequence of idealism. Garaudy firmly insists that objectification need not be alienated. That it appears so in our experience is the *result* of alienation and not its cause. It was this ancient docetic heresy in philosophical garb that Marx sought to counter with his historical materialism.

The path from Hegel to Marx passed by way of Feuerbach,[15] who effected a general reversal of the Hegelian system, replacing "Spirit" by "material," and "God" by "man." Thus, man is no longer, as with Hegel, an alienation of the Spirit, of God; rather it is God who is an alienation of man. Here we broach upon the two major contributions of Feuerbach: projection and alienation. The master idea of alienation can be expressed in this way: "For man, alienation consisted in regarding what was in truth his own work, the fruit of his creativeness, as a reality exterior and superior to himself."[16] The remarkable similarity between this definition and that given at the beginning of the chapter illustrates the Marxist debt to Feuerbach at this point. According to Garaudy, Hegel's chief problem stemmed from his idealist perspective in which the entire material world was an "alienation" of the Spirit. On the other hand, for Feuerbach it is the transcendence of God that constitutes the alienation, and this by way of projection. In reversing the Hegelian formula, man becomes the subject and God the predicate. The human species projects its ideals beyond itself and generates its own "God." The ensuing alienation is a consequence of man's "duality," the estrangement of man from himself. Hence, while for Hegel it was the Spirit that was alienated, for Feuerbach it is man in the abstract.

Feuerbach's purpose is to liberate man from the alienation of religion and reunite him with his fellowmen. To do this he would replace traditional religion with a materialistic and atheistic humanism.[17] Garaudy asserts that this is but a reversal of the Hegelian *system*, and as such does not change its nature. It changes an idealist system into a materialist system, but remains equally dogmatic. "The metaphysics of Hegel becomes anthropology, and real man is an alienated religious man."[18] This anthropology is, for Feuerbach, the kernel of truth within religion. Its goal is the reconciliation of man with man in love.

Marx, says Garaudy, saw that a simple reversal of the Hegelian system was useless; the only option lay in discarding entirely the system, keeping only the *method*. Marx retained Feuerbach's ideas of projection and alienation, and indeed, they appear frequently in his early writings. But he saw that Feuerbach's critique of religion touched only the theoretical side of alienation; its was necessary to attack the practical side as well. Thus Marx moved from the criticism of heaven to the criticism of earth, from religious alienation to political and economic alienation.

### The Historical and Social Character of Alienation

In summarizing the Hegelian and Feuerbachian concepts of alienation, Garaudy isolates three basic misconceptions which must be clarified before going further. (1) Contrary to the understanding of Feuerbach, alienation cannot be characteristic of abstract, generalized mankind. As Marx clearly showed, alienation is not a metaphysical concept, an eternal quality written into the structure of reality as such, but the direct result of the estrangement of labor in the capitalistic form of economy. (2) Contrary to the idealism of Hegel, alienation is not a religious phenomenon, the result of the objectification of the Spirit. Rather than finding its source in the internal necessities of an idealist system, Marx locates its origin in the context of concrete economic transactions. Thus alienation cannot be an abstract, a priori category. (3) Finally, alienation must not be viewed fatalistically as some sort of inherent evil afflicting human existence. Rather, it is an historical phenomenon which will vanish when the economic conditions from which it arises have been eliminated. Conversely, simply because men find alienation unjust and evil and cry out against it does not bring about its end. Only a change in the socioeconomic system leading to a resolution of its internal conflicts will eliminate alienation.

These three negative comments should be enough to indicate the specifically historical character of alienation. "For Marx and Marxists, alienation is . . . an historical category: the subjective contradictions within man are not separable from his social contradictions."[19] Any attempt to consider man outside his social context necessarily leads to the abstraction of alienation. But alienation, insists Garaudy, is more than an abstract theory; it is first and foremost an estrangement from real life. Thus it necessitates a careful examination of the illusions springing from this fundamental estrangement.

The consequences of the fundamental alienation of man's labor are evident throughout all of his social existence. The interpersonal relationships of men are scarred and warped; men are no longer united by what is specifically human: the possibility of projecting the desired ends of labor. Everything that springs from man—relations, creations, technology—is caught up in the relentless grinding of the capitalist economy and dehumanized. "Man has become an object. The relations between men have become relations between things."[20] The result is a fundamental and pervasive estrangement in the subjective life of man. When people are deprived of the right to free and real creativity in the work they perform, they are alienated from and mutilated by a world which is no longer the product of their labor, but a threatening and destructive external force.

To speak in this way of the objects of our creation turning on us and threatening our very existence brings us close to the distinction of Gabriel Marcel between "having" and "being."[21] Marcel found the source of alienation in man's perpetual attempt to possess the world around him, both objects and people. The danger, according to Marcel, is found in the inherent risk involved in "having." That which is possessed might be stolen, destroyed, or simply used up—there is no certainty or security in "having." Of course, this is even more true when the object of possession is a person, subject to all the vicissitudes of human existence. In "having," reality becomes objectified and estranged.

Garaudy finds Marcel's distinction very useful, and even traces its origin to Marx himself:

> We refer intentionally to this opposition of *being* and *having,* not only because those are the terms currently used by Gabriel Marcel, but because they are the very words of Marx in his Manuscripts of 1844. . . .[22]

Marx, like Marcel, draws a direct line from *having* to alienation. "The less you *are* . . . so much the more you *have,* and so much the more is your life alienated."[23] The worker invests his life in the objects of his labor, and from that moment on his life belongs not to himself, but to the object. The alienated, objectified world of "having" becomes reality; the world of "being" seems no more than an imaginary escape from the "real world." Man is alienated from himself.

There is only one way to escape from this situation of estrangement: "Man cannot *be* except in breaking the iron laws of *having.*"[24] Herein lies the motivation behind the proletarian revolutionary fervor. The only way to achieve a fully human existence is via the route of struggle against, and overthrow of, the economic system which dehumanizes and subhumanizes its victims. In other words, the only solution possible for the Marxist is the collective ownership of the means of production, since only a change in the concrete socioeconomic conditions in which we live can change the alienation we endure.

The social and economic conditions prevailing in capitalist, class-dominated societies lead to a split in the initially unified act of labor. Ideally, the work of men is distinguished from that of other creatures—ants or termites, for example—in that man first posits a project and then proceeds to achieve the end he has set for himself. Thus work which is truly human holds together in a unity the initial project, the means for accomplishing it, and the final result. This state of affairs can be said to exist for the primitive man who makes, say, his own shoes. The original pattern, design, creation, and use all appertain to the same individual, and the labor is not alienated.

The first fracture in this ideal situation occurs with the division of labor. As Marx and Engels point out in *The German Ideology*, such a division is by no means an exclusive product of capitalism. Originally, it was

> nothing but the division of labor in the sexual act, then that division of labor which develops spontaneously or "naturally" by virtue of natural predispositions (e.g., physical strength), needs, accidents, etc.[25]

This becomes a true division of labor only when it is possible to separate physical and mental work, a division moreover that reflects the implicit contradictions within a society. Finally, this division leads to an unequal distribution of labor, its products, and, ultimately, to property. Property develops within the nucleus of the family, and takes its crudest form in the slavery of the wife and children to the husband. Thus it is that Marx and Engels could say that "division of labor and private property are . . . identical expressions."

Garaudy asserts in *Humanisme marxiste* that the piecemeal character of human existence found in modern society grows out of the division of labor, but that this social division characterizes merchandise production in general, and is hence anterior to capitalism *per se*. In effect, division of labor points to the conflict between individual interest and the interest of society at large. In capitalist societies, this contradiction reaches its maximum dimensions, since the apportioning of tasks is not done voluntarily and consciously, but "according to the blind and spontaneous demands of the market,"[26] thus crushing the natural creative activity of man.

Garaudy seems to have undergone an evolution in his thinking since *Humanisme marxiste* (1957). His most recent works scarcely mention division of labor, preferring to focus on private property and the private ownership of the means of production as the chief source of social alienation. This is, of course, justifiable on the basis of the foregoing citation from Marx and Engels; the division of labor can be described in terms of private ownership, the one referring to the activity of production and the other to the product of that activity.

In any case, it is the private ownership of the instruments of production that Garaudy blames for the triple alienations of dispossession, depersonalization, and dehumanization of the worker. The first of these alienations is, in fact, still associated with the division of labor: "With the division of labor, when a product enters by sale into the exchange cycle, it leaves its producer, it becomes a commodity. . . ."[27] But the critique of the division of labor rapidly slips into the critique of private property, since the real problem is that the product of labor no longer belongs to the worker to dispose of as he sees fit. Although the worker is reimbursed an amount theoretically equal to the work performed Marx demonstrated that there is always a disparity between the salary received and the labor appropriated by the owner of the means of production. This Marx referred to as "surplus value."

The simple meaning of all this is that the worker is forced to provide maximum effort for minimum earnings, with the result that "the disparity unceasingly grows between the wealth produced by the worker and his own misery."[28] The work performed is no longer the expression of the needs and goals of the worker, but a task imposed upon him. The organic relationship is broken between the desired end and the means used to attain it. The product of the work done belongs to the owner of the means of production. Thus the humanity of the worker, found in the projection of specific projects and goals, is lost, and man becomes a cog in a machine, a means of producing merchandise and surplus value for the capitalist. This specific form of alienation is simple *dispossession*.

However, it is not only the product of his efforts that is estranged from the laborer; it is the work itself. The owner of the instruments of production imposes the means and methods for accomplishing his purposes. The worker's very movements and speed are directed from outside and depend on where he is placed in the production line. In the early days of the Industrial Revolution, the pace and rhythm were often such as to reduce the worker to a state of drugged stupor. To quote the expression of Marx, the worker becomes "a flesh and blood appendage in a machine of steel."[29] This form of alienation is called *depersonalization*.

The third and ultimate social expression of alienation is directly related to the concept of "species-life." The "generic" or "species-life" is represented by the technological and cultural heritage of mankind as a whole. Over the millenia since man first invented the tool, there has been a gradual accumulation of the fruits of human thought and labor. It is this cumulative body of knowledge and experience that makes possible modern industry, society, and culture. When a man performs any kind of work, his labor is a direct expression of this species-life. However, when the means of production rest in private hands, as under capitalism, all this heritage is at the personal whim and disposal of a few men who control the objectified creativity of thousands of years of human labor and genius. "Capital is the alienated power of mankind getting itself up above men as a foreign and inhuman power."[30] This private control of the creativity of the whole of mankind as species-being represents the ultimate form of alienation. This alienation is no less than *dehumanization.*

The tragedy of alienation is further amplified by the false separation in the worker's mind of creative labor and alienated labor. Truly human work, in which man realizes ends which he himself has determined, is cut off from normal, everyday effort, appearing either as a class privilege or under the guise of art. Because men are totally immersed in an environment of alienation, alienated labor appears as the natural and necessary form. This kind of dehumanization appears "in, with, and under" the capitalist economic system, and will disappear only when the system disappears.

### Communism and the End of Alienation

Garaudy, as we have seen, places great emphasis on the historical and social character of alienation. Since alienation is not an abstract or spiritual phenomenon, its demise will not be the result of some sort of self-illumination, seeing the world "as it really is"; speculation and criticism are not in themselves sufficient to overcome the estrangement of men. "To overcome alienation, it is not enough to *become aware* of alienation; it is first necessary to *transform* the world which engenders it."[31] This is the task of revolution.

Alienation, Garaudy insists, is the direct result of the private ownership of production. Man can return to himself only through the total elimination of this kind of private property. Thus, it is communism which holds out the only promise for the true liberation of mankind. As for our discussion of "having" and "being," Garaudy points to the genius of Marx in having discovered that communism is not simply a generalization of "having," thus remaining within alienation, but rather that it is the realization of the true nature of man, of "being." "With communism, not only all the alienations of labor, but every other form of alienation will come to an end."[32] Since communism is defined as the union of free men, working together toward a common goal while sharing among themselves the means of production, all forms of alienation are thereby robbed of their significance and power. The optical illusion of alienated labor as the only real form of work is then destroyed.

This totally new form of social existence can come into being only through the struggle of the class which suffers most brutally under the present system: the working class or proletariat. In rising up and overthrowing the regime of private property, the workers would put an end to those forms of alienation engendered by it. The liberation of the working class from the alienation of labor would then lead directly to the liberation of society from other forms of alienation.

A word of caution is in order at this point, lest Garaudy be unjustly accused of utopianism. At no point does he deny the continued existence of certain forms of alienation, even under a socialist regime.[33] He recognizes that insistence on total de-alienation would mean adopting an apologetic for the socialist system that would, of necessity, be blind to its weak points, and thus emasculate any efforts at social development. It would, in effect, "rob the building up of socialism of the leaven provided by the critical spirit."[34] Finally, and far from least, it would make it impossible to deal with the question of the continued existence of religion in socialist societies. Such a stance refuses to deal with the objective conditions behind the development of religion, and treats belief as no more than an anachronistic vestige, soon to "wither away."

The question of the continued existence of alienation, even within the theoretically "de-alienated" society, has also been raised by a number of theologians, and has been characterized by Marxist James Klugmann as the "Pannenberg Problem."[35] Pannenberg questioned whether it is reasonable to expect that man, who, "it is recognized, is alienated from his true nature—will at the same time be able to overcome his alienation by himself."[36] Pannenberg suggests that the promise of a non-alienated humanity enters our situation from the outside, and operates there in spite of man's continued estrangement from himself. It is, in other words, the promise of a new future in God.

Actually, the "Pannenberg Problem" is a misnomer. The question is not original to Pannenberg; it was raised by J. B. Metz at the Salzburg Colloquium of Christians and Marxists in 1965. Garaudy was also present at the seminar and later took up Metz's question in *From Anathema to Dialogue*. Essentially, the question was the following:

> Are there really only those alienations which—as Marxism supposes—can be conquered by social progress, and which we Christians canonize by a theology of the beyond and an anthropology of original sin?[37]

Metz went on to ask if there are not also forms of "auto-alienation" that no degree of socioeconomic freedom can eliminate. What of the problem of sin and guilt? What of the problem of evil?

Garaudy tries to respond constructively to these questions, acknowledging that the issues raised by religion are legitimate and, indeed, are the same as those raised by Marxism. The alienation of religion is said to be in the absolute answers it attempts to give to the fundamental demands of life. Marxism "asks the same questions as the Christian does, is influenced by the same exigency, lives under the same tension toward the future."[38] The significant difference is that Marxism does not feel entitled to transform the question of existence into an answer. Therefore Marxism cannot simply dismiss religion as another form of alienation: "alienation is in the answers, but not in the questions."[39]

Garaudy's response is evasive, since it does not really deal with the basic question of Metz and Pannenberg: how can there be any confidence in the promised future of human fulfillment when this future represents a project of alienated men? Garaudy nowhere gives a direct reply to the question, and one can only presume that the answer proffered by Klugmann correctly represents the Marxist position. For Klugmann, man is neither "good" nor "evil." He is both influenced by, and influences, his environment. Man is always and everywhere in a state of flux, ceaselessly changing. In the struggle to change the external environment of nature and society men conquer both the alienation around them *and* the alienation within them. "Marxists see all things in their process of change: not only the cosmos, the earth, nature, society, thought, but also men and women and their characters."[40]

This answer still does not explain by what standard of values men can judge the right direction for this process of change nor, indeed, whether they can alter its direction to any significant degree. Thus, the overcoming of alienation implies the question of transcendence, to which we shall return in Chapter Two.

## ATHEISM

*Atheism as a Consequence of Marxist Humanism*

Unlike Feuerbach, Marxism does not begin from a theoretical atheism; rather, atheism is the logical consequence of a humanism that exalts man to supreme importance and denies the existence of any reality that might stand over against and transcend him. Of course, one cannot deny within Marxism the heritage of the various theoretical atheisms of the last several centuries, any more than one could deny the Marxist debt to Hegel, Fichte, and Feuerbach. This humanist heritage was summed up in Marx's preface to his doctoral dissertation of 1841: "Philosophy adopts as its own Prometheus' profession of faith: 'I hate all the gods!' "[41]

As we saw, Feuerbach's atheism is tied to his speculative theory of man. Religion is, for him, the real expression of man's relationship to his own nature, but it is not recognized as such. Since the predicates normally assigned to God by man are purely human concepts—love, mercy, forgiveness—there is no reason to assume that the object to which they are applied is any less human. Man is thus his own God; or rather, God is nothing more than the projection of man's own unconditionality onto a fictitious supernatural being.[42] Marx rejected Feuerbach's atheism because of his conviction that atheism by itself is insufficient to eliminate the alienation of man; only revolution can accomplish that. He was, however, by no means averse to using Feuerbach's basic concepts of projection and religious alienation.

Similarly, the philosophical atheisms of the last two centuries, while suffering from various shortcomings, are not unrelated to contemporary Marxism. The atheism of the eighteenth century, Garaudy tells us, was essentially political. Since the Church was at that time an arm of the state, sanctioning by dogma and tradition the continuity of despotism, the struggle against religion was, in reality, a struggle against tyranny. Garaudy cites such prominent figures as the Baron d'Holbach and Meslier as representatives of this *political atheism*. Unfortunately, this form of atheism, limited by the intrinsically polemical nature of its purpose, viewed religion as "nothing but an arbitrary invention, without asking either what human needs it met or what human values had been created in this religious form."[43]

Nineteenth-century atheism was constructed on a positivist basis, as a critique of religion's prescientific world view. Garaudy sees a valuable contribution here as well, in atheism's struggle against superstition and irrationalism. But once again, the failure lay in the exclusively negative character of this kind of atheism. Auguste Comte is cited as the most important proponent of *"scientist" atheism,* and also as the one most clearly demonstrating the limitations of the nineteenth century. He not only attacks religion; he refuses any consideration of final ends or meanings, or indeed, any truth beyond "facts" and the relationships between them. This world view is just as destructive of Marxist humanism as it is of religion. Philosophy, theology, and metaphysics are all dismissed with a wave of the hand.

*Marxist atheism,* called twentieth-century atheism by Garaudy, is basically humanist. That is to say, it is grounded not in political or scientific negations of religion, but squarely in the affirmation of human autonomy. Only as a consequence of this affirmation can Marxism be said to be hostile to the idea of a transcendent God. Moreover, since religious alienation is a reflection of the alienation of society, atheism cannot be considered as an end in itself:

> Humanism is no more to be defined by the negation of religion (and so still by relationship to religion) than communism is to be defined as the negation of private ownership (and so still by its relationship to the latter).[44]

This central emphasis on the positive side of humanism, with atheism as a logical consequence, distinguished Marx and Engels from other atheist thinkers. It also distinguishes them from the neo-Hegelians and their anti-theism, as well as the utopian socialists who were diverted from the primary task of changing society into an anti-religious crusade.

Marx, in the *Manuscripts of 1844,* and later Engels in his writings of 1874, both rejected the primitive and altogether negative character of the word *a-theism.* Once one has adopted a completely materialist point of view, opposition to belief is no longer theoretical, but practical. In the battle for a fully human society the Marxist is led by simple logic to spurn any religious formulation which does not give answers worthy of the questions posed by man. The dignity of man is the motivation behind the rejection of religion's irrationality and resignation, and not any theoretical atheism.

The Marxist is first and foremost a materialist, and materialism, we are told, is not a negation. Quite the contrary, it is a full and positive affirmation of man. Atheism is but a corollary. Thus Garaudy could be understood as saying that there is no *necessary* rejection of religion inherent in Marxism. Theoretically, one could imagine a form of religion which would not imply any mutilation of man and would, by the logic of this argument, be perfectly acceptable to Marxism.

It would be a mistake, however, to be lulled into a false sense of rapprochement between Christianity and Marxism on the strength of these encouraging remarks. As open as he appears to be, Garaudy remains a Marxist, and for the Marxist, religion is symptomatic of a social disease. Very little comfort can be drawn from the fact that Garaudy considers religion the expression of real distress, since he does not take seriously the content of the expression. Rather, the symptom will disappear when the disease is cured. Theism is always a questionable ally in the struggle for a truly communist society, even though atheism alone is insufficient to produce such a society.

### Roots of Marxist Atheism

The social and economic roots of man's alienation have been amply discussed. It remains to investigate the meaning for religion of this estrangement at the very heart of the social process. Using Feuerbach's concept of projection, Marx wrote at length (particularly in his earlier work) demonstrating that religion is but one expression of man's real alienation. Man takes refuge in a fantasy world of heaven and hell, sin and forgiveness, because he is profoundly frustrated in this earthly, pragmatic world. Thus, as Garaudy is quick to point out, it is impossible to say that "the elimination of religious beliefs is a *sine qua non* for the building up of socialism."[45] The construction of communism is rather the real *sine qua non* for the elimination of the social roots of religion. Unlike Feuerbach, who believed that simple consciousness of alienation would suffice to overcome it, the Marxist cannot say that a good, scientific education will spell the end of religious alienation. Nevertheless, although religion will survive as long as its social roots continue to exist in the form of the state, the eventual and certain withering away of the state in the "second stage" of communism will usher in an age when all the really significant alienations of man have been liquidated—including religion.

Religious alienation takes a variety of forms, according to Garaudy, and conflicts with human autonomy on several fronts. One significant point of conflict centers on the idea of creation, an issue important to both Christianity and Marxism. For the Marxist, man is essentially a creator. This assertion derives directly from Garaudy's definition of human labor: work which a free, responsible human being initiates and pursues. The relationship between work and creativity is so close that at times Garaudy seems to dull the distinction between labor and art.[46] Alienation is then the very opposite of creation, since it divides creativity at its source: man himself. The creative act is torn from man and appears in its alienated form as a transcendent force or reality. In the chapter in *Capital* on "Fetishism of Merchandise," Marx "compares the alienation of labor to the religious alienation which stems from it and which attributes to God the properly human act: that of creation."[47] The whole of the Marxist critique is dominated by the effort to end the alienations which strip man of his role as creator; religion is one of these alienations.

Human creativity is closely tied to what Garaudy calls "transcendence." It must be clearly understood that when Garaudy employs this term, he is not speaking theologically. There are certain aspects of the concept which can be adapted to a Marxist view of man, but the term must first be stripped of all "alienations" and "mystifications" which attribute to a supernatural or divine being powers which truly belong to man. In essence this is a restatement of Feuerbach's critique of religion: the qualities normally predicated to God are really man's own characteristics, projected on the experience of his own unconditionality. Because of this unconditional element in man, the image projected takes the form of a divine figure or symbol. Certainly, the need to have any projection at all is located by Marx in the experience of social alienation, but this in no way justifies the false separation of man's essentially whole nature into human and divine elements. Garaudy would like to rescue transcendence, defined as man's own capacity to supersede and go beyond himself, while rejecting any transcendence "over against" man which would imply a limiting of man's creative powers. The first form of transcendence is but the recognition of man's true humanity; the second is a heteronomy[48] which denies that man is for man the supreme being. We will return to this problem in Chapter Two.

In all fairness one cannot simply dismiss Garaudy's argument out of hand, for the threat to man's autonomy from an objective, transcendent God is one that has been explored from within the Christian camp as well as outside it. Roger Mehl, in an address to the Protestant Historical Society of Paris, isolated the roots of such disparate groups as the Sartrian existentialists on the one hand and the "God is dead" theologians on the other, in their mutual fear of the oppressive power of a transcendent God over man's autonomy.

> If there is a transcendence which presses all its weight on our existence, if the subject who wishes to engage himself in an adventure of freedom without which he would lose all humanness is subjected to a transcendence which offers no handholds, which constitutes an external limit on his freedom, does he not risk being completely alienated?[49]

On the side of Christianity, this denial of the existence of a being (*Seiendes*) endowed with omnipotence is seen by some as the direct result of the theological argument for the absolute sovereignty of God, typified by Karl-Barth. The claim that God is not a being like other beings, and is thus totally beyond the grasp of human reason, is a response to Feuerbach's materialist concept of God as projection. It is interesting to note that such an argument eventually meets with the proponents of the "atheism of freedom" (Pannenberg) which, following Nietzsche, is found today in such thinkers as Sartre, Ernst Bloch, and, of course, Roger Garaudy. Pannenberg finds the principal difference between the new "theologians of hope" and the proponents of an atheism of freedom in that "one group completely dismisses every statement about God while the other, the theologians, tries to find new possibilities for talking about God."[50]

But there are dangers in placing the nature of God totally and absolutely outside the grasp of reason. Carl Braaten may well have struck upon an important factor in the progress of modern theology when he related the "God is dead" theologies to the work of Karl Barth, even to the point of making the one the consequence of the other.[51] Although Barth answered the critique of Feuerbach by making God (at least in his early writings) *"Totaliter Aliter,"* and thus not subject to rational investigation, the ultimate result of this course was to eliminate all possibility of talking about God except as he manifests and reveals himself in Jesus Christ. Theology is reduced to Christology, and it is then a moot point whether the crisis of transcendence is responsible for this Christocentricity (as Mehl indicates) or whether, indeed, it is the very overemphasis on Christology that has produced the crisis. For if natural theology is all but eliminated, and the only possible way of speaking about God is indirectly, through Christology, the logical conclusion, should this train of thought be carried to the bitter end, is that there is no reason to discuss transcendence at all. Either it is impossible to grasp rationally, or it is irrelevant.

In either case, the forms of radical theology which deny or ignore the problem of transcendence play directly into the hands of Marxist critics who see transcendence as infringing on man's intrinsic humanity. A more constructive approach, as already hinted by Pannenberg, would be to follow the theological developments in the so-called school of hope. Here Karl Rahner, among others, is struggling with the very real problem of finding new ways to speak about transcendence which do not emasculate either man or God. At the Salzburg colloquium between Marxists and Christians in 1965 (in which Garaudy participated) Rahner suggested that God is not an object of understanding which can be cataloged in our minds alongside of other objects. God is rather the One who gives consistency to our plans and projects for the future. If the creativity of man is found in his ability to formulate a project and pursue a future goal, "the knowledge of God is thus implied in the elaboration of the personal project to which man gives himself in regarding the future."[52] Rahner would insist that modern man has become atheistic only with regard to a God who has been reduced to another aspect of the world, even if it be the greatest and final aspect.

Garaudy responds affirmatively to this understanding of God as "Absolute Future" and sees the possibility of Marxist atheism making a positive contribution to Christianity at this point. If human history is composed of free decisions made possible through the pressure of a transcendent and Absolute Future, and if this active and demanding presence is found in everyone, then atheism constitutes a critique of all efforts to replace the absolute quality of this future by a historically conditioned and limited future. Atheism in this sense could even have the effect of returning to God his transcendence. The concept of transcendence as Absolute Future carries the possibility of putting an end to a religion which "offers ersatz totalities and ersatz infinities, which sterilizes and humiliates thought and action."[53]

There is yet another stumbling block to a true rapprochement of Christianity and Marxism, one that appears insuperable since it is part of the fundamental Marxist methodology: the concept of praxis.[54] Praxis enables Marxism to hold both sides of human reality—nature and consciousness—simultaneously present. All other interpretations of man or nature, endeavoring to explain either consciousness or nature independently of one another, are a priori false. Garaudy repeatedly emphasizes this essentially dialectical nature of Marxist epistemology. Knowledge is both reflection and projection, passivity and activity.[55] The errors in previous dogmatic distortions of Marxism were in neglecting the active side of knowledge. The real basis of knowledge is not in a simple reproduction or representation of nature; rather, it is the result of a long process of constructing successive projects, models, hypotheses, and using them to challenge our understanding of reality.

As a consequence of this practical approach to the theory of knowledge, both idealism and metaphysical materialism are rejected as "ideological." In the former, consciousness is seen as the only active element; in the latter, nature is considered independently of consciousness. The only way to avoid such pitfalls is to make practice the sole criterion for all truth and value. In the words of Garaudy, Marxism is not a *philosophy of being*, in which consciousness is but an impoverished image of the reality which produces it. The identification of truth and being leads to a suppression of authentic historicity. Quite the contrary, Marxism is seen as a *philosophy of act*.

> . . . that is, one which makes of the consciousness and the human practice which engenders it and constantly enriches it a true reality, rooted in earlier activity and in the real, and reflecting them, but constantly going beyond the given and continually adding to reality by a creative act, which is not yet given at the level of pre-human nature and the success of which nothing can guarantee in advance.[56]

Thus, the only true philosophy is one of action, since the truth of man is found in what he does, not what he knows or thinks he knows independently of his active relationship to nature.

This is why Marx dismisses pure atheism as ideology; it is not based on praxis and, hence, is only speculation. Such a theoretical atheism ignores the practical origin of knowledge, assuming that ideas are independent of the social conditions out of which they arise. But in reality, man's activity is primary, and his creativity and freedom are essentially related to *doing*, not to *being*. Atheism as a denial of supernatural reality refers only to the freedom of man's *being*; such freedom is really a direct implication of his freedom of acting. Except for this ontological implication of the autonomous praxis, Marx need not even have bothered to term himself an atheist. Atheism is but a corollary to praxis, since any epistemology not rooted and grounded in man's relations to nature and society is nonsense. In this manner Marx disposes of all speculative systems, atheism and naïve materialism as well as religion.

Hence, we see the three primary sources of Marxist atheism in its assertion of human creativity, its fear of a transcendent heteronomy, and its concept of praxis. The first two of these are by no means final and insuperable barriers to a true dialogue between Marxists and Christians, since recent theological developments have tended toward a definition of transcendence as futurity which is neither alienating nor heteronomous, but which preserves the full thrust and significance of man's creative spirit. The third problem is more serious, since it denies the possibility of any transcendent reality whatsoever. As long as the ultimate explanation of all meaning and value rests within the historical process, it is difficult to see how Garaudy can salvage a true humanism from Marxism, or on what grounds a rapprochement is possible between Christians and Marxists.[57]

### The Legitimacy of Religion

In spite of its systematic and methodological bias against religion, Marxist atheism nevertheless remains distinct from other forms of atheism. Marx certainly considered the split between heaven and earth a reflection of the division within society of exploiter and exploited. But neither Marx nor Engels stated that religious faith was in itself the reason for submission to exploitation. In fact, as Garaudy hastens to point out, "what characterizes specifically Marxist atheism is that . . . it does not regard religion simply as a lie fabricated by despots or as a pure and simple illusion born of ignorance."[58] There are actually three factors involved in the religious drive: religious conceptions are an *expression* or a reflection of real afflictions, they are a form of *protest*

against these afflictions, and as mere conceptualizations, they are the
*opium* of the people.

As reflection, religion is an ideological explanation and justification
of man's alienated condition. Hence, it is guilty of indefinitely post-
poning into the distant future man's rightful claim to freedom and
justice. In this sense, says Garaudy, the concept of original sin has
been used by theologians from Augustine to Luther as a means of
justifying the continued existence of institutions such as slavery and
feudal servitude. But at the same time that it expresses the alienation
of man, religion also forms a mystified protest against it, and implies
the possibility of overcoming the present condition of mankind. To
protest against something means that matters could change; the existing
social order is not the will of God, but a false and evil condition to be
resisted, even if only in the imagination. "The essential moment here
is when man refuses to accept life as a given, when he disengages himself from reality, searches possibilities and creates them."[59] Thus it is
false to consider religion *only* as a form of alienation. Inasmuch as it
protests human misery, religion rightly questions the structures of
society; it is alienated in its answers, but not in its questions.

The problem of religion, for Garaudy, is not in the legitimate
protest against the injustices of society, but in the way the protest is
formulated and the answer given. The grandeur of religion is found
in its drive to respond to the question of human existence. The fault
is in a dogmatic reply which offers a definite solution on the basis of
a certain, limited understanding of reality. Insofar as religion is a
*mystified* protest against the exploration of man by man, it remains in-
effective and misleading, for it does not move toward the only possible
resolution of the human predicament acknowledged by the Marxist
revolution. Religion is still the existence of a "lack" in man, which
will be displaced when the social justifications for its continued existence are eliminated.

It is at this point that the third characteristic of religion enters:
"religion is the opium of the people." The protest made by religion is
misdirected and futile. It is a protest only in the sense that the Chinese
coolie protests when he reaches for his opium pipe. The very manner
in which religion raises the question of man's suffering and alienation
implies a wrong answer at the start. Thus, even though positive elements do exist in religion, they are insufficient to counterbalance the

inherently misguided and escapist elements. Religion must, in the end, disappear, for it cannot give the right answer to man's dilemma—that is, the Marxist answer—as long as its protest remains "religious." It will continue to act as a brake on human advancement and freedom as long as it exists. It is only reasonable, therefore, that the first step in the liberation of man is to abandon a form of posing the question which can only inhibit a solution.

There are numerous problems in Marx's approach to religion, in particular the basis upon which he constructed his critique. As Gollwitzer has pointed out,[60] research in the field of comparative religion at the time of Marx tended to view Christianity as simply one example among others of the religious phenomenon. Religion was defended by demonstrating that it is a universal human possibility and, indeed, a human need to worship the Creator. Christianity was then cited as the supreme manifestation of the religious instinct in man. Marx took over this point of view uncritically, and in so doing he made a specific, if unconscious, theological decision. Thus, it becomes a matter of importance to consider the *kind* of theology adopted by Marx.

Actually, the idea of religion "in general" is a product of modern times; such a conception would have been impossible in the first century or during the Middle Ages. This is why Marx could so confidently assert in 1844 that "the criticism of religion is in the main complete."[61] Virtually all of his ideas on the subject had been taken over uncritically from the rationalist school of religion. The credibility of such views today can be judged by the relative weight given to the religious theories of Bruno Bauer and D. F. Strauss in contemporary theology. Garaudy is aware of the historically limited nature of Marx's critique, and attempts to divest himself of it accordingly. Interestingly enough, he does so by an appeal to Marxist principles: "It would be contrary to the fundamental principles of Marxism to approach this problem of "Christians" in general, or of "religion" in general."[62] Such generalizations would have the effect of reducing religion to a kind of immutable Platonic Idea, and Christians to a single homogeneous group unrelated to social class, national background, or historical period. This is entirely incompatible with the Marxist assertion that existence determines consciousness and not vice versa. Religious ideas and communities, like other superstructures, are products of specific historical conditions, subject to change when those conditions change.

In saying this, of course, Garaudy conflicts directly with Marx, who founded his critique on just such gross and naïve generalizations.

*Theism and Atheism*

While disqualifying Christianity from making any ultimate contribution to the Marxist struggle, Garaudy is quick to suggest that Marxist atheism might well offer a valuable corrective to Christianity: "The protest of atheism has thus a purifying value."[63] This is a most interesting reversal of the problem, particularly since there are a number of theologians whose opinion is not radically different from that of Garaudy. In fact, Garaudy himself cites the work of such scholars as Leslie Dewart, Teilhard de Chardin, Dietrich Bonhoeffer, Rudolph Bultmann, and Paul Ricoeur. Faced with such a battery of theological erudition, we are compelled to consider Garaudy's suggestion seriously and in some detail.

Perhaps the most instructive name for our purposes is that of Paul Ricoeur.[64] On the subject of atheism versus theism, Garaudy reduces Ricoeur to two essential statements. If we define the "horizon" as "the metaphor for what approaches without ever becoming a possessed object,"[65] we can then say that "an idol is the reification of the horizon into a thing";[66] when the "Wholly Other," the transcendent absolute who forms the horizons of our past and future, is objectified and thus disposed of, "this diabolic transformation makes religion the reification and alienation of faith."[67] Garaudy takes firm hold of the idea that religion represents a form of idolatry, the acculturation of "pure faith." But he neglects to carry the thought of Ricoeur through to its completion, for no serious attempt is made to deal with the object of faith: faith in whom?

The horizon for Ricoeur is the "alpha" and the "omega" of all purely immanent reflection, but to what does this horizon refer? It is the Wholly Other who is objectified and ossified into concepts such as Supreme Being, First Substance, or Absolute Thought. In this sense the idol is the reification of the horizon function, "the fall of the sign into a supernatural and supracultural object."[68] Hence the never ending task of separating faith from religion: faith in the Other who comes to us must be cleansed from belief in the religious object which forms simply another part of our cultural milieu. But—and here is where Garaudy has left a deliberate lacuna—the Wholly Other represented by the horizon-function is both real and personal. It is he who addresses us in the kerygma, in the Gospel. This Absolute is totally beyond my knowing; "but, by its very manner of approaching, of coming, it shows itself to be Wholly Other than the *arché* and the *telos* which I can conceptualize in reflective thought."[69] The place of battle between this Other and his cultural objectifications is the realm of the sacred.

> The sacred can be the meaningful bearer of what we describe as the structure of horizon peculiar to the Wholly Other which draws near, or it can be the idolatrous reality to which we assign a separate place in our culture, thus giving rise to religious alienation.[70]

Thus for Ricoeur, religious alienation is indeed a form of projection; it is the construction of human cultural forms for that One who must forever remain beyond description. To the extent that atheism is an attack on these "religious objects," it is legitimate, and indeed biblically grounded.[71] But at this point Ricoeur goes far beyond the critique of Feuerbach, Marx, and Garaudy; for Ricoeur, the death of the idol is necessary in order that the *true* God may live.

The claim that "the protest of atheism has therefore a cathartic value" because it wages war "against all the caricatural images of the infinite, which are the crime *par excellence* against the spirit,"[72] has received support from a number of other voices. One of the clearest expressions of this support is found in the writings of Karl Rahner. He too has spoken out against the idea of a God reduced to simply another aspect of the world, even if it be the supreme and ultimate aspect. For Rahner, then, "atheism today could have the effect of restoring to God his transcendence,"[73] and from this possibility stems the idea of the "anonymous" or "implicit" Christian. Rahner builds on the Thomistic presupposition that every moral act has a supernatural formal object, even if such an object is not recognized. Thence the distinction between "categorical atheism," for which the content of the moral act is insufficiently or falsely understood, and "transcendental atheism"— actually the experience of God—for which the content of the act is a presupposition for obedience to one's conscience. The two types of atheism are not of necessity mutually exclusive. Rahner identifies the "presupposition" behind the moral act as the "objective" constitution of human existence by the Christ event, even prior to our appropriation of that event. Because God's saving grace is extended to man even be-

fore the hearing of the Gospel, and because his love appears in everyone, even when unrecognized, then to obey one's conscience in an act
of love places man in a state of grace, apart from any conscious recognition of the work of Christ. In other words, for Rahner, faith is seen
as implicit in every situation.

This point of view is clearly more far reaching than simple icono-
clasm. It runs the risk of violating the warning of Wilhelm Dantine
who, speaking at the Salzburg Colloquium, suggested that atheism
"must be respected by the Christian faith, and counted among the possible modes of using freedom."[74] For if the end result of Rahner's
position is to effect a synthesis of the world such as it is with the coming salvation of God, have we not in fact baptized the Marxist against
his will? It is possible, as Harvey Cox suggests, that God may be on
the side of those who deny his existence;[75] this is not the same as
saying that the atheist is a "hidden Christian" who has no need for the
explicit *fides ex auditu*. Others have perhaps seen the danger of over-
stating the case more clearly than Rahner.[76]

There is without doubt a definite anti-religious bias inherent in even
the most avant-garde Marxism, in spite of Garaudy's protests that
atheism is not in itself a presupposition of dialectical materialism.
Politically, the fear of organized religion is understandable, for the
Church, as institution, has often been allied with the forces of social
conservatism in history; philosophically, it is equally easy to sympathize
with a certain wariness of heteronomous conceptions of God which
have, in some situations, led to a diminution of human responsibility
and autonomy. Thus there is an imperative on Christian theology to
deal seriously with these atheistic objections, and to work toward the
enunciation of a doctrine of God which supports the creative and free
initiative of man. Specifically, this leads us to a consideration of the
question of transcendence, for it is here that the greatest problem as
well as the greatest hope exists for a mutual and constructive understanding between Christians and Marxists.

## NOTES

1. HM, p. 15.

2. This term is used more frequently by the young Marx, e.g., in the *Manuscripts of 1844* and *The German Ideology*. Later, in *Capital*, Marx turned to a more economically oriented discourse, replacing the term *alienation* by *fetishism of merchandise*. Although Garaudy makes note of the development in Marx's thinking (cf. HM, pp. 30–31), he tends to prefer the broader term *alienation*, and relates the fetishism of merchandise to a purely economic form of alienation.

3. MTC, p. 99.

4. Marx, cited by Garaudy in HM, p. 21.

5. HM, p. 22.

6. QMM, p. 132.

7. HM, p. 60. Cf. "Theses on Feuerbach IV," in *Marx and Engels: Basic Writings on Politics and Philosophy*, ed. L. S. Feuer (New York: Doubleday & Co., 1959), p. 284. (Hereafter referred to as "Feuer.")

8. The dialectic between religion as cause and religion as effect of alienation is closely related to the understanding of religion as both *reflection* of real, historical distress, and as *protest* against that distress. Cf. *infra*, Chapter Five, the section entitled "Christianity as Reflection and as Protest."

9. *Dieu est mort* (God Is Dead). Cf. pp. 416 ff.

10. DEM, p. 416.

11. DEM, p. 417.

12. HM, p. 92.

13. Quoted by Garaudy in DEM, p. 7.

14. HM, p. 92.

15. For an analysis of the relationship of Hegel, Feuerbach, and Marx, see also KM, pp. 24–33.

16. KM, p. 26.

17. Garaudy applies the term *materialist* very loosely to Feuerbach. To what extent Feuerbach's system could be called materialist depends very much on what Garaudy means by the word. Paul Tillich points out that historical materialism is a far cry from "ontological" or "metaphysical" materialism: "You find this in Feuerbach who derives everything in nature from the movements of atoms in terms of calculable mechanical causality." Tillich, *Perspectives*, p. 183. This Feuerbachian materialism is really closer to the French dogmatic materialism which Garaudy scorns. See MTC, pp. 40 ff.

18. KM, p. 27.

19. MTC, p. 122.

20. QMM, p. 128.

21. For a detailed analysis, see "Outlines of a Phenomenology of Having," in Gabriel Marcel, *Being and Having*, trans. A. & C. Black (London: Collins, 1965), pp. 168–189.

22. PH, p. 266.

23. Marx, cited by Garaudy in PH, p. 266.

24. QMM, p. 154.

25. This and the following citation are from *The German Ideology,* in Feuer, pp. 293–294.

26. HM, p. 28.

27. KM, p. 59.

28. HM, p. 38.

29. Cited by Garaudy in MTC, p. 181. This kind of depersonalization is taken up by Jean-Paul Sartre in *Critique de la raison dialectique* (Paris: Gallimard, 1960), pp. 290–291: "In the earliest days of semi-automatic machines, investigations showed that specialized female workers let themselves go, while working, into a kind of sexual fantasy. . . . But it was the machine in her that dreamed of caresses . . . the machine demands and creates in man an inverted semi-automatism. . . ." See also Herbert Marcuse, *One Dimensional Man* (Boston: Beacon Press, 1968), pp. 24–27.

30. PH, pp. 381–382. Cf. also MTC, p. 182.

31. QMM, p. 151.

32. HM, p. 58.

33. Moreover, Garaudy is quite careful to state that alienations of one sort or another will persist *even within communism!* "Not only socialism, the first step of communism, but even communism itself will not put an end to all alienations. Certainly the most monstrous, spawned by class societies, political oppressions, and cultural manipulations, can for the most part be conquered. But at no time will it be possible for us to turn to our work and say, like a God too quickly satisfied on the seventh day of creation: it is good!" RE, p. 132.

34. MTC, p. 123.

35. Jack Klugmann, "The Marxist Hope," in *The Christian Hope* (London: S.P.C.K. Theological Collections 13, 1970), p. 59.

36. Wolfhart Pannenberg, "Can Christianity Do Without an Eschatology?" in *The Christian Hope* (London: S.P.C.K. Theological Collections 13, 1970), p. 29.

37. Johannes Metz, MCES, p. 121.

38. ATD, p. 92.

39. ATD, p. 89.

40. Klugmann, "The Marxist Hope," p. 61.

41. Quoted by Garaudy in MTC, p. 108.

42. See the excellent discussion of projection and alienation in Helmut Gollwitzer, "The Marxist Critique of Religion and the Christian Faith," in *Study Encounter* (WCC), vol. 4, no. 1 (1968), pp. 6–19. Also see Tillich, *Perspectives,* esp. pp. 139–141, where the author offers a very positive appraisal of Feuerbach's idea of projection, emphasizing the uniqueness of his insight that the infinite screen on which man projects God is the awareness of man's

own unconditional nature. This is a much more profound understanding of the projection mechanism than, say, Freud's, since it explains why the image projected takes on infinite qualities identified with God.

43. MTC, p. 107.

44. MTC, p. 108. On the other hand, cf. Wilhelm Dantine, "The Dialogical Character of Human Existence," in *The Gospel and Human Destiny,* ed. Vilmos Vajta (Minneapolis: Augsburg Publishing House, 1971), p. 168: "For although atheism is a phenomenon that appears in all cultures, its western form—the only one to have created a tradition—was conceived from the start *in opposition to a theism* which to a large extent determined and characterized Christianity. Not only historically, however, but also in view of the matter itself, *atheism proves to be an intra-theological problem.* Insofar as the theistic idea of God is foreign to the essence of Christian faith, the anti-theistic front of atheism can also call upon certain theological arguments" (italics mine).

45. HCHM, p. 64.

46. E.g., MTC, p. 183.

47. MR, p. 16.

48. The term *heteronomy,* composed of the two Greek words *heteros* and *nomos,* was coined by Paul Tillich, and refers to the imposition of an alien will or law on human autonomy.

49. Roger Mehl, "La Crise actuelle de la théologie," in *Etude théologiques et religieuses,* vol. 45, no. 4 (1970), p. 359.

50. Wolfhart Pannenberg, "The God of Hope," in *Crosscurrents,* vol. 18, no. 3 (summer 1968), p. 29.

51. Dr. Braaten discussed this thesis during a seminar in systematic theology in 1966–67.

52. Karl Rahner, MCES, p. 225.

53. MR, p. 7.

54. Here we are drawing on the argument of Louis Duprés, "Marx and Religion: An Impossible Marriage," in *New Theology Number 6,* ed. Martin Marty and Dean Peerman (New York: Macmillan, 1969).

55. Cf. e.g., MTC, p. 53: "Knowledge is at the same time both *reflection* inasmuch as it is science already formed, and *projection* inasmuch as it is science in process of formation."

56. MTC, p. 84.

57. In his most recent book, Garaudy asserts that "there is no necessary relationship between materialism, atheism, and revolution" (RE, p. 121), and that "all that science and any Marxism wishing to call itself scientific can require is a "methodological atheism," i.e., the refusal to make God either an "explanation" or a "force" intervening in the fabric of natural phenomena" (RE, p. 124).

58. MTC, p. 108.

59. MR, p. 17.

60. Gollwitzer, "The Marxist Critique," pp. 7–8.

61. Marx, excerpt from *Toward the Critique of Hegel's Philosophy of Right*, in Feuer, p. 303.

62. PMFS, p. 357.

63. Roger Garaudy and Gilbert Mury, "Des éléments nouveaux dans la dialogue chrétiens-marxistes," in *Témoignage chrétien*, no. 1167 (17 November 1966), pp. 12–13.

64. See Paul Ricoeur, *Freud and Philosophy: An Essay on Interpretation*, trans. Denis Savage (New Haven: Yale University Press, 1970), esp. the section on "Faith and Religion: The Ambiguity of the Sacred," pp. 524–531.

65. Ibid., p. 526.

66. Ibid., p. 530.

67. Ibid.

68. Ibid.

69. Ibid., p. 525.

70. Ibid., p. 531.

71. Cf. e.g., Isa. 44:16–18.

72. Roger Garaudy, MCES, p. 90.

73. Karl Rahner, MCES, p. 225.

74. Wilhelm Dantine, MCES, p. 75.

75. Harvey Cox, quoted in PMFS, p. 368.

76. E.g., Johannes Metz, MCES, pp. 125–126. See also Vilmos Vajta, "Theology in Dialog," in *The Gospel and Unity*, ed. Vilmos Vajta (Minneapolis: Augsburg Publishing House, 1971), p. 35: "The world must remain the world, even when it becomes a subject of theology. A 'Christianized world' would no longer be in perspective, even if by that we mean no more than an offer to the world. To presuppose an 'anonymous Christianity' as a basis for dialogue would mean no more than a churchification of the world in modern disguise. Secularization has rightly arisen as a protest against this. . . ."

TWO

# *Transcendence*

## TRANSCENDENCE AS AN ATTRIBUTE OF MAN

As might be expected, Garaudy's approach to the problem of transcendence rests upon a social analysis. Building on the epistemology developed by Marx and Engels in *The German Ideology*, he asserts that the most fundamental human experience is not solitude, but community. "The 'we' comes first in relation to the 'I' "[1] Marx and Engels based this axiom on their analysis of speech. Specifically, it is clear that from infancy men are deluged by the complex pattern of sounds we call language. Since no self-reflection is possible without verbalization, becoming conscious of oneself is a social process; it presupposes a language which is certainly not the invention of the self, but the inheritance of the whole history of mankind. From the very beginning consciousness is a social product. Men become conscious of themselves only in dialogue with other men.

However, if consciousness of self originates only in relationship with others, it then represents a kind of interiorized dialogue; it implies that within myself there is a tension between "me" and the other. In the dialectic between the self and the not-self, something new comes into existence.

> The act by which I become conscious of what I am is possible only inasmuch as it entails and produces a being who is already no longer what I am now: reflection holds within itself a genesis.[2]

Here we discover the root of Garaudy's understanding of transcendence, for the very process of reflection already entails a kind of transcendence. Consciousness means at every moment to stand at a distance from one's self. "There is thus a transcendence of mankind in relation to itself."[3] Here transcendence is a totally human phenomenon, a "dialectical supersession" of man by himself.

This transcendence is not absolute, however, but is rather grounded in immanence. It is man's self-transcendence, and as such it is identified with the presence of an "other" within my self. Garaudy goes so far as to say that I and the other are one. This totalization of human experience in which man is defined as the sum of his social relationships is not a form of alienation, as a first glance might indicate, since I can always decide whether or not to accept as my own the will which was at first in opposition to me. Thus this tension between my self and the other—what Garaudy refers to as the tension between the finite and the infinite, i.e., between the "I" and the totality of others—"makes possible the reciprocal involvement of transcendence and immanence."[4]

In this way Garaudy is able to define transcendence in a way that empties it of any *"Totaliter Aliter"* and orients it around the purely human phenomenon of man reaching beyond himself. "To investigate the dimension of transcendence . . . is simply to investigate all the dimensions of human reality."[5] Garaudy asserts that any attempt to refer transcendence to an Absolute, to God, would be to limit man by imposing an antiquated world view on him. To the Marxist, transcendence is not a presence, but an absence. It is a demand, an exigency, a driving force, but a force that cannot be conceived, named, or expected. Nor can it be hypostasized under the heading of transcendence. Such an exigency simply is, and what it is, is always growing, always incomplete, like man himself.

With such a humanistic approach to transcendence Garaudy seeks to enrich Marxist thought. Unlike religious transcendence, which begins by affirming the existence of God, this understanding might better be termed "negative," because it "opposes itself to the sufficiency of man; it demands that he be open to the infinite. To affirm transcendence is to deny that man can fully realize himself in his empirical life."[6] Only Marxism can correctly grasp this openness toward the infinite, since it views man as always incomplete, always unfinished.

In this way the dialectical, Marxist approach to transcendence is asserted to be richer and more demanding than the Christian understanding, "because if nothing is promised to us and if nobody is waiting for us, the responsibility of man is total; the sense that he will give to his history depends only on him."[7] This concern for the autonomy and responsibility of man is a recurrent theme in Garaudy's thought, as is his criticism of Christianity on the grounds that it is an evasion of man's responsibility and a betrayal of his freedom. For the Marxist, the autonomy of man is absolute; there is nothing outside of him which could limit his free self-development, his unrestricted auto-creation.

> Everything depends therefore on us. Everything. The whole of our history and of its meaning. Everything is played out in the intelligence, the heart, and the will of man, and nowhere else.[8]

From this perspective, transcendence ceases to be an attribute of God and becomes a dimension of human action and experience. It is what is specifically human in man, as opposed to what is animal and alienated in him.

At this point it would be wise to issue a caveat concerning Garaudy's use of the term *transcendence*. There is something suspiciously finite about the infinity of presence for which he reproaches Christians. Actually, what Garaudy denies is not really what Christianity affirms. For Garaudy, the presence of God is seen as a limit, a restraint on the otherwise unlimited field of possibilities that opens out before man. If God is (*An Deus sit*) then man is not absolutely free and self-determined. But such an understanding overlooks the very nature of transcendence, since a true infinite cannot serve as a limit on the finite; it is situated on another level. Similarly, to acknowledge the transcendence of God does not imply any restriction on the transcendence of man. In fact, from the Christian point of view, the infinite transcendence of God, in the last instance, grounds the infinite possibilities of human freedom and responsibility. In other words, the freedom, responsibility, and transcendence of man are rooted and grounded in the transcendence of the One in which he lives and moves and has his being.

Roger Garaudy uses the term *transcendence* in at least three different ways; none of these are mutually exclusive, but each requires some individual attention and elucidation. We will examine each of them in turn.

*Transcendence as Discontinuity*

Garaudy distinguishes the Marxist from both the existentialist and the metaphysical materialist. The former sees the meaning of life and history as the creation of the individual; the latter sees this meaning as finally established for all time by a history which unfolds according to certain immutable laws. Marxism, however, asserts that "the meaning of history is man's work, or rather the work of men in the totality of their history."[9] Contrary to all existentialist philosophies, states Garaudy, Marxism affirms that history has meaning prior to and outside of us, simply because the historical initiatives of our ancestors have been objectified into today's ideologies, products, and institutions. These objectifications are the historical preconditions for our own initiatives, thus limiting the number of options open to us. On the other hand, the meaning of history remains open and free; the future must still be created, even though its creation begins from conditions inherited from the past. The game is still open and all bets are off.

Thus, while Garaudy insists on an exhaustive conceptual analysis of the preconditions of our historical initiatives and decisions, such an analysis in no way exempts us from the necessity of choice and risk. History depends on us and on our action. And herein lies the first sense of transcendence for Garaudy: it is simply the disjunction between the present state of reality and the human creative act. "This 'transcendence'—which is simply this discontinuity between creative human *act* and *being*—is not the attribute of a God, but the specifically human dimension of action."[10] This human dimension involves the relative discontinuity between our actions, decisions, and choices, and the conditions and concepts which form their context.

Christianity, writes Garaudy, is no stranger to this form of transcendence, or discontinuity. From the Marxist point of view, faith can be described as the commitment for which the meaning of the world, and our responsibility *for* that meaning, are indistinguishable. The dialectical interaction of act and being is then paralleled in the dialectical nature of faith. Religious faith

> is at once knowledge and action, being and act; it is both assurance and uncertainty, commitment and awareness of risk, dependence on the past and a break-away which creates the future; and it is under the constant threat of alienation.[11]

A cursory examination of Garaudy's thinking at this point could easily convey the impression of a rapprochement with the Christian faith. But while faith shares Marxism's experience of break and discontinuity, Garaudy adds that it does so in an alienated manner. The "constant threat of alienation" cannot be detached from the essence of religious faith; religion must be approached in such a way as to "disclose the *authentically human reality* and the *real content it conceals* and which Marxism has to incorporate" (italics added).[12] The question is then whether the "authentic humanity" and "real content" Garaudy wishes to expose really constitute the essential nucleus of the faith. If not, is the surgery he proposes actually the amputation of what is truly central to Christian faith? While there is certainly a dialectical character to faith, is this all that can be said about it? Since the Christian views faith as a *relationship* with God, is it not necessary to deal with the One to whom he relates? Garaudy's understanding of faith is one-dimensional; it completely overlooks the most important question: faith in whom?

*Transcendence as Exigency*

Garaudy's second method of characterizing transcendence also finds its origins in the creative act. According to Marxism, man is continually involved in self-creation. Moreover, there is a direction and a sense to this auto-creation; the ends and goals of man always exceed his empirical existence. To affirm transcendence is to affirm a meaning to human history that goes beyond every empirical and provisional realization of man. But whence comes this direction and meaning? If we cannot posit an absolute Transcendence in which to ground the meaning of existence, how is it possible to say anything about the meaning and goal of history? And if such a meaning is affirmed, does Garaudy not fall into the very theism he so vigorously condemns?

Garaudy's response is that man finds an absolute axis of reference in the process of becoming more fully himself, more fully human. But this frame of reference remains always in the form of a question, not a response.

> Hence, that is what makes the two points of view irreductible: to refuse transcendence is to refuse to transform into a *response* what is only a *question;* it is to refuse to make an *exigency* into a presence.[13]

To the extent that faith poses the *question* of the meaning of human existence, it acts as an agent of historical change; insofar as it attempts to give *answers*, it is inevitably bound up in alienation. In other words, Garaudy bases the Marxist understanding of history on the sense of urgency rising out of the sheer contingency and questionability of existence.

It is the radical contingency of history that drives man to search for what Garaudy calls "totalization,"

> that demand for a totality which transcends all experience; that exigency that the universe make up a totality, compose a harmony; that certainty that the synthesis is other than and more than the multiplicity of its conditions; that is the postulate of both knowledge and action.[14]

Here man is pictured as an incomplete being, a creature in the process of formation. The goal of this self-creation is an ever fuller social consciousness, a more complete social integration, and an absolute domination of the physical world. In other words, the exigency of which Garaudy speaks is future oriented—it is the demand for an ever more complete realization of the potential of man. Man's "essence," then, is always becoming, always deferred, since for the Marxist "nothing is promised and no one is waiting."[15]

This emphasis on human autonomy drives Garaudy to reject traditional expressions of divine transcendence. Here he follows in the footsteps of Fichte, for whom the essence of reality is absolute freedom, a freedom that must resist all efforts to limit or restrain it. The choice is simple: either we are annihilated in our capacity as deciding, responsible individuals, or we annihilate God as an external reality. Either free will or God, but not both. Marxist humanism is similarly Promethean or Faustian in that it ascribes final authority and responsibility to man. Thus it must vehemently deny any form of transcendence as a reality outside of man. Such a reality is, in the words of both Fichte and Feuerbach, a "projection" of purely human needs.

From this we see that Garaudy's main purpose in reducing transcendence to simple exigency, or demand, is the preservation of human responsibility—a laudable end in itself. For this very reason Marx labeled religion the "opium" of the people; it appeared to be the source of man's resignation and acceptance of unbearable social conditions. And indeed, if the world is preplanned by God, if God's will is inevitable and inexorable, a mighty juggernaut relentlessly grinding out history, then it is easy to see how man could lose a sense of hope and responsibility for the world.

> If he had to accept so many primary "givens" in his life because they were not his own work, man would have neither the sense of his total responsibility, nor the ambition of his total creation.[16]

Nevertheless, such a view of the transcendence of God is a grave perversion of the truth, for it is precisely Christianity which offers man release from the heteronomous "powers and principalities of this dark world." In himself, man is not free; he is a prisoner of his own passions and a stranger to himself. To use Marxist terminology, he is alienated. In point of fact, the Marxist position is a caricature of Christianity. Freedom is not excluded by the divine nature; rather, the relationship with God, broken by human sin, is restored as a free gift of grace. Our response is purely voluntary. If anything, one might say that the divine initiative has the effect of sustaining as response the free initiative of man, and this is what drives us to be effective collaborators of God in history.[17]

A final point bears some additional comment. Garaudy's argument is built on the criticism that God is a projection—an idea that has been disputed by many Christian apologists. But honesty compels us to agree with Feuerbach: God *is* a human idea! Whatever man says about God, we can never forget that it is *man* who says it. Every theological statement is and must be expressed in human language and suffers from the inadequacies inherent in all such discourse. The point overlooked by Feuerbach, however, is, in the words of Pannenberg, that "God is a *necessary* idea for man, and that *there* is where the real problem is."[18] It is a necessary idea because it is inherent in human nature to look for meaning and fundamental reality outside and beyond the phenomenal world. This reality, beyond all that we can measure, predict, and control, meets man and transcends everything sensible.

### Transcendence as New Future

If we speak of transcendence as projection, we are driven to ask about the nature of the "screen" upon which the idea of God is thrown. Projection could be interpreted as pertaining to the future as the ever receding screen against which the image of man's hopes and plans is cast. In this way we might approach Garaudy's third understanding of transcendence: the possibility of a new and freely created future. Indeed, Garaudy goes so far as to say that "this future, open on the infinite, is the only transcendence which is known to us as atheists."[19]

Such a broad statement is possible because the idea of transcendence as futurity includes the understandings of transcendence both as discontinuity and as exigency. Thus the future may signify the radical break between reality experienced *now* and the human creative act as a *future* possibility. This future is not a simple extrapolation of the present, but represents something totally new. It must not be simply predicted, but invented. There is a fundamental transformation, since the future is a creation of man achieved in anguish and in hope.

Conversely, while our hopes and expectations for the future always exceed our experience of present reality, the achievement of the future also reveals more than the original projection had anticipated. The finished labor is always more than the projected labor. At the same time that the future rolls back the horizon of man, it creates new horizons in the form of new tasks to satisfy new demands. Thus, "this future is already here . . . as the leaven of our action in the present."[20] In this way the dialectic is maintained in man between what he *is* and what he *is not yet*. The transcendence of the future in this instance takes on the form of a discontinuity between *act* and *being*.

The future also approaches man as radical demand, or what Garaudy refers to as "exigency." It confronts man with the radical contingency of existence. It calls into question his self-assurance and security by constantly overthrowing his achievements, and it offers unlimited possibilities for creative action. "The future is situated on the level of question, not on that of response. The future is an exigency, not a promise. . . ."[21] This exigency of the future is without bounds. An unlimited perspective opens up before the creative activity of man. Garaudy concedes that Christianity, too, has claimed to offer this unlimited field of possibilities, and that such an aspiration had its value and greatness in a world of class antagonism and exploitation. However, he is quick to add that in speaking of transcendence there is no question of retaining either the word or the idea in the traditional sense of the "supernatural." Garaudy's "transcendence" of the future is purely immanent; it is no more than the power of man to go beyond the situation imposed on him by nature or society.

The immanental character of Garaudy's transcendent future raises serious questions. How is it possible to speak about the transcendence of an immanent process? Either the transcendence is purely relative—what the French refer to as *dépassement*, or supersession—or it implies some absolute or finality which gives history a direction and goal. In the first case it hardly seems worthwhile to use the word *transcendence* at all. But Garaudy clearly resists the alternative which would, in effect, "reify" the future. That is the very reason he stresses the creative activity of man.

Garaudy seems to view the future as an "opening" or "window" before man, which exercises an attractive force on man's creative activity. And he refuses to speculate on the nature of that window, or even to say that it exists. Here he follows closely the thought of Ernst Bloch. Bloch prefers to speak of the future in terms of a "vacuum," the "pull of the future," which is forever drawing men into the unknown before them. Yet Bloch, like Garaudy, refuses to take the last, crucial step of saying who or what is the nature of this inbreaking future.

But how is it possible to find meaning in a future without content? What does it mean to talk of the "pull" of a vacuum, of nothingness? And if the future *is* pure transcendence, devoid of content, how can one have any confidence in the successful emergence of the "novum"? What guarantee do we have that such a future even exists? And what meaning can be drawn from it? The question has been aptly put by George Cottier: "If one wishes to expel finality, does not the indefinite opening of the future become a continuous deferment which opens on nothing?"[22]

We have already hinted at some of the problems presented by Garaudy's humanistic definition of transcendence. These problems do not prevent us from appreciating the new avenues for mutual understanding that have been opened through this novel point of departure. The beginnings of this breakthrough go back at least as far as the 1965 Salzburg colloquy between Christians and Marxists sponsored by the *Paulus Gesellschaft*. It was at that conference that Karl Rahner put forward his idea of the "Absolute Future" as the essential focus of the Christian faith.

> The perspective of the future is essential both to Christianity and to the understanding of Christianity. The future which waits for man and mankind is for Christianity an absolute future.[23]

Man interprets the past in the light of the future to the extent that the latter reveals itself; the present cannot be understood except in releasing our grip on it and opening ourselves to the advent of the Absolute Future.

Garaudy was impressed by this new theological formulation, and saw immediately the rapport between Rahner's position and his own: "Here is a language which unites us as brothers, since the future is the only transcendence recognized by us, atheists as we claim to be from Marxism."[24] But here again the question arises of just what Garaudy means when he endorses Rahner's future-centered terminology. Because, although Marxism is said to ask the same questions as Christianity, and to live under the same tension toward the future, there appears to be a wide divergence between the two understandings of futurity. Rahner is speaking of an Absolute which transcends history itself, while Garaudy's new future is *immanent in the historical process* and *devoid of content*. In other words, it is a question of where the center of transcending activity is located. For the Christian, the future is the power of God which *comes to* man and evokes a response, whereas for the Marxist, the future is the *creation of* man—it is an act of self-transcendence. Garaudy himself is crystal clear on this point.

> For a Christian, transcendence is the act of God who comes toward him and summons him. For a Marxist, it is a dimension of man's activity which goes out beyond itself toward its far-off being.[25]

### The Marxist Future as Immanent

Garaudy's understanding of transcendence as futurity is *immanent* in the historical process; it is a dimension of each of our creative acts. Marxist man is never simply the result of past and present conditions, but the totalization and overcoming of that past and those conditions. Thus Garaudy always speaks of transcendence as a fundamental dimension of man, and not an attribute of God. What Christianity has designated under the heading "transcendence" (the emergence of the divine in human action), Garaudy calls *"dépassement dialectique"*— dialectical supersession of the present state of man through historical initiative and creative action. Thus, while expressing appreciation of Rahner's idea of the Absolute Future, Garaudy would qualify it by adding that "for us it is a human future, and as such it is not a set future . . . but a future always moving and expanding, a future which grows *in direct proportion to our progress*" (italics added).[26] It is man and man's activity that give meaning to this transcendence, and not some Absolute Transcendent which forms the goal of man's activity. And this constitutes the radical difference between the two concepts: for the Christian, transcendence gives meaning to history; for the Marxist, it is history that gives meaning to transcendence.

Consequently, it would appear that there is an ultimate block to any complete accord and understanding between Christians and Marxists on this issue. The conception of transcendence Garaudy proposes cannot change the Marxist attitude toward religion, since that transcendence must always remain *within* the immanence of historical possibility. But here the warning of J. B. Metz must be taken seriously, for the future is *not* our own—from the beginning we are "expropriated" into it. And our struggle to control the future must ultimately lead to the recognition of this fact. "The more creatively, the more operatively and militantly we act toward the world and its future, the more grievously we experience this expropriation."[27] The Marxist transcendence is not a true transcendence, for it is finally limited by the totality of human possibilities, however numerous these may be. It allows us to project beyond our present, but not beyond our future. In the last analysis, therefore, the Marxist transcendence cannot be God. Garaudy himself notes this when he points out that "it is impossible to conceive of a God who is always in process of making himself, in process of being born."[28] This is the very nature of a humanist transcendence. A true absolute is out of the question. The Marxist transcendent remains within the totality of human historical possibility.

## The Marxist Future as Empty

This way of understanding transcendence in terms of the future is not only immanental, but it opens on a future which is essentially empty. One must admire the frankness with which Garaudy acknowledges this criticism. He insists that it is not human hubris that impels the Marxist to assert that the future is experienced as absence rather than presence, but simple honesty. He holds to an agnostic position. "We are incapable of saying that God, as the absolute future of man, is already present, and that we move already within him."[29] Marxism does not deprive man of the fullness of transcendence, but only the illusion of certainty.

Garaudy supports his view with references to two of his favorite Christian thinkers: St. John of the Cross and Teilhard de Chardin. From Teilhard Garaudy draws the fundamental axiom that the movement toward God is not exclusive of a concern for and interest in this world. Rather, each of us shares in our own transformation and creation. Such a point of view rules out a God who is either a "being" or even the "totality of being." Here, of course, Garaudy agrees not only with Teilhard, but with contemporary theologians from Barth to Bonhoeffer to Tillich, who have all emphasized, each in his own way, that faith is not the possession of an object by knowledge. Garaudy asserts that St. John of the Cross made this claim long ago when he wrote that faith does not reach out to grasp an object, but that it meets "nothing." This experience of the "absence of God" has, to be sure, long been an element of the mystical "*via negativa*" which asserts that "God's transcendence implies his constant negation, since God is beyond all essence and existence; he is constant creation."[30]

If Garaudy were saying simply that doubt is an integral part of faith, he would be difficult to refute. Tillich himself has said as much. The problem arises when we try to determine just what Garaudy means by the "nothing" which he identifies as the object of faith. For St. John of the Cross, the "nothing" had a comparative value. It referred to the radical inadequacy of all attempts to grasp intellectually the nature and being of God, and the impossibility of relating to God except in faith. This hardly seems to be what Garaudy has in mind!

Finally then, we are compelled to admit that Garaudy's "future open on the infinite" suffers certain limitations stemming from its anthropocentric character. It may transcend our historical present but not our future, since it remains a "*dépassement indéfini*" at the root of human initiative. Moreover, by refusing to characterize the nature of this infinite future, Garaudy leaves man plunging headlong into an empty and meaningless abyss. No doubt man's creative initiative possesses a certain degree of transcendence, but only to the extent that it partakes of and points to an Absolute Transcendence from which it draws its significance. Without such an Absolute the human struggle lacks not only the assurance of a goal for the historical process, but it is bereft of a meaning for the struggle itself.

### TRANSCENDENCE AS AN ATTRIBUTE OF GOD

In formulating an acceptable response to Garaudy's concept of transcendence, we might well start from the idea of "horizon," to use the term of Paul Ricoeur, or "limit," "boundary." In so doing, of course, we must be careful that this horizon-limit in no way restricts the free creative responsibility of man. Ricoeur's term meets this requirement perfectly, since it is "the metaphor of what comes closer without ever becoming an object possessed."[31] Only when the "horizon-function" degenerates into an "object-function" does religion become the alienation of faith. The true man of faith, whether Marxist or Christian, is eternally "on the march" toward this ever receding horizon.[32] All attempts to reify the horizon of the future, either through the establishment of a final "socialist utopia" or through a static and hierarchical concept of God, are betrayals of the true nature of man and "bad faith."

The word *horizon* is not the crucial issue here. Moltmann, for example, prefers to use the expressions *boundary* or *limit*. But he correctly perceives that some such idea is imperative, for "it is this experience alone which ever made it possible to speak of 'transcendence' and 'immanence.' "[33] Even more, if we deny the experience of boundary and limit, not only do we refuse the possibility of transcendence, but it is then no longer possible to speak of immanence either. In order to have a valid perspective from which to view immanence, we must be able to transcend that immanence.[34] Otherwise, "the difference between them experienced 'on the boundary' disappears. All is one, and Yes is No."[35]

In view of what we have just said, it is incumbent upon us to investigate this notion of limit. Here is a starting point upon which both Marxists and Christians can agree. When in the course of evolution man first emerged to full self-consciousness, that self-consciousness was experienced as limited, as finite. Thus it was inevitable that man would try to give some significance to this experience of finitude. Although early interpretations were invariably primitive and mythological, the question which gave rise to those interpretations was a valid one, and still remains so today. Following the discussion of this phenomenon by Gordon Kaufman, we will try to see how "the idea of God functions as a limiting concept,"[36] that is, as the ultimate limit to all our experience.

### God as Ultimate Limit

In attempting to deal with the ultimate meaning of existence in the light of his finitude man is driven up against the notion of "God."[37] Attempts to speak about an Other who is greater than and beyond all that we can know or experience arise because of our encounter with the ultimate limits of all knowledge and experience.

> If there were no experiences within the world which brought us in this way up against the Limit of our world . . . then there would be no justification whatsoever for the use of "God-language.[38]

Thus, this approach to the problem of God is anthropocentric. It is oriented around man's awareness of finitude and refuses to say anything about God which cannot be ultimately related to human experience. Here we are firmly in agreement with Garaudy when he says that we must begin with man, for "no matter what we say about God, it is man who says it."[39]

This is a warning to the theologian to avoid the temptation to ground a doctrine of God in some metaphysical Absolute that cannot be related to human consciousness. Limit means limit, and to be honest and consistent in our discussion of God in the context of our experience of limitedness, we cannot arbitrarily transcend that limitedness to describe the structure of a reality beyond it.[40]

In other words, man is an historical creature; all he ever experiences are particular events such as suffering and death (of others), joy and peace, and so on. When we attempt to understand ourselves in the light of these experiences we encounter the limits to our being which surround us. But this is a reflective act. The notion of restriction, of limit, is not an immediate datum of experience, but is rather a deduction based on our encounter with reality. In other words, we move by generalization from particular checks and limits to the idea of ultimate or absolute Limit. Through this process of deduction the self comes to an awareness of its finitude.

> Thus, the so-called experience of finitude or contingency, however powerful the emotions which accompany and deepen and reinforce it, has an intellectual root, and it is possible only because man is a reflective being.[41]

The origin of the notion of limit is found in concrete experiences of real limits. This is quite different from, for example, the idea of mathematical limit, which has no tangible physical identity. The only way we can conceive of the idea of absolute Limit is by use of certain analogies or images drawn from the actual experience of being limited. Kaufman sees four basic categories or types of limiting experience, from which models may be drawn for approaching the idea of Ultimate Limit.[42] As human beings we know the experience of external *physical* limit, the internal *organic* limitation of our human resources, the external *personal* limitation of other human beings, and finally, the *normative* restrictions with which we must grapple, such as conceptions of beauty, etc. The third type of limiting model—the personal limitation—is most interesting for our purposes. Because the limits and constraints imposed on us by others are subjective acts of volition and intention, the experience of these restraints is interpersonal and social. It is the only one of the four categories that permits us to interact with the source of the limitation, and thus opens the possibility of a personal relationship with the limiter.

Kaufman uses this personal limiter as an analogical basis for understanding the Ultimate Limit of all human action and experience. Such a model leads directly to the notion of God. Ultimate Limit is then conceived of in personal terms and understood by means of terminology drawn from the realm of interpersonal experience. Thus certain traditional attributes of God—for example, his absolute freedom and transcendence—can be understood in analogy to human freedom and transcendence. For Kaufman, then, the root of the idea of God is simply the awareness of limit or finitude, an experience known in some fashion by all men. Any Marxist would be quick to point out, of course, that in and of itself this awareness does not imply any infinite or absolute reality. Kaufman would agree.

> Indeed, only when it is grasped and interpreted in concrete personalistic terms does the Limit become understood as the expression of a being transcending the world, i.e., of an active God.[43]

Thus, the fundamental experience underlying the idea of God is limitation; the basic image which gives the term its peculiar transcendent character is personal. The two together provide the root referent for the word *God*.

There is much to recommend this approach to a concept of God. First of all, the universal experience of limit permits a certain consensus between Christians and Marxists regarding the starting point of any such discussion. Then too, the decision to work exclusively within the realm of human experience—and particularly at boundaries of that experience—allows us to maintain an anthropological center to our theological speculation, which is only being honest with ourselves in light of the limited character of all experience. Nevertheless, certain difficulties with Kaufman's argument must be dealt with before we can use it as a departure point in formulating a concept of transcendence. In his list of limiting models Kaufman makes no mention of temporal limitation, certainly one of the most basic human experiences: I can in no way retrieve the past or foresee the future. This failure to see the dynamic possibilities of a temporal limiter leads Kaufman to reify the personal limiter analogy into a God who stands over against me and limits my transcendence with his. But this is only a return to a mythological, medieval view of God as another being, infinite perhaps, but still of the same nature as his creation. There is then no absolute transcendence of God over the world, but merely a matter of degree. This sort of super-being is precisely what Garaudy is resisting: a static conception acting as an absolute and fixed limit on the possibilities open to man. For this reason Garaudy rejects the idea of God, "because the name implies a presence, a reality, whereas it is only an exigency which we live, a never-satisfied exigency of totality and absoluteness. . . ."[44]

A possible solution to this apparent impasse is found in Ricoeur's idea of horizon. The horizon is the metaphor or analogy of what comes closer without ever becoming an object possessed. Any attempt to objectify this horizon is idolatry. Such a concept might well be combined with the notion of limit suggested by Kaufman. The horizon of the future is then still the Ultimate Limit, but it is no longer a static limit. It is a constantly receding limit that gives full play to the dynamic of man's initiative and possibilities while nevertheless remaining the final and complete horizon of existence. Then we could agree with Garaudy to the extent that he simply says of this absolute: "It is. For what it is is always deferred, and always growing, like man himself."[45]

This horizon of the future is an Ultimate Limit which in no way restricts the full play of man's responsibility and creativity. It is what Karl Rahner calls the "Absolute Future."[46] If such an absolute, dynamic horizon is conceived of on the basis of a personalist model, as Kaufman suggests, we have an image of God which might well be a response to Garaudy's criticisms. The idea of divine transcendence would then be modeled on the real experience of human transcendence, insofar as that experience is a movement toward the future. To use the expression of Garaudy, "while man belongs to nature he differs from things and animals and . . . with his capacity continually to outstrip himself, he is never a completed being."[47] Such a model emphasizes the freedom and possibility of man. When used in analogy with God as the final horizon of all experience, transcendence takes on the character of unlimited freedom and unbounded possibility. Then the horizon-limit of the future is that personal experience of constantly new possibilities appearing before us and the freedom to create a new future without limit. It is the Absolute Future which absolutely transcends all our limited, projected futures, continually calling them into question, while forever beckoning us on toward the mystery of its receding horizon.

*Transcendence, Immanence, and the Future*

In identifying transcendence with the horizon of the Absolute Future, "transcendence" is really a relative word. It implies a going beyond and rising above some existing immanence. "To conceive a transcendence always involves experiencing some reality as immanent."[48] Conversely, as we have already hinted, there is no way to speak about immanence without relating it to a corresponding concept of transcendence. The two are related and present "a distinction and a relationship within the experience of 'boundary.' "[49] Moltmann has recognized the centrality of the idea of boundary or limit, and points out that if something is bounded, "the possibility of negation arises at its boundaries. Transcendence is then defined negatively as the un-bounded, unlimited, infinite."[50]

The problem of the boundary between transcendence and immanence is heir to a long history of development. Greek metaphysics wrestled with the problem and formulated a variety of ways of describing the phenomenon. Parmenides saw the universe as spherical with transcendence as the outermost, all-inclusive periphery and the finite perfection of immanence. The Stoics, on the other hand, conceived of the divine and transcendent as the obverse of all that is cosmic and immanent, corresponding to the order of *logos* and *nomos*. This leads one to ask just where the Greek mind encountered the experience of limitedness. The answer, according to Moltmann, is found in Greek philosophy's attempt to answer the fundamental metaphysical question of existence. All that exists is vulnerable, for the Greek, because of its finitude and temporality. The boundary is thus between immanence "experienced as finite, transitory, and threatened by chaos," and transcendence which "takes the form of what is infinite, imperishable, a source of order, and one."[51]

Today we have left behind the idea of the universe as the "house of being," and modern man sees the world as the material to be molded to the purposes of his own mind. Man is master of nature and the world. This objectifying of the universe has the effect of making transcendence not the outermost, all-inclusive periphery of the cosmos, but an aspect of the subjectivity of man.[52] The boundary between immanence and transcendence is then found in man himself. But this model of personal existence as transcendence, so popular with the existentialist philosophies of the thirties, has its own pitfalls, and is rapidly becoming untenable.[53] Man's world is becoming less and less the natural order of creation, and more and more the world of his own creations. This modern, technological, and industrialized world is increasingly difficult for man to understand and control.

> In this way, man once again comes up against a new experience of boundary and limit . . . the experience of his own powerlessness in a hard shell of reified products of his own creation and in a "closed society."[54]

The question is then where man can find a transcendence that is not alienating, but liberating.

In the face of this apparent dilemma, a new possibility arises: the idea of immanence as history. Garaudy himself points out that in ancient metaphysical systems, history was of no special significance. The greatest virtue was to recognize the inevitability of the natural order, and to conform oneself to it.

> In this philosophy of *being,* man is greater the more he is *what is,* through his consciousness of this being, through his participation in this order, the order of the cosmos and of the city.[55]

For Greek metaphysics, history was the incalculable and the chaotic. The only transcendence was in the destiny and order of the cosmos. And even in the modern, existential model of transcendental subjectivity, where the boundary is located within man's personality, history is meaningful only through personal decisions and encounters. But today, as Moltmann points out, "social, technical, and political history is becoming the field of interaction between man and nature."[56]

The mutual relationship between men and their objectified creations is becoming the central theme of history. "The world of man is the work of man."[57] Thus far Marx. But what Marx did not suspect, and what Garaudy does not admit, is that the objects of man's creativity could turn on their creator and exercise a tryrannical control over him. Herbert Marcuse, for example, has painted a terrifying portrait of this enslavement of men by their creations.[58] Faced with such a situation, man can no longer maintain the traditional idea of the neutrality of technology. Technology itself cannot be isolated from the use to which it is put, and the technological society "is a system of domination which operates already in the concept and construction of the techniques."[59] In this regard, Marcuse sees no difference between capitalistic and socialistic systems.

Thus, we face a new boundary situation for which the possibility of transcendence is in relation to the existing system. It is therefore a transcendence directed toward the future. It is found only where this situation of domination is resolved in a qualitatively different, transforming new future.

> Transcendence is experienced where perspectives of discerning choice open out for the present discord, where new and significant possibilities appear for concrete human expression, and for giving a human character to alienated conditions. . . .[60]

Here, however, a note of caution must be sounded, for this transcendent future has nothing to do with a mere extrapolation of present trends; it is not simply a planned and programmed future. Such a projection holds out no promise for genuine change and freedom from alienation.[61] Rather, what we mean here must be the appearance of a qualitatively new future. This new future is present where the conflicts which make us experience present reality as history are transcended in the direction of their suppression or reconciliation.

There exists a dialectical relationship between this new future and present historical reality. The future of history is qualitatively new and different, yet it gives its character to the actual shaping of history here and now. Moltmann points out two kinds of deviation that must be avoided in this dialectical relationship of the "now" and the "not-yet." On the one hand, it is possible to overemphasize the difference between history and eschatological future. This leads to a negation of history and the world and, in the end, to resignation. On the other hand, if an adequate distinction is not maintained, transcendence becomes identified with history, in a continual unfolding of the future in the present. This also leads to resignation, because "every act of transcending creates yet another present to be transcended."[62] The correct dialectical tension is possible only when transcendence *above* history is associated with the process *of* history.

Karl Rahner has also pointed out the dialectical relationship of historicity to futurity:

> The two propositions concerning, on the one hand, the definitive character of history, and on the other, its radical transformation, remain for us at the present time in a dialectical oscillation, which leaves the future open and at the same time gives the present its decisive importance.[63]

History and change are both hermeneutical principles and objective affirmations. Rahner hints that this dialectic may be the silent manifestation of the Absolute Future. He bases his belief squarely on the Incarnation, "because the Logos of God himself acted and suffered historically."[64] The humanity of the God-Man is not a simple costume or disguise used temporarily, but it remains his *own* humanity. Any other position would tend to separate body and soul, the noumenal and the phenomenal. Consequently, Rahner does not see any divine reality behind history (or above it as in Heilsgeschichte theology), but rather "it is . . . necessary that history itself have a definitive meaning. . . ."[65]

Several leading contemporary Marxists have noted with interest the new Christian understanding of transcendence as futurity, and have responded affirmatively. Ernst Bloch, one of those most responsible for the rebirth of interest in eschatology, sees the tendency as a "sign of genuineness" and hopes that it signals a new era of Christianity in which the Kingdom will no longer be seen as something above, but as something ahead. "If the salvation in the Gospel is to become flesh—for us or for men who follow—there must not be merely something above, but also something before us."[66] Garaudy seconds this endorsement, and sees it as the only real possibility for a Christian-Marxist dialogue. In an interesting paraphrase of Teilhard de Chardin, he says: "The synthesis of the (Christian) God of the Above and the (Marxist) God of the Ahead: this is the only God whom we shall in the future be able to adore in spirit and in truth."[67]

Any attempt to join transcendence and futurity must, however, first accept the fact that history is the locus of conflict. This is not simply the recognition of the transitory character of all things, or the necessity for man to make decisions. It is, to use the words of Moltmann, "the insight that man, his society, and his world are an experiment, a hazardous enterprise. . . ."[68] Transcendence is then the possibility of overcoming the present risky situation in a successful solution. But even the projection of a possible resolution of the present experiment is itself a project involving risk and danger.

The point is that "future" has nothing to do with "transcendence" as long as we think solely in terms of an historically immanent future. A dotted-line extrapolation from the present situation is no more certain or sure than is our experience of reality and history; in other words, it provides no real assurance or certainty of success. "Only a future which transcends the experiment of history can become a paradigm of transcendence and give a meaning to that experiment."[69] Thus the utopias that men create break through the structure of reality and offer the prospect of the totally new. Harvey Cox has said essentially the same thing using the language of fantasy. Such fantasy "can inspire new civilizations and bring empires to their knees . . . it does so through that particular form of fantasy we might call 'utopian thought.' "[70] Such utopic or fantasizing thought envisions new kinds of social existence without first asking if they are feasible, and thus it provides the impetus for the breaking open of existing societies and orders. The possibility of a new earth is the source of the drive to transform *this* earth.

This new earth is portrayed by Rahner as the eschatological gift of God and not simply as the final outcome of earthly progress. On the other hand, it is necessary to emphasize that the new earth is not discontinuous with this one: "neither is it simply something which replaces the preceding state, contenting itself in repelling and suppressing it; rather it is a transformation of the former world. . . ."[71] The dialectic between the radical newness of the future and the historical reality of the present is what gives impetus to social change and, finally, to what Garaudy calls the creation of man by himself. Speaking at Salzburg, Metz put it in this way: "Only a future which is more than the projection of our own latent possibilities can really call us to go beyond ourselves. . . ."[72] The gap between the promise of a new future and the present unredeemed state of mankind is the source of the drive to change the pattern and systems of this world. The Absolute Future is the power of God acting in the midst of history to transcend history toward a new future.

### God and the Future

We have not yet faced the final and possibly most difficult question in this attempt to find a way of speaking about God in a manner acceptable to both Christians and Marxists. Thus far we have examined the notion of Ultimate Limit as the horizon of the future, constantly receding from us and beckoning to us; we have discussed the idea of the future as the only acceptable form of transcendence for the alienation of twentieth-century man; and we have suggested some guidelines for the practical implementation of a transcendence of the future in history. Nevertheless, the critical question remains, as recognized by Pannenberg: "To what extent did we have the right to call the power of the future . . . God?"[73]

Indeed, this is no insignificant question. What is being suggested here is not that the future is a means by which God comes to man, simply one manifestation among others of the power of God; rather, we are suggesting (with Carl Braaten) that "the future [is] a divine mode of being."[74] The future then would not simply be the possibility, or the exigency, for man to transcend present reality. Quite the contrary, it would be "ontologically grounded in God's own mode of being."[75]

There would then be a direct ontological relationship between God and future. The consequences of such an identification are considerable. For example, as Braaten goes on to point out, any notion of God as the power of the future removes the force from traditional formulations of God as *summum ens* or *ens perfectissimum*.

This idea of the future as a mode of God's being has not yet been seriously considered in theology in spite of its obvious biblical precedents. The eschatological message of Jesus rests squarely on the revelation of God's power and might as a future event. The hopes and expectations of Israel, the claims of Jesus, have yet to be vindicated. The Resurrection is but a foretaste, an anticipation of the coming Reign of God. But this Reign of God *is* only to the extent that the future has power over the present. ". . . the future decides what will become of that which is present at the present time."[76] It is the God of the future who is the object of the hopes of Israel.

The experience of the Absolute Future which calls into question all our limited and projected futures is nothing less than what Christians put under the name of God. It is not, however, necessary to name this Absolute Future in order to experience its power and demand. Rahner has expressed it in this way: ". . . it is the same thing to believe in an absolute future and to believe in God."[77] It is Rahner's contention that this Absolute Future (Rahner's own term) is no less than God himself. Such an Absolute cannot be constructed theoretically by a compilation of attributes and qualities added together into a static whole. It cannot be anything less than the absolute fullness of being. "It is . . . the term and the motor of the dynamism that drives the world and man toward the future."[78] To describe the future in such a way is to speak of God.

A number of advantages accrue to such a conception of God. For one, God cannot in any way, shape, or form be an object of understanding or reason, placed alongside other such objects. Rather, he is the One who gives consistency to our future plans. This ties in directly with Garaudy's understanding of "project." "A project is an anticipation of the real. Starting from conditions in which it is born, and as a function of them, consciousness projects its own ends."[79] This is the Marxist conception of the specifically human form of labor, as opposed to the industry of, say, ants or bees. Man begins by positing the ends toward which he is working. But Rahner's idea of God as the Absolute Future is part and parcel of any human effort to project the future. "The knowledge of God is thus implied in the elaboration of the project from itself to which man gives himself in regarding the future,"[80] even if man takes no account of this source of reality undergirding all human dynamics.

### JESUS OF NAZARETH AND THE ABSOLUTE FUTURE

No discussion of God and transcendence can be complete without attempting to deal with the person of Christ. For if the claim of Christians is to be taken in all seriousness, it means that the mystery of the Absolute Future has appeared in history at a definite place and time, an event which cannot help but have repercussions for every effort to understand and describe the nature of transcendence. Marxism, too, has acknowledged the significance of the person of Jesus and, while denying his divinity, has spoken enthusiastically of his contribution to man's sense of freedom and responsibility. In the light of this common regard for Jesus of Nazareth, and the apparently contradictory interpretations offered by Christians and Marxists, we will explore Roger Garaudy's understanding of the historical significance of Jesus, and then attempt to relate that understanding to a theological interpretation based on the idea of Absolute Future.

### A Marxist Interpretation

Garaudy speaks of Jesus only with the highest admiration and praise. Indeed, it would seem that, for Garaudy, Jesus is one of the most creative and important men who ever lived. This admiration has nothing to do with Christian claims about the nature of Christ, but is directed toward the contribution of Jesus to human self-understanding and development. Jesus—or the early community gathered around him— opened up the perspective of an infinite horizon for man. Men were no longer prisoners of fate, as the Greeks had believed; it was the birth of the idea of freedom. Indeed, Jesus lived his entire life with a style that announced to all the world: "Each of us can, at every moment, begin a new future."[81] He exposed the error of confusing reason with necessity in a Greek concept of destiny. He was the very opposite of destiny; he was freedom, creation, life itself! History was de-fatalized in the event of Jesus.

Contrasting Jesus to Adam in a Marxist exegesis of Rom. 5, Garaudy identifies the original sin with heteronomy.[82] Adam sinned because he allowed his conduct to be determined by exterior forces, by a will other than his own—by a snake! In other words, if we take Garaudy seriously at this point, the sin of Adam was not in wrestling his independence from God by opposing his will to the Supreme Will; rather, it was a surrender of freedom and responsibility to another: it was alienation. This is a most interesting interpretation of Adam, because Adam's sin is depicted in Rom. 5:14 as "disobeying God's command." But if disobeying the will of God is described by Garaudy as heteronomy, as a loss of freedom and responsibility, we have nothing less than an Augustinian understanding of free will: man is only truly free when his will corresponds to the Divine Will; the attempt to go counter to the Will of God is tantamount to slavery! It is to be questioned whether Garaudy intended this reading of his remarks on Adam, but it remains highly instructive nonetheless, since it fits in so well with what he has to say about Jesus.

In the same passage, Garaudy describes Jesus as affirming the basic prerogative of man, that by which man lifts himself above the level of the animal. The message of Jesus is then that man's destiny is not predetermined; we stand in freedom before an open future. The "powers and principalities" of the world—economic forces, class relationships; instinctual and physiological pressures, psychological inclinations, family, group, and national mores—none of these have any ultimate power over man. There are no natural or societal structures that totally predetermine man, even though these structures provide the basic framework within which we act and think. Jesus has pointed the way to the de-fatalization of history and the de-alienation of man.

> Is not the essence of the message of Jesus the message of this transcendence, of this dialectical supersession, freeing man from the tyranny of intrapersonal or suprapersonal forces?[83]

What Christian could disagree with this understanding of Jesus, as far as it goes? Certainly Jesus, by his Resurrection, has liberated men from the forces of death, even, as Garaudy himself points out, from the power of death itself. Jesus, "by his resurrection, announces that all limits, even the supreme limit of death itself, have been conquered. . . ."[84] It is interesting to contrast this interpretation of Jesus with what Garaudy had to say about Adam. If Adam's sin was in surrendering his freedom (by disobeying the commandments of God, according to St.

Paul), the victory of Jesus was in living a life of absolute freedom, in accordance with the will of God. "And just as many men were made sinners as the result of the disobedience of one man, in the same way many will be put right with God as the result of the obedience of the one man" (Rom. 5:19). In other words, if this idea of Garaudy were carried through to its logical consequences, we would have a very well-developed Augustinian (and Lutheran)[85] doctrine of freedom of the will. A man, then, is only truly free to the extent that his will is in accordance with the will of God; to the extent that men seek to defy the will of God, they subject themselves to heteronomous forces which dictate their actions and deny them true freedom. "Freedom is what we have—Christ has set us free" (Gal. 5:1).

The contribution of Jesus to human self-understanding is not the only point at which Christians might agree with Garaudy. Just as atheism was said to be a corrective to the idolatrous tendency to reify God, so Marxist materialism, it is suggested, could serve to remind Christians of the centrality of the Incarnation. Christians have often forgotten or ignored the historical and social dimensions of mankind in a docetic tendency toward spiritualization of the Gospel. Viewed in this (heretical) way, the Christian message is a call to turn away from the problems of this world toward the future life to come. Here, perhaps, Garaudy may be close to the truth when he asks: "Is it not possible that Marxism is nothing other than a serious call for the Christian to meditate on the Incarnation?"[86] A little "materialism" might well aid a balanced understanding of this central doctrine of the Faith.

Of course, there are numerous problems with this understanding of Jesus. For one, it is relatively unimportant to Garaudy if Jesus really lived or not. The point is that a certain conception of man came into existence, a new community was born. "What is important is that about twenty centuries ago men conceived the idea of a limitless human community. . . ."[87] Jesus, if he existed at all, is represented as a human hero—a Prometheus carrying to mankind its proper self-image. In other words, Jesus is valued only insofar as he represents a prefiguration of the Marxist conception of man. In that Jesus offers a model of this ideal Marxist man, Garaudy is more than happy to give him a central role in human history. Needless to say, there is no question here of seeing in Jesus a transcendence above and beyond the human capacity for self-transcendence.[88] Moreover, such an interpretation is incapable of aiding men in today's struggle for free and authentic responsibility. If Jesus were but a concept or an ideal, the unyielding Marxist critique tells us that such ideals and concepts are incapable of changing the historical conditions that enslave us.[89] And if Jesus is simply a man who somehow managed to live a life of absolute freedom and self-determination, this freak historical occurrence is powerless to aid *us* in our struggle. In other words, as long as Jesus remains either an ideal or an isolated event, he is at best a good example and at worst irrelevant. Man remains trapped by the psychological, social, and economic forces which oppress and destroy him.

### A Christian Interpretation

It is only if the future of Jesus can somehow also become *our* future that his existence has any relevance for us. It is only if his life is stamped with the character of the Absolute Future—that which is future to every present—that he can free us to face our future with hope. Human beings are historical creatures. Rahner sees this historicity as the basis of man's question:

> if he could not find someone in his history whom he could believe had been perfectly open to the coming of the Absolute Future in him, not only for himself, but also as a promise for us.[90]

Such a person exists: the biblical texts testify to a common horizon of concern between the Christ event and the future of Christ, between the Christ event and the kingdom of freedom. In other words, Jesus Christ is the person in whom God gives himself to be *our* Absolute Future.

This is not, however, to equate the person of Jesus with absolute transcendence, with God. Pannenberg has correctly noted that christological doctrine, as it developed, spoke of the deity of Jesus, but as that of the "Son" as opposed to the "Father."[91] This difference of the Son from the Father corresponds to the difference between the "futurity of the Reign of God" and its realization and actualization in the life and ministry of Jesus. In other words, in the ministry of Jesus, the Absolute Future has broken into the present without ceasing to remain future. Jesus, it is to be noted, never claimed divine authority for himself; rather, he subjected himself to the One he called the Father. Pannenberg interprets the "Father" to mean the coming "Reign of God"— inseparable from God himself—which is completely and conclusively present in Jesus and yet remains different from him. The finality of the ministry of Jesus is thus based on its eschatological character; through this ministry the final future of God becomes determinative of the present and thus becomes present. Here Pannenberg presents a novel formulation of the doctrine of the two natures of Christ; any mixing of the divine and the human in the appearance of God in Jesus is rejected. It was in pointing away from himself that Jesus made it possible for the Absolute Future to become present in and through him. This event is unique, once and for all, and final.

But if the freedom of the Absolute Future has become present in a particular time and place, we find ourselves confronted by the paradox of the continued existence of suffering and slavery. We are forced to ask ourselves how the biblical "horizon of freedom"[92] can be mediated to the oppression and unfreedom of the present. Here the suffering of Christ is instructive, for it points to what is really evil in the world: the radical contingency of reality and the chaos boiling away beneath the veneer of existence. And it is at this point that the Resurrection kindles the spark of hope, for the Resurrection is in radical tension with the world of experience. The discrepancy between righteousness and sin, good and evil, life and death, forces us to look to the Absolute Future of Christ for a transcendent resolution of the contradiction.

Here is where Garaudy's Promethean and humanist image of Jesus runs counter to the historical facts, as well as the whole history of Christian thought. As J. B. Metz pointed out in his address to the Salzburg colloquium, the message of Jesus is inseparable from the proclamation of Cross and Resurrection.[93] It is a message of hope, of hope crucified in the world. Through the event of the Resurrection our eyes are directed not to the past, but to the future. The object of the Resurrection proclamation is the promise of the final victory and vindication of hope. Without the eschatological act of the Resurrection, the message of Jesus would, indeed, be no more than Garaudy portrays it: the birth of a new philosophical concept. But the Resurrection signifies more than an ideal; it is the sign of the inbreaking of a new future.

The significance of the Resurrection for the early Church is more clearly evident in the light of the Jewish apocalyptic. It is a well-known fact that in post-exilic apocalypticism the idea of the resurrection of the dead is an element in the theology of universal history.[94] It appears again in the debate between the Pharisees and the Sadducees in the

Synoptic Gospels.[95] Thus, when the early Christians spoke of the Resurrection of Jesus, they spoke within the context of a general expectation of the resurrection of the dead at the end of time. They knew they were speaking eschatologically. In other words, the question was not whether the Resurrection could happen, but whether it had happened.

The interrelationship between the Resurrection of Jesus and the general resurrection of the dead becomes clearer in the light of St. Paul's discourse in 1 Cor. 15. Witness this significant passage in verses 12 to 16:

> Now, since our message is that Christ has been raised from death, how can some of you say that the dead will not be raised to life? If that is true, it means that Christ was not raised; and if Christ has not been raised from death, then we have nothing to preach, and you have nothing to believe. More than that, we are shown to be lying against God, because we said of him that he raised Christ from death—but he did not raise him, if it is true that the dead are not raised to life. For if the dead are not raised, neither has Christ been raised.

Here it is obvious that Paul is not arguing from the event of Jesus' Resurrection to the possibility of a general resurrection, but exactly the reverse. It is the general resurrection which provides the context and the meaning for the Resurrection of Jesus, "for if the dead are not raised, neither has Christ been raised."

The importance of the distinction is immense. If the resurrection of the dead is one of the *eschata,* belonging to the end of history, then the Resurrection of Jesus is the *pre-actualization* of the eschaton. "The end of history is present proleptically in Jesus of Nazareth. In his Resurrection the final end of universal history has been anticipated; it has occurred beforehand."[96] Thus, all of the present is eschatologically conditioned, because the final and Absolute Future has become present definitely in the Resurrection of Jesus. This is the view of Pannenberg, who insists that it is only from the perspective of the end of history— that is, the eschaton—that one has the right or even the possibility to talk about history as a whole. Any understanding of the direction and meaning of history depends on this perspective from the end, since history will only have its final shape and form when it is consummated.[97]

Moltmann criticizes Pannenberg's idea on the following grounds:[98] If the Resurrection of Jesus is the anticipated end of all history, then the risen Christ has already attained the end and he himself no longer has a future. Then believers would not wait in anticipation of the future of the risen Christ, but only in hope that their future would resemble what happened to him. Moltmann sees the Resurrection not simply as the first example of the final resurrection of the dead, but as the source of resurrection life for all believers. Believers find their future *in* Christ and not only in a final event that resembles his. What is at stake here is the very meaning and purpose of history in the time between the Resurrection of Jesus and the general resurrection of the dead. The purpose of the Church during the interim is not merely to interpret history (to paraphrase Marx's eleventh thesis on Feuerbach) but to change the world in anticipation of the Absolute Future of God.

## NOTES

1. MTC, p. 96.
2. MTC, p. 97.
3. Ibid.
4. MTC, p. 104.
5. Ibid.
6. HCHM, p. 28.
7. Ibid.
8. HCHM, p. 29.
9. MTC, p. 208.
10. MTC, p. 209.
11. MTC, p. 210.
12. MTC, pp. 211–212.
13. HCHM, p. 30.
14. HCHM, p. 31.
15. ATD, p. 95.
16. QMM, p. 59.
17. Cf. George Cottier, *Chrétiens et marxistes—dialogue avec Roger Garaudy* (Paris: Maison Mame, 1967), pp. 133–134.
18. Wolfhart Pannenberg, *Disputation zwischen Christen und Marxisten* (Munich: Kaiser Verlag, 1966), p. 187; cited in A. J. van der Bent, "Le dialogue entre chrétiens et marxistes," in *IDOC International,* no. 18 (February 15, 1970), pp. 62–63.
19. ATD, p. 94.

20. Roger Garaudy, MCES, p. 346.

21. Ibid.

22. Cottier, *Chrétiens et marxistes,* p. 99.

23. Karl Rahner, MCES, p. 221.

24. Roger Garaudy, MCES, p. 345.

25. ATD, p. 92.

26. ATD, pp. 92–93 (Italics mine).

27. Johannes Metz, "God Before Us Instead of a Theological Argument," in *Crosscurrents,* vol. 18, no. 3 (summer 1968), p. 48.

28. ATD, p. 95.

29. Ibid.

30. MTC, p. 160.

31. Ricoeur, *Freud and Philosophy,* p. 526. Garaudy cites this definition in MTC, p. 63.

32. A word of caution is in order. Ricoeur is of course referring to an epistemological or hermeneutical horizon, while Garaudy uses the term to describe the "horizon" of the future. The basic idea, however, is the same.

33. Jürgen Moltmann, "The Future as a New Paradigm of Transcendence," in *Concurrence,* vol. 1, no. 4 (fall 1969), p. 334.

34. This is the essence of the Kantian critique. In order for philosophy to even speak of finitude, there must be a point at which it transcends the finite. For Kant, the point of unconditional validity was the categorical imperative. For Moltmann, it is the possibility of hope.

35. Moltmann, "New Paradigm," p. 334.

36. Gordon Kaufman, "On the Meaning of 'God': Transcendence Without Mythology," in *New Theology Number 4,* ed. Martin Marty and Dean Peerman (New York: Macmillan, 1967), p. 75.

37. Cf. Tillich, *Perspectives,* p. 99: "This is the essence of what is called religious experience, the presence of something unconditional beyond the knowing and acting of which we are aware."

38. Kaufman, "On the Meaning of God," p. 77.

39. Garaudy credits Barth with this Kantian critique of theology. Cf. PMFS, p. 360: "Whatever I say about God, it is a man who says it." Karl Rahner puts it in slightly different terms when he asks if it is not necessary to say, "Whatever is said about man is said from the point of view of man himself, and not from the point of view of God, who cannot be known except from the point of view of man." Karl Rahner, "Humanisme chrétien," in *Ecrits théologiques 10* (Paris: Desclée de Brouwer/Mame, 1970), p. 56.

40. Once again we return to Kant's first Critique. Ricoeur has shown that the Kantian doctrine of the "transcendental illusion" founded a critique radically different from that of Feuerbach or Nietzsche. The transcendental illusion "does not arise from the projection of the human onto the divine, but on the contrary from the fulfillment of the thought of the unconditional according to the mode of the empirical object; this is why Kant can say: "It is not experience that limits reason, but reason that limits the pretention to extend

our time-space, empirical, phenomenal understanding to the order of the noumenal." From Paul Ricoeur, "Approche philosophique du concept de liberté religieuse," in *L'herméneutique de la liberté religieuse* (Paris: Aubier, 1968), p. 226. It might be added that the same critique is equally devastating to the "anthopological illusion" that denies a priori the existence of a noumenal order beyond man's phenomenal world.

41. Kaufman, "On the Meaning of God," p. 81.

42. See ibid., pp. 84 ff.

43. Ibid., p. 95.

44. ATD, p. 94.

45. ATD, p. 95.

46. See Karl Rahner, MCES, pp. 220 ff.

47. MTC, p. 133.

48. Moltmann, "New Paradigm," p. 334. Garaudy can well appreciate this insight. In his latest, as yet unpublished, work, he explains that "Marx is not the successor to Spinoza, wrapping himself in pure immanence. Like Spinoza he refuses all external finality: man creates, in this world, his meaning and his freedom. But he *creates* them; he does not discover them ready made. Marx does not only resist a certain dogmatic theology which would oppose transcendence and immanence. He also resists Hegel's philosophy of history and positivist evolutionism. Transcendence and immanence do not oppose each other, according to him, like the yes and no of classical logic. They are dialectically related, in tension. They exclude each other and imply each other at the same time. Transcendence is the interior struggle of immanence." Garaudy, private communication.

49. Moltmann, "New Paradigm," p. 334.

50. Ibid.

51. Ibid., p. 335. Carl Braaten, in a discussion of Paul Tillich's concept of transcendence, questions whether it is even possible for Christian theology to borrow neo-Platonic, mystical categories to develop a doctrine of transcendence, since by so doing, "transcendence" passes over into the immanence of the eternal Now, understood as an ecstatic moment extending into its own depths. See "The Gospel of the Kingdom of God and the Church" in *The Gospel and the Ambiguity of the Church*, ed. Vilmos Vajta (Philadelphia: Fortress Press, 1974).

52. Or the subjectivity of God. Moltmann sees these two trends in modern theology typified by Barth (theology of the transcendental subjectivity of God) and Bultmann (theology of the transcendental subjectivity of man). Cf. Jürgen Moltmann, *Theology of Hope* (New York: Harper & Row, 1967), pp. 50–57. In the first case, God can only be known through his gracious self-revelation, a subjective experience achieved through the God-man encounter (Ebeling). In the latter case, God is known through an existential encounter with the kerygmatic word. In both cases the experience of transcendence is purely subjective. Neither Barth nor Bultmann leave room for any sort of "natural theology."

53. Garaudy's remarks are instructive. Referring to Heidegger, he says, "From what was the situation of men in a certain nation and a certain class of that

nation at a moment of crisis, Heidegger made the human condition, the tragic characteristic of all existence." (PH, p. 53).

54. Moltmann, "New Paradigm," pp. 336–337.

55. MTC, p. 130.

56. Moltmann, "New Paradigm," p. 339.

57. KM, p. 68.

58. See e.g., Marcuse, *One Dimensional Man*, pp. 1 ff.

59. Ibid., p. xvi. Cf. also Jacques Ellul, *The Technological Society*, trans. J. Wilkerson (London: Jonathan Cape, 1965), pp. 387–427.

60. Moltmann, "New Paradigm," p. 340.

61. Karl Rahner, speaking at the Salzburg colloquium, issued a categorical rejection of "the utopian vision of a future based on an ideology, the pretension to mix the absolute future with an essentially earthly future made of 'categorical' elements. . . ." (MCES, p. 229).

62. Moltmann, "New Paradigm," p. 344.

63. Karl Rahner, "La 'nouvelle terre,' " in *Ecrits théologiques 10* (Paris: Desclée de Brouwer/Mame, 1970), p. 117.

64. Ibid., p. 118.

65. Ibid.

66. Ernst Bloch, "Man as Possibility," in *Crosscurrents,* vol. 18, no. 3 (summer 1968), p. 27.

67. ATD, p. 54.

68. Moltmann, "New Paradigm," p. 343.

69. Ibid., pp. 343–344.

70. Harvey Cox, *The Feast of Fools* (Cambridge: Harvard University Press, 1969), p. 82.

71. Rahner, "La 'nouvelle terre,' " p. 112.

72. Johannes Metz, MCES, p. 120.

73. Pannenberg, "The God of Hope," p. 35.

74. Carl Braaten, "Toward a Theology of Hope," in *New Theology Number 5,* ed. Martin Marty and Dean Peerman (New York: Macmillan, 1968), p. 108.

75. Ibid.

76. Pannenberg, "The God of Hope," p. 34.

77. Karl Rahner, MCES, p. 220.

78. Ibid., p. 225.

79. MTC, pp. 125–126.

80. Karl Rahner, MCES, p. 225.

81. GPG, p. 165.

82. See PMFS, pp. 373 ff.

83. PMFS, p. 374.

84. GPG, p. 166.

85. Cf. esp. Martin Luther, *Bondage of the Will*, trans. Philip S. Watson in collaboration with Benjamin Drewery, Luther's Works, vol. 33 (Philadelphia: Fortress Press, 1972).

86. Roger Garaudy, MCES, p. 348.

87. MR, p. 7.

88. George Cottier has also noted this selective interpretation of the biblical record; anything in the life of Christ which suggests the presence of God is rejected as an infringement on human freedom and responsibility. "As if, in its idolatrous desire to divinize man, Marxism can see in God nothing but another word for man" (*Chrétiens et marxistes*, p. 130).

89. Cf. Friedrich Engels, who makes this quite explicit: "The ultimate causes of all social changes and political revolutions are to be sought, not in the minds of men, in their increasing insight into eternal truth and justice, but in changes in the mode of production and exchange. . . ." *Anti-Dühring*, in *Reader in Marxist Philosophy*, ed. H. Selsam and M. Martel (New York: International Publishers, 1963), p. 219. (Hereafter referred to as "Selsam and Martel.")

90. Karl Rahner, "Autour du concept de l'avenir," in *Ecrits théologiques 10* (Paris: Desclée de Brouwer/Mame, 1970), p. 103.

91. Wolfhart Pannenberg, "Appearance as the Arrival of the Future," in *New Theology Number 5,* ed. M. Marty and D. Peerman (New York: Macmillan, 1968), esp. pp. 118–122.

92. Jürgen Moltmann, "Toward a Political Hermeneutic of the Gospel," in *New Theology Number 6,* ed. M. Marty and D. Peerman, (New York: Macmillan, 1969), p. 80.

93. Cf. Johannes Metz, MCES, pp. 120–121. Garaudy's latest thinking has tended toward a revaluation of the significance of the Resurrection, as witness the following stirring phrases: "The Resurrection is not a 'fact' in the positivistic sense of the word; it is a creative act, an affirmation of the impossible by which history opens the future to all possibilities. It signifies that our future cannot be derived from a series of facts, based on the extension of past givens. This emergence of the totally unexpected, not based on any extrapolation, is the recognition that man is not born to die, but to begin." Roger Garaudy, private communication.

94. Cf. Braaten, "Toward a Theology of Hope," p. 102.

95. Cf. esp. Luke 20:27–40 and parallel passages.

96. Braaten, "Toward a Theology of Hope," p. 105.

97. See Wolfhart Pannenberg's discussion of this theme in "Redemptive Event and History," in *Essays on Old Testament Hermeneutics,* ed. C. Westermann (Richmond: John Knox Press, 1964).

98. Braaten, "Toward a Theology of Hope," pp. 106–107.

# THREE

# Creation and History

## MARXISM AND CREATIVITY

Chapter Two brought together a number of strands of thought in an attempt to speak of transcendence in a way acceptable to both Christians and Marxists. The concept of transcendence as futurity was suggested as the best possibility for mutual understanding between these two disparate traditions. This chapter will explore some of the ramifications of such a concept in the areas of creativity and historical initiative. These activities are directly related to both transcendence and the future in their mutual orientation toward the "not-yet" of human cultural and political development. If we recall Garaudy's fundamental proposition that "Marxism's specific difference from all earlier forms of materialism lies in the fact that Marxism takes as its point of departure the *creative act of man,*"[1] we will see how important it is to relate transcendence to creation. If transcendence is seen as man's capacity to continually supersede himself through the creation of a new future, then it is clear that creativity, transcendence, and futurity are inextricably bound together. This fundamental relationship will govern our discussion in this chapter.

### Creativity and the Transcendence of Man

Transcendence, as we have already noted, is for the Marxist an attribute of man; indeed, Garaudy identifies transcendence as that which is specifically human in man. It is "the presence of the future as the leaven of the present."[2] For the Marxist, all human activity, from technology to religion to art, stems from the act of labor. Labor is distinguished from purely instinctual or animal activity in that its end preexists in the

79

mind of man, and serves as a guide for action. This "project" is more than simple anticipation of the desired end; it is the active presence of the future in man, and it lies at the root of all human endeavor. Reality is not a set of givens which man must accept and suffer; rather, it is a "task that has to be accomplished," "an awakening of responsibility."[3] Man is not fully human except when he strives to go beyond himself, to become what he is not yet, to forge his own identity in the struggle with nature and existence.

The socialist revolution is neither an end-in-itself, nor an ultimate goal; rather, the final end and *telos* of the Marxist struggle is to make of each man a man. Garaudy specifies that this means to make of each a creator: a center of historical initiative. "This is the goal of our struggle: to create in the world the social conditions man needs really to be man, creative man."[4] But the creativity of man extends far beyond even the control of nature and history. It reaches to his very nature. The task before man is to create himself, and in this auto-creation Garaudy finds the essence of transcendence.

What has been referred to as "Faustian" or "Promethean" humanism differs from what Garaudy calls the "Apollonian," or Greek conception of man.[5] For the Greek, reality was a closed totality of which man represented a tiny microcosm, his destiny controlled by the fates. History was itself a closed, cyclic unity, forever destined to repeat itself. The highest achievement to which the Greek mind could attain was an understanding of fate, and conformance with it. In contrast to this Apollonian view of reality, Garaudy opposes the Promethean, or Marxist view. The Marxist rejects all givens, whether tangible or intellectual, for a continued creation of man by man. A Promethean or Faustian humanism calls into constant question all absolutes, all temporally conditioned conceptualizations, all values. It automatically excludes a transcendence imposed from below, in the sense of absolute and definitive knowledge, as well as a transcendence from above, in the sense of an absolute Good, a God, or an unquestionable Revelation. In place of these arbitrary and false transcendents, Garaudy affirms man's self-transcendence. "Man is nothing other than his own creations, his products, his institutions, as well as his projects."[6] There is no closed totality before us; reality is open and subject to change in accordance with the purposes and goals of men.

The question naturally arises at this point: how is this self-transformation and self-transcendence realized? What is the process by which man is able to alter his essential character and being? Garaudy responds that in transforming nature, man transforms himself. Human historical action consists in altering nature according to a plan conceived in the light of a conscious end or goal. The teleologically conditioned creation of new "objects" corresponds to the creation of a new "subject." "Labor therefore constitutes the essence of man, the act by which he constantly engenders and develops himself."[7] This point of view is radically different from either the idealism of a Fichte, who saw the subject as creating in isolation, or the dogmatic materialism of a d'Holbach, who believed that the subject was no more than a passive reflection of the object.

The creation of new objects parallels the creation of new demands. As the initial, instinctive needs for food, sex, and shelter are met, man is able to expand his interests and develop new needs which then become as necessary as the first. This is similar to the well-known American experience that what is introduced as a luxury rapidly comes to be considered a necessity. Thus one can still find families in backward rural areas living in the most severe poverty, and yet possessing a television set. Garaudy sees these artificially created needs as a sign of man's humanity: "The more man creates for himself needs which are specifically human, the more he raises himself above his original animality."[8] The needs thus created are more than expressions of an immediate and unilateral relationship with nature; rather, they imply a multiplication of man's relations with the world, leading directly to the form of knowledge known as science. To develop himself properly, man has to be freed from his immediate biological needs. This new freedom allows the conscious development of projects, the means for realizing them, and finally, conceptualization.

Garaudy's anthopology is open to numerous criticisms. Among these is the critique of anthopologist Lewis Mumford, who has frequently called for a rethinking of the nature and condition of man.[9] Mumford believes that the constant multiplication of needs and artifacts to meet those needs is a vicious and never-ending circle which leads to the eventual suppression of the genuinely human qualities of culture, art, and religion by a mechanized and mechanizing technology. The Marxist idea of true life, at least according to this view, consists in having ever increasing wants and in finding ways to vary and expand those wants. If that were truly the case, modern technological society should be an unqualified success because of its immense productivity and activity; but the actual result, both in America and in the Soviet Union, is confusion, frustration, and disappointment.

> The mechanical expansion of human appetites, the appetite for goods, the appetite for power, the appetite for sensation, has no relation whatever to the ordering of the means of existence for the satisfaction of human needs. The latter requires a humane scale of values and a priority schedule for their fulfillment which puts first things first.[10]

We might add that Mumford is not the only one to have seen the flaw in the process of reasoning which moves from man's needs to a definition of man, rather than from an understanding of the true nature of humanity to an analysis of needs. The radical Marxist Herbert Marcuse has denounced both American capitalism and Soviet socialism as betrayals of the true nature of man.[11] Both systems, according to Marcuse, have used an all-pervasive technological environment to strip man of his depth and his critical powers. With his needs, both immediate and projected, met by an ever-expanding technology, man cannot see that he is essentially a prisoner of a system over which he has no control.

Garaudy's error is a direct consequence of his materialist definition of man. It is axiomatic for him that material and tangible factors are of more importance than ideas and concepts. The latter are, in fact, derivatives of man's manipulation of nature.[12] This bias is clearly evident in Garaudy's remarks on the origins of man. Man is defined by labor, and labor is an action moving from man to nature. But this movement becomes specifically human only when it passes by way of an intermediary: the tool. "Human history is, at its starting point, founded on tools. . . ."[13] Throughout the prehistory of man, the presence of human beings is evident only by extrapolation from the existence of tools. Man is preeminently the tool-making animal.

Once again it is Mumford who attacks this widely accepted materialist myth.[14] Without in any way underestimating the importance of technics in the history and development of humanity, Mumford points out that other species of animals had proved themselves more technically proficient than man, far in advance of human technology, for example, in the fabrication of geometric beehives, urbanized anthills and termitaria, beaver lodges, etc. Rather than placing the entire burden on technics, Mumford emphasizes the role of the human mind.

> The consequence of this perception should be plain: namely, that there was nothing uniquely human in tool-making until it was modified by linguistic symbols, esthetic designs, and socially transmitted knowledge.[15]

Nevertheless, the description of man as a tool-making animal has been so widely accepted in popular thought that Garaudy's definition seems altogether reasonable. Thus, while not disparaging the role of language, and certainly emphasizing the importance of society, Garaudy has effected a subtle and destructive inversion of logic. Tools are the mark of specifically human labor, as well as the product of the collective work of many generations. As the presence of tools raises the complexity of social relationships, a new, higher form of social life is produced, characterized by the presence of language. "Language is born of social labor, of the coordination of efforts by the 'cry' whose complexity grows with the complexity of work."[16] This in no way negates the subsequent dialectical action of language on the labor which gave birth to it, but it definitely establishes the logical and ontological priority of labor over language. Such a mechanical understanding of the nature of man not only does violence to any sensitive study of the origins of human civilization, but it leads to an inverted set of values that tends to put production and material satisfaction ahead of the inner life of man.

One of the persons who has dealt with this question in great detail is Paul Ricoeur. Observing that Marxism has equated work with thought, physical labor, and even man himself, Ricoeur remarks that "a notion that signifies everything no longer signifies anything."[17] In other words, Garaudy has made the term *labor* so vague and all-inclusive that it is possible to prove virtually anything from it. The fact remains, however, that when Garaudy speaks of man creating himself in the act of labor, it is manual labor which carries the brunt of the argument. Pure thought, as Marx and Engels specifically assert in *The German Ideology,* is subordinate to physical work, since it is the latter that produces the former. And yet, asks Ricoeur, is this equation of true existence with labor not tantamount to the elimination of pure contemplation, pure thought from the human condition?

Ricoeur goes on to question Garaudy's understanding of the origins of language. If it is true that language began as a kind of imperative cry in association with some physical gesture or action, it is not altogether clear that such a cry of command can be reduced to the level of gesture, simply serving to facilitate work. This reduction of language to praxis would in the end make all culture nothing but a "long detour which starts with action and returns to action."[18] Ricoeur suggests, rather, that even at the point of origin, language moves beyond the limits of gestures; the imperative command is more than an emotional appendix to the act: it moves to control, to supervise, to transcend the act. It gives significance and meaning to gesture. In other words, there is a constant and primordial dialectic between language and labor, between word and work. It is speaking man who creates and transforms his tools. By itself, the tool is but an extension of the human body.[19] Thus even at its most primitive level, the imperative word is already a critique of labor. The essential nature of language cannot be reduced to the nature of labor. Language is not productive in the materialist sense; it is significative. Without the undergirding of thought as expressed in language, labor would indeed be nothing more than an instinctive and pre-reflexive action similar to the work of bees or ants. In making language ontologically subordinate to labor, Garaudy has attacked the very essence of what it means to be human!

*Toward a Christian Anthropology*

Although a number of contemporary theologians have dealt with the question of the future as a determining factor in the life of man, Karl Rahner has focused most concretely on the relation of human creativity to the future. Returning to the concept of the Absolute Future, and using that image to characterize the Christian faith, Rahner sees Christianity as a religion of becoming, of history, and of auto-transcendence.[20] Each situation imposes a task to be accomplished, since what "is not yet" determines the sense of what "is." Rahner even uses the terminology of Garaudy in speaking of the "project" established by man over against the future. The question he raises, however, is this: Is the project established with respect to a "categorical" future, made of "singular and distinct elements, limited in space and time, making up an eventually planned and fabricated whole whose complexity grows without limit?"[21] Or is the project grounded in and directed toward that Absolute Future which is the transcendental basis for *all* limited futures? The only real future, the only authentically human future, is the Absolute Future. The supreme task before man is to accept the challenge and the destiny of that Absolute Future.

It is the pull of the Absolute Future that beckons man to act historically in the creation of himself and his world. This is, however, more than a simple extrinsic exigency, a postulate of the spirit which drives man to create his earthly future. Rather, the Absolute Future comes to man and becomes a reality within man. The real issue is then that of the relationship between the Christian, eschatological hope and the Marxist, utopic future. Marxism provides a valuable challenge to Christianity at this point, for it impels us to consider what kind of world we propose to create. But Christianity must, in turn, criticize the tendency in Marxism to absolutize the "categorical" future of man, the tendency to see in the creativity of man only an immanent urge to transcend himself. The Absolute Future must stand over against all man's limited, finite, categorical futures, judging them in their very provisionality, while eternally calling man to reach beyond himself toward its absolute horizon. Here man is called to "prolong the work of the Creator," for

> the real act, which is not simply thought theoretically, and which consists in being open to the Absolute Future of God, cannot produce itself except in the concrete act of anticipating the concrete future to be created. . . .[22]

Thus man, for Rahner, is indeed man the creator: creator of history, and creator of himself. The world as seen from a Christian perspective is the arena for the creative activity of man; but it is more. It is a world "raised to the second power: man himself causes it to be born."[23] In this way the divine creation is accomplished through the process of historical development. Consequently, men find themselves before the possibility—even the responsibility—to turn themselves actively toward the future. And the Christian should be conscious of this new possibility which is even now coming into existence in the world. It is the Christian task to make this clear: the creation of a truly human future cannot be carried out except in making ourselves open and available to the Absolute Future of God.

## HISTORICAL INITIATIVE

The creation of a truly human future is obviously not a task to be carried out in a vacuum; rather, it is in the context of history that man's creativity is most fully realized. For the Marxist, this means that ". . . the very spirit of Marxism . . . is essentially *a methodology of historical initiative*. . . ."[24] This emphasis of Garaudy on the specifically human ability to create projects and posit ends does not in any way allow these activities to be mere products of the conditions surrounding their origins. Quite the contrary, he emphasizes that real history requires the emergence of the radically new; without this new element there would be no history at all. Thus creative human activity in history must be seen as something more and other than the simple summation of its preconditions. In fact, Garaudy credits this emphasis on the new for having freed Marxism from the metaphysical or theological claim of regarding history "from above." Such pretensions to an overarching and authoritative perspective are shattered by a Marxism which is "the awareness and the driving force for action by which man transforms things and himself, and builds his own history."[25] It is with the positing of projects and ends toward which men strive that true history begins, no longer a natural history, but that of the creation of man by himself.

But men do not act in history alone. Man is a social being, and his acts have social significance. In fact, history is not simply an account of certain great men, such as Napoleon or Julius Caesar. It is the unfolding of the drama of humanity as it constructs its future. Thus the social interrelationships of men are of central importance in any discussion of historical initiative. Garaudy would use the language of Marx's sixth thesis on Feuerbach in stating that

> since, through the accumulation of social labor, man acts as a species, and no longer as an individual, he is no longer just a fragment of nature; he becomes the ensemble of his social relations.[26]

Thus, no living creature can be conceived or imagined outside of the web of reciprocal relations upon which it depends for its existence. This is of critical significance if we are to understand Marx's view of the autonomy and freedom of man. Marx does not conceive of man in the same sense as, for example, Hegel, for whom an isolated subject was entirely responsible for the construction of its object; on the other hand, it would be erroneous to see man reduced to the simple resultant of social relations. Nowhere does Garaudy even imply that men are not the subject of history or that in Marx there is no subject who creates meaning and makes history. In fact, the relationship of man to society is on the level of contradiction between the personal life of man and the economic and social system in which he lives.[27]

History, it must be added, is not simply a meaningless movement, born out of the dialectical confrontation of the creativity of man with the restriction of his societal context. In the very act of projecting ends toward which he strives, asserts Garaudy, man gives a sense to human action, whether conscious or not. The "significations" of human conduct are not to be grasped analytically by moving from cause to effect; rather we are compelled to "understand, that is, to grasp synthetically the signification of each particular act starting from the concrete totality of the end pursued. . . ."[28] Man is indeed the source of meaning, but man within the context of history. Moreover, these significations are neither the product of the individual man, nor of some sort of transcendental subject, but rather they are the work of the whole history of man as a "species-being," "the work of the ensemble of social relations in their historical becoming."[29]

For Garaudy, man is the measure of all things, but man as a social and historical being, taken within the context of the whole of his social relationships. The significance of historical man is so great that we can even speak of a new rhythm and a new meaning for time itself. Historical time is not an empty framework into which men and events are thrust; that would be no more than a modification of nature's time, measured by mechanical and mathematical relationships. Man's time "is measured by his decisions and creations."[30] The understanding of time here is based upon a distinction similar to that of the Greek notion of *kairos* and *chronos*.[31] *Chronos*, or clocktime, is the endless and invariable succession of natural events, typified by the movement and transformations of matter. *Kairos*, on the other hand, is measured by meaning-filled events and historical initiatives. It is the time of decision. Thus, according to Garaudy, "a man's life is really 'historical' (and not biological) when it is made up of free decisions."[32] Such decisions are by no means arbitrary; they are conditioned by all previous human decisions and creations. On the other hand, as we have already indicated, this does not necessarily reduce man to a valueless link between past and future. "The present is the time of decision."[33] Man takes responsibility for the outcome of human history in the present moment, conscious of the past from which he can in no wise cut himself off, but aware of inaugurating a new beginning in his conscious acts. This dialectical interaction of the creative faculties of man with the historical givens of his actions is the essence of historical initiative.

The historical consequences of Garaudy's understanding of human creativity and initiative are well summed up in his response to Father Giulio Girardi. Speaking at the Salzburg colloquium, Father Girardi stated that Marxism, to the extent that it finds this earth enough for man, constitutes an impoverishment of humanity.[34] Garaudy responds to this critique with the statement that "Marxists are so little content with the earth that they assume the primary task of transforming it."[35] Insisting that his response is neither a play on words nor an evasion, Garaudy goes on to affirm that the development of new and more humane social, economic, and political relations is itself a basic spiritual transformation of man. It is, to use the term of Teilhard de Chardin, a step in the process of *hominization*.[36] The development of human productivity is not founded on the exploitation of man, but "to the contrary, on the blossoming in each worker of what is specifically human in him: the critical spirit and the spirit of initiative, of creation."[37] Historical initiative is only the social manifestation of the free and untrammeled creativity of man as he transcends himself toward a new and open future.

*Philosophical Origins*

Garaudy acknowledges the great debt owed by Marx to the Hegelian concept of history. Unlike all other philosophies of history, the master idea of Hegel was that men make their own history and in the process create themselves through their labor. "History is not the work of a few individuals, heroes, great men, or solitary geniuses, but of the labor of the masses."[38] But Marx went far beyond Hegelian idealism with his concept of *praxis,* of practice. Not content simply to put back on its feet the philosophy that idealism had turned upside down, Marx attacked the optical illusion of idealism itself. The apparent split between practice and thought which characterizes idealism is rooted in a rupture in the very structure of society. The fatal error of idealistic philosophy was to ground the relationships between men and objects not in social reality, but in thought itself. This led to the mistaken belief that philosophy is the "motor of the world." It was this philosophical radicalism —in reality the worst form of conservatism—that led Marx to formulate his eleventh thesis on Feuerbach: "The philosophers have only *interpreted* the world in various ways; the point, however, is to *change* it."[39]

Thus the originality of Marx was to effect the transition from the world of thought to the real world by way of practice, that is, through effective action to transform the world. The failing of speculative philosophy had been to separate consciousness and reality, thus leading to a general acceptance of the world as it is. The Marxist doctrine of praxis, on the other hand, leaves the future open for historical initiative and development precisely because it does not attempt to construct a system exterior to and abstract from reality. Marxist philosophy is immersed in the historical process itself: "it becomes coextensive with the reality of things in continuous becoming and with the practice of men in perpetual development."[40]

Idealism was not the only philosophy to fall before the Marxist criterion of praxis; Garaudy points out that all earlier forms of materialism were similarly criticized as dogmatic perversions of reality. This is abundantly clear in the *Theses on Feuerbach* with their emphasis on the active element of knowledge. Any authentic epistemology must be based on the criterion of praxis; man deals with reality by constructing hypotheses and models, and then verifying the feasibility of his artificial construction in practice. "Knowledge is a construction of 'models' and the only criterion of their value is practice."[41] This emphasis on the active role of the intellect in grasping and understanding reality is meant to offset the possible misinterpretation of the Marxist attack on idealism. All dogmatic philosophies, including both abstract idealism and abstract materialism, are subjected to the critique of praxis.

The active participation of man in the creation of his own history is transparently clear in the third thesis on Feuerbach:

> The materialist doctrine that men are products of circumstances and upbringing, and that, therefore, changed men are products of other circumstances and changed upbringing, forgets that *it is men that change circumstances.* . . .[42]

Marx goes on to state that the relationship of social change to human activity is conceivable only within the matrix of revolutionary praxis. In *The Holy Family* he states explicitly that history is no external, abstract force, but the creation of men themselves:

> It is man, the real, living man, who is the maker, the possessor, the fighter. It is not history that uses man to become real: history is simply the activity of man pursuing his end.[43]

Engels only reinforced this praxis-oriented view of history when he wrote in *The Eighteenth Brumaire of Louis Bonaparte* that "men make their own history, but they do not make it just as they please. . . ."[44] In fact, for both Marx and Engels, men have been making their own history since the invention of the tool, and in the process they have been transforming themselves. This is not intuitively evident, according to Engels, because up to now "men make their history themselves, but not as yet with a collective will or according to a collective plan. . . ."[45] This tension between the creativity of man and the conditions determined by the past arises from the dialectical interaction of the two poles of historical development, and marks the starting point for any Marxist exploration of the meaning of history.

Lenin, asserts Garaudy, followed in the footsteps of both Marx and Engels in considering historical initiative the prime virtue of a political revolutionary. Thus the fundamental criterion for the formation of party cells is the capacity for initiative, the aptitude for taking hold of the new and developing it. Garaudy insists that in this way the party illustrates in its life and actions the example of a real and working democracy.[46] Unlike formal, bourgeois democracies, real freedom does not consist solely in the right to say no, tolerance of the opposition, or majority rule; rather, freedom is found in the possibility of creation and historical initiative in all areas of life: economic, political, and cultural. In this return to the fundamentals of Marxist philosophy, we are told, Lenin laid the groundwork for an authentic methodology of historical initiative.

The Marxist concept of historical initiative is thus distinguished from both idealism and materialism by its philosophical basis in praxis. Unlike the ideological illusion, Marxist materialism represents a call to a more modest attitude, affirming the independence of reality from consciousness. Reality remains inexhaustible and irreducible to the knowledge we have of it. On the other hand, and contrary to all non-critical materialisms, dialectical materialism asserts that every man is greater than the conditions out of which he arises. Marx coupled historical science with historical initiative,

> without *sacrificing either the rational to an abstract "freedom," or human choice to the concept in which what already exists and what has already been accomplished are summed up and illuminated.[47]

### Historical Initiative and Christianity

What Garaudy identifies as historical initiative, i.e., the dialectical interaction between the historically given conditions and the creative potential of man, is far from alien to Christian thought. In fact, more than one contemporary theologian has attempted to deal with history in similar dialectical terms.[48] The relationship of Christianity and Marxism at this point is not merely superficial; in fact, the Marxist approach to history is built on Christian foundations, antecedents which Garaudy in no way denies: "We cannot, without impoverishing ourselves, forget Christianity's basic contribution: the change in man's attitude toward the world. . . ."[49] Christianity and the Judeo-Christian tradition in general stood in sharp contrast to Greco-Roman antiquity. While the Greek mind had as its highest ideal the rational mastery of the world, the biblical tradition was essentially a search for an authentically human historical initiative. These two emphases form the basis of all consequent Western humanism, and Garaudy insists that both contributions must be maintained; the two ends of the chain must be kept hold of, even if we are torn apart in the process.[50]

The ultimate consequence of the Judeo-Christian heritage, according to Garaudy, is participation in the struggle for the liberty and dignity of man. Man is not miserably and helplessly thrown into a prefabricated world; rather, he participates in its birth. "When He had created man, God rested the seventh day, since He then had someone to take charge of the rest."[51] Thus the first task of the Christian must be to discern the "signs of the times"—the signs of the presence of God in the world— and to follow where He leads. Garaudy maintains that Christians and Marxists live under the imperative of the future, and that God, for the Christian, is to be found wherever the new is coming into existence. This is a direct consequence of the Christian faith, for if man meets God only in the world; if the world is the only theater of this dialogue between God and man; if it is true that the biblical God manifests himself only in history, that is, in human actions, in man's victories and defeats, his exiles or his revolutions; if the Word of God is always an act; and if God calls men through events of social change —can one not then say that God is wherever something new is in the process of being born. . . ?[52]

God is active where man reflects the images of God in his creativity: in science and technology, art and poetry, freedom movements and social revolutions, and in every aspect of life. This is by no means an abstract, theoretical concept; it concerns Christian action in an immediate, concrete, and practical sense. The Christian is one who is oriented toward the new future of God. To the extent that he opens himself to the "not-yet" and cooperates in its birth, he is faithful to the biblical tradition; to the extent that he closes himself to this new reality, flees from change, and tries to hide in a static, unchanging universe, he has betrayed the essential Christian mission.

This is the point at which Christians must accept the Marxist critique of their traditional response to the challenge of history. Marx demonstrated the disastrous influence on Christian social practice of the doctrine of the immutability of God.[53] A basically static theological stance is no longer a live option today, and if Marxists can teach Christians the essential character of historical change, we will have learned a great deal indeed. Hence, a future-directed theology, such as Karl Rahner, Jürgen Moltmann, and Johannes Metz suggest, is not only a healthy response to the Marxist critique, but represents in itself a return to a more authentic expression of the Judeo-Christian tradition. Rahner insists that the world is not only the creation of God, but a task, "the action and objectification of man himself, as a world made and to be made, projected by man toward the future, a world of which man himself is a part as he acts on himself."[54] But is this radical-sounding position not really the rediscovery of a truth as old as Abraham? Is not the entire Bible a record of God's continually new and unexpected action in history, and man's attempt to respond faithfully to it? The modern epigram "Exodus Church" is in its very language a return to an earlier conception of the people of God as a community continually on the march, a community led toward the future of God which stands always beyond and beckoning.[55]

Garaudy uses much of the language of theologians like Rahner, Moltmann, and Metz. He sees transcendence as the possibility of an absolutely new beginning for human life, and the Christian "myth" as a call for man to exercise his power of historical initiative. Speaking at Salzburg, Metz responded to Garaudy's use of the term *historical initiative* by asking if Christianity has not always been such a theory of historical initiative or, rather, a theory of historical initiatives for the transformation of the world in accordance with biblical promise. Expanding on this idea, Metz suggested that

> it was precisely the biblical message that made us recognize the "world" as a history, that for the first time made us recognize the world as the space offered to human initiative.[56]

The world is itself in movement toward the new future of God, and men must take responsibility for its transformation.

Metz is not the only theologian to have responded affirmatively to the Marxist challenge. Carl Braaten has also warned against a concept of the Kingdom of God which is reduced to a symbol of eternal life beyond history. The Kingdom of God is an active dynamic *in* history manifesting itself in political and social issues, in the struggle for peace, justice, and freedom.[57] For Braaten, then, as for Rahner and Metz, "the category of the future provides the basic perspective for all theological and ethical reflection."[58] Here the Marxist critique is taken with utter seriousness. Only an ethic driven by hope in the Absolute Future can really change the world, can really alter the course of history. A theology of historical initiatives, offering a valid option to Marxism, is only possible through faith in the God of the future who says, "Behold, I make all things new."

Such a faith requires at the same time, however, that we ask if Garaudy's dependence on dialectical materialism has not devalued the role of the human spirit in historical initiative. The experiences of freedom and creation arise from the spiritual depths of mankind; they are the true meaning of the Christian claim that man is created in the image of God. If God is essentially futurity, this means that man, as his image, is a creature fundamentally oriented toward the future in faith and hope. Thus, openness to God means openness to the not-yet, it means spontaneity, creativity, and freedom. These qualities do not emerge with the creative spirit of man; rather, that creative spirit is itself a gift of the Absolute Future who *comes* to man and calls him toward a future which is even now coming into being. Garaudy insists that history does not give meaning to man, but rather man gives meaning to history. Perhaps it would be better to say that man finds meaning and significance in response to the call of God in history, and on the basis of this experience he can begin to construct a new and more human future.

## CREATIVITY AND AESTHETICS

It has been stated that the purpose of human creativity is the transformation of man. As a form of human labor, indeed the highest form, art participates in this process of transformation. Thus art is really much more than "mere aesthetics"; it is a teaching device by which man learns this specifically human act of creation "thanks to which he overcomes by creative work and historical initiative his own definition, his past, his constraints, his alienations."[59] Such a learning process is possible only because aesthetics is basically and intrinsically the recognition and appropriation of the new. A truly significant work of art will, because of this essential future orientation, pose the question of final ends. To use the terminology of Paul Tillich, it will point beyond itself to an "Ultimate Concern." To be sure, Garaudy would accept such terminology only insofar as "Ultimate Concern" refers to the immanent transcendence of man over himself. Nevertheless, there are important points of convergence in the aesthetics of Garaudy and Tillich, to which we shall presently return.

On the basis of this understanding of art, Garaudy goes on to assert that aesthetic education is perfectly complementary to the technological civilization in which we find ourselves. This complementarity is not taken in the sense of an escape from modern society, but as an essential component of it. Here Garaudy appropriates a view of the critical function of art similar to that of Marcuse and Tillich. This perspective sees art as a "translating medium" enabling man to become aware of the interaction between himself and his social environment, an interaction otherwise unrecognized.[60] Marcuse has described the "irrational" character of "rationality" in modern, industrial societies.[61] When the intrinsically irrational ideas of unlimited production and consumption, a military-dominated economy, and the potential destruction of the race are accepted by the majority as rational, then art must supply what

Whitehead termed the "element of determinate negation" within society. Art creates another universe of thought and practice over against the existing one. "The more blatantly irrational the society becomes, the greater the rationality of the artistic universe."[62] Garaudy acknowledges this contribution from Marcuse, suggesting that the criterion of openness in a society rests on whether it can accept the rupture with reality by which art maintains the tension between actuality and possibility.[63] This ability to stand "alongside of reality and criticize it is the transcendent element of human creativity. Man does not simply accept a foreordained and given reality; he creates a radically new reality through labor, historical initiative, and art.

The critical and educative functions of aesthetics are amply described by Garaudy. Art renders the absent present, it makes the invisible visible. Art is in essence not an escape from reality (at least not when it is true to itself) but rather "that which makes present alienations more intolerable through consciousness of alienation. . . .[64] The highest form of art is that which constitutes a call to man to go beyond himself; it is the negation of present reality and the anticipation of possible reality, the incessant call to transcendence. Thus every great work of art bears witness to a creative act transcending the given situation and summoning us to be other than what we are.

This understanding of the critical and anticipatory character of art closely resembles the aesthetics of Paul Tillich. Art, for Tillich, is prophetic insofar as it equips us to participate in a level of reality otherwise beyond our reach. Consequently, the artist is always calling people to a clearer understanding of reality. Tillich's "Protestant Principle," for example, represents a critique of all cultural forms;[65] it searches for the Ultimate Concern expressed within limited artistic styles. For Tillich this Ultimate Concern is communicated to us today most effectively through modern painting.

> The disruptedness of expressionism, surrealism, and all the other recent forms of styles, such as cubism and futurism, is really nothing else than an attempt to look into the depths of reality. . . . It is the attempt to see elements of reality as the fundamental powers of being out of which reality is constructed.[66]

The resemblance between this profound artistic insight and the aesthetics of Garaudy is more than superficial. Both thinkers see that reality is often not what it appears; both recognize the capacity of art to penetrate beneath the veneer of the real, to plumb the depths of the human experience. But at this point a divergence appears.

For Garaudy, art has both a critical, negative function and a positive, constructive function. In fact, the two are complementary; the negative aspect acts as a challenge to the creative self-transcendence of man, of which the positive aspect is an expression. Thus while art makes us aware of the intolerable alienations of our existence, it also gives birth to "the unforgettable hopes which it is able to sustain."[67] This second function—by far the most important for Garaudy—is a direct result of Marxist Promethean humanism. "Such might be the role of aesthetic education for the formation of the new man who must be taught to be born. . . ."[68]

Such a positive interpretation of the constructive possibilities of art is at direct variance with Tillichian aesthetics. Tillich's existential stance, as well as his Christian understanding of the role of sin in human affairs, prohibits him from accepting such a Promethean theory of art. Although Tillich readily admits the critical element in all true art, he is skeptical of the possibility of giving an answer to the questions raised by aesthetic perception. This was not necessarily always so. The combination of a religious style of painting with a specifically religious content is capable of responding to the existential question of existence.[69] Matthias Grünewald's Gothic "Crucifixion" from the Isenheim altarpiece is perhaps a supreme example of this kind of art. However, Tillich is pessimistic about the possibilities of such a response being formulated by today's art. He believes that contemporary art must confine itself to a purely critical function for modern man.

The consequences of Garaudy's Promethean aesthetics and the subsequent divergence with Tillich are readily discernible in the respective analyses of Picasso undertaken by the two men. It is not accidental that both philosophers see the ultimate artistic expression of the twentieth century in Picasso's "Guernica." For Tillich, "Guernica" is the epitome of the Protestant Principle in art. He points out that Picasso painted this horror—the fragments of reality, men and animals and unorganic pieces of houses all together—in such a way that the fragmentary character of our existence is frighteningly visible. It shows the human situation without any deception: the disruptedness, anguish, emptiness, and meaninglessness of modern existence. It is not, of course, the final word, since it is not an affirmative work of art. It raises the question of human alienation, but gives no answer.

Garaudy only partially agrees with Tillich. The human situation in all its misery is only one pole of the internal dialectic in Picasso. Art is indivisibly both reflection on the human predicament and creation of a new reality. The secret for Garaudy's understanding of Picasso is found in the artist's 1945 statement that "the 'against' comes before the 'for.' "[70] This is taken to be the statement of the dialectical law of all artistic expression, including Picasso's.

The precipitating event behind "Guernica" was the outbreak of the Spanish Civil War and the destruction of the Basque village for which the painting is named. The painting was thus a response to the agony of a specific historical and political situation. "Once again the 'against' came before the 'for.' "[71] With this brief introductory remark, Garaudy has already affirmed his understanding of "Guernica." Unlike Tillich, he does not see it as a purely negative insight into the depths of alienation, but as carrying within itself the seeds of a new historical initiative. The painting is mythic. Its meaning is not external, reductible to logical explanation. The color is uniformly grim, the lines convey terror or anger. But then the startling interpretation: "The work is indivisibly a verdict and the cry of man, *he who will conquer.*"[72] Garaudy sees the work as a call to human responsibility, expressing an unquenchable confidence in the ultimate victory of man. Whence comes this confidence? Based upon Picasso's adherence to the Communist party, his frequent declarations of the creative role of art, and the very nature of cubism itself, Garaudy has chosen to see in "Guernica," as in all of the work of Picasso, the progress of human hope. "He knew how to make the dream serve the future and how to put the mythic power of the gods in the hands, the vision, and the heart of man."[73] This remains the goal of all Marxist endeavor, whether in art, science, or politics: to give to man the ultimate authority and power over his own destiny and future.

NOTES

1. ATD, p. 70.

2. MTC, p. 166.

3. MTC, p. 172.

4. Roger Garaudy, MCES, p. 69.

5. See HCHM, pp. 25–27 for a discussion of this distinction.

6. HCHM, p. 26.

7. QMM, p. 103.

8. MTC, pp. 177–178.

9. See Lewis Mumford, *The Condition of Man* (New York: Harcourt, Brace & World, 1944), esp. chap. IX, "The Progress of Prometheus," pp. 301–342.

10. Ibid., p. 303.

11. Cf. Marcuse, *One Dimensional Man*. Garaudy has also noted the failure of contemporary socialism, although he does not follow Marcuse in condemning technological society *per se*. Cf. e.g., GPG, pp. 44–47: *"Le socialisme perverti,"* and RE, pp. 9–35: *"Le socialisme n'est pas cela!"*

12. Cf. Marx and Engels, *The German Ideology,* in Feuer, p. 288. "Men are producers of their conceptions, ideas, etc.—real, active men, as they are conditioned by a definite development of their productive forces and of the intercourse corresponding to these, up to its furthest forms." Helmut Gollwitzer has noted that this position corresponds to that of the nominalists in the medieval debate over universals. "But it must be noted that the production of these conceptions was no arbitrary process either . . . the history of these conceptions is the history of the conditions which produced them and are reflected in them" ("The Marxist Critique," p. 9).

13. QMM, p. 103.

14. Lewis Mumford, *The Myth of the Machine* (New York: Harcourt, Brace & World, 1967), esp. "Prologue," pp. 3–13.

15. Ibid., p. 5.

16. QMM, p. 104. The birth of language through the primitive cry of command is the theory of Pierre Janet. Cf. Paul Ricoeur, *History and Truth,* trans. C. A. Kelbley (Evanston, Ill.: Northwestern University Press, 1965), p. 200.

17. Paul Ricoeur, *History and Truth,* p. 198.

18. Ibid., p. 200.

19. This is the basic idea behind Marshall McLuhan's *Understanding Media* (New York: McGraw-Hill, 1964). He states, e.g., that "any extension whether of skin, hand, or foot, affects the whole psychic and social complex," Introduction, p. 4. The only way to control these extensions and prevent their destructive and unconscious action on the human psyche is to *understand* the process of extension. Understanding presupposes thought and language, thus confirming Ricoeur's thesis in an unexpected way.

20. Cf. Karl Rahner, MCES, pp. 221–235.

21. Karl Rahner, MCES, p. 223, n. 8.

22. Karl Rahner, "Humanisme chrétien," p. 64.

23. Karl Rahner, "La 'nouvelle terre,' " p. 113.

24. ATD, p. 73.

25. MTC, p. 38.

26. HM, p. 98. Cf. *Theses on Feuerbach VI,* in Feuer, p. 285.

27. The confusion on this point is a consequence of the Marxist dialectical understanding of freedom and necessity, which has frequently devolved into its second term (cf. Chapter Four). E.g., Roger Garaudy, "L'homme révélé," in *Réforme,* no. 1394 (4 December 1971), p. 10: "This equivocation has weighed heavily on the development of Marxism which has sometimes juxtaposed voluntarism and a positivist interpretation of the Hegelian formula: freedom is the consciousness of necessity, and sometimes oscillated between the two."

28. QMM, p. 107. Moltmann observes that for Marx the theoretical meaning of history is recognized "to the extent that men make themselves ready to perceive this significance practically. . . ." This means that "the makability of history itself becomes the goal of the making of history," and we find ourselves in an infinite regress. Jürgen Moltmann, "Hoping and Planning," in *Crosscurrents,* vol. 18, no. 3 (summer 1968), p. 58.

29. QMM, p. 108.

30. MTC, p. 194.

31. Cf. the parallel discussion in Paul Tillich, *Systematic Theology,* vol. 3 (Chicago: University of Chicago Press, 1951), pp. 369–372. Referring to *kairos,* he says: "Its original meaning—the right time, the time in which something can be done—must be contrasted with *chronos,* measured or clock time. The former is qualitative, the latter quantitative" (p. 369).

32. MTC, p. 195.

33. MTC, p. 194.

34. Jules Girardi, MCES, p. 54.

35. ATD, p. 93.

36. See Pierre Teilhard de Chardin, *The Phenomenon of Man,* trans. B. Wall (New York: Harper & Row, 1959), esp. pp. 163–189.

37. QMM, p. 110.

38. DEM, p. 371.

39. Feuer, p. 286.

40. HM, p. 83.

41. MTC, p. 41.

42. Feuer, p. 284.

43. *The Holy Family,* quoted by Roger Garaudy in MTC, pp. 149–150.

44. Feuer, p. 360.

45. "Letter to Heinz Starkenburg," dated 25 January 1894, in Selsam and Martel, p. 203.

46. PMFS, p. 20.

47. MTC, p. 200.

48. Leslie Dewart, for example, asserts that a true responsibility for history requires two postulates: "the absolutely radical freedom of the history that we create," and the apparently contradictory belief that "man is not the only creator." (Leslie Dewart et al, *Initiative in History: A Christian-Marxist Exchange* (Cambridge, Mass.: Harvard University Press, 1967), p. 7.) There remains a significant difference between Dewart and Garaudy, however, since the former limits the creativity of man less by historical and natural preconditions than by the creative power of God. This dialectical interaction is necessary, according to Dewart, to do justice to the human reality itself which, if it were the only creative power, would be unable to overcome the intransigence of history, i.e., evil.

49. ATD, p. 112.

50. Cf. Paul Lehmann, "Discussion: Communist-Christian Dialogue," in *Union Seminary Quarterly Review,* vol. 22, no. 3 (March 1967), pp. 205–212. In response to Garaudy's presentation, Lehmann asserts his willingness to accept Garaudy's identification of the two demands of humanism in the Western tradition, and the necessity of holding onto both ends of the chain.

51. QMM, p. 61.

52. PMFS, p. 366.

53. See Lehmann, "Discussion," p. 222, for further amplification of this point.

54. Karl Rahner, "Théologie pratique et tâches sociales," in *Ecrits théologiques* 10 (Paris: Desclée de Brouwer/Mame, 1970), p. 76.

55. Cf. the chapter "Exodus Church," pp. 304–338, in Moltmann, *Theology of Hope.*

56. Johannes Metz, MCES, p. 133.

57. See Braaten, *The Future of God,* p. 106.

58. Braaten, "Toward a Theology of Hope," p. 106.

59. GPG, p. 197. See also the discussion of aesthetic education in GPG, pp. 197–207.

60. Not only is this interaction unrecognized, but Marshall McLuhan has suggested that technology has an explicit numbing effect on man which conceals the "auto-amputation" of the extension effected through media. The results are disastrous, says McLuhan, since if we are not aware of this "numbing," we cannot understand what is happening, and if we do not understand, it is the technology that controls man, and not man the technology. *Understanding Media,* pp. 41–47.

61. See e.g., Marcuse, *One Dimensional Man,* pp. 225 ff.

62. Ibid., p. 239.

63. Cf. GPG, p. 204.

64. GPG, p. 205.

65. Cf. Paul Tillich, "The Protestant Principle and the Proletarian Situation," in *The Protestant Era* (Chicago: University of Chicago Press, 1963), pp. 161–181. Cf. esp. p. 163: "The Protestant Principle is the judge of every religious and cultural reality, including the religion and culture which calls itself 'Protestant.' "

66. Paul Tillich, "Existentialist Aspects of Modern Art," in *Christianity and the Existentialists*, ed. C. Michaelson (New York: Charles Scribner's Sons, 1956), p. 137.

67. GPG, p. 205.

68. GPG, p. 207.

69. Tillich, "Existentialist Aspects," pp. 143–144.

70. RSR, p. 27.

71. RSR, p. 84.

72. RSR, p. 86 (italics mine).

73. RSR, p. 113.

# FOUR

# Freedom and Dialectical Materialism

## FREEDOM AND MATERIALISM

Having examined Roger Garaudy's concept of transcendence and its practical application in the realm of creativity and historical initiative, we must now confront what is without doubt the central problem for any theory that claims to be Marxist. Garaudy himself recognizes this as "the heart of the problem, the problem of freedom. . . ."[1] For the repeated assertions by Marx and Engels that the laws of historical development are "necessary" and inflexible seem to contradict the very basis of a free and open future. Garaudy deals with the problem by redefining freedom as more than the simple disengagement of an individual from his own past or simple indeterminate choice. Rather, he views freedom as a "going beyond," a "transcendence" of the historical situation. It is a majestic and necessary "supersession" of the objective world order, "the creative participation of the militant revolutionary in the dialectic of historical necessity."[2] This dialectical overcoming of the tension of freedom and necessity through the idea of human autonomy has been a powerful chord in the history of Western humanism since Kant and Fichte. In order to understand Garaudy's solution to the problematic of freedom, we must now turn to this humanist heritage as it was received and adapted by Marx and Engels.

### The Concept of Autonomy in Kant and Fichte

Garaudy sees the entire humanist tradition in the West resting on the twin foundations of Greco-Roman and Judeo-Christian antiquity. From these two ancient traditions came the essential requirements of humanism: "the demand for a rational mastery of the world, and that for a specifically human historical initiative."[3] Although these dual emphases have interacted with each other throughout the history of Western thought, it was not until Kant and Fichte that any real attempt at synthesis was made. The key concept of autonomy provided the basis for the effort, incorporating

> the necessity of the rational law, without which there is no science and no world, and the freedom of man's creative act, without which there is no moral initiative and responsibility and no history.[4]

The attempt of Kant and Fichte was destined to failure, and the long sought for synthesis was never completed. Kant tried without success, Garaudy believes, to unify reason and freedom, pure and practical reason. Nevertheless, the struggle to hold on to "both ends of the chain" remained a driving force in Western humanism.

Garaudy finds the concept of human autonomy to be Kant's most original contribution, especially as it applies to ethics.[5] For Kant, moral judgments do not stem from forces and principles exterior to man, whether nature or God. To claim any such moral law, says Garaudy, is to "subject man to an external law and, consequently, to deprive him of his autonomy, of his responsibility."[6] Ultimately this would eliminate all possibility of true moral judgment or action. A natural moral law would reduce all moral decisions to judgments of fact; a morality dictated by God would equally remove the possibility of making value judgments, since we would be faced with the simple choice between obedience or rebellion. Thus, Kant's concern for the authenticity of human autonomy forces him to reject all such heteronomies, whether divine or natural. At the heart of the Kantian critique is the affirmation of a profound humanism: man is the measure of all things.

Garaudy has correctly perceived the importance of autonomy in Kantian thought. Autonomy, for Kant, was closely tied to his understanding of enlightenment (*Aufklärung*). The latter was defined in the eighteenth century as the conquest of man's immaturity through the free use of reason. Since immaturity is that lack of character and personal courage which allows another to guide one's reasoning, the free use of reason is the essence of enlightenment. It is also a good way of describing autonomy. Kant wanted to remove the security that people experience under the guidance of others. Security contradicts the true nature of man; it contradicts his autonomy. Thus far Garaudy has correctly interpreted Kant. But the assertion that moral law reduces all judgments to factual decisions, or that the law of God faces us with a simple choice between obedience or rebellion, is to overlook the tremendously complex nature of moral decisions. The preexistence of moral truth does not obviate the necessity to make moral judgments, since real decisions cannot be separated from the ambiguities intrinsic in every situation. This is no less true of revealed moral law. Luther's discussion of the Ten Commandments in the Large Catechism amply demonstrates the far-reaching consequences of Christian morality. The choice between obedience and rebellion is never simple. Finally, it might be noted that Kant himself did not rule out the existence of moral law, the "categorical imperative," but related that law to man's autonomy itself.

Kant's emphasis on human autonomy is blunted, continues Garaudy, by a certain idealist tendency to view man in abstraction. In place of real, concrete, and total man, Kant introduces what Garaudy refers to as a "theological" conception of man: "a double man, cut in two: reason and feeling, nature and spirit."[7] The activity of the subject is reduced to formal thought.[8] Here Marxism is credited with enriching the Kantian conception of human activity with the totality of concrete and living praxis. But there is a second sense in which Kant falls victim to an abstract conception of man. Garaudy sees throughout the Kantian critique a certain confusion of objective reality with the knowledge we have of it. The truth in Kantian epistemology "that experience is the result of reciprocal action between subject and object" leads easily to the idealist perversion "that there is no object without a subject."[9] In actuality, the activity of man is responsible for the elaboration of our understanding of reality, but not for the elaboration of reality itself.

Kant escaped from the idealist trap of making external reality dependent on our subjective activity, but at a high price. The essence of the external phenomenon, the noumenal behind the phenomenal as it were, was the *Ding an sich*, the thing-in-itself; but this thing-in-itself is totally beyond human knowing. Engels, referring to the neo-Kantian school, summed up the problem this way: "We may correctly perceive the qualities of a thing, but we cannot by any sensible or mental process grasp the thing-in-itself."[10] One cannot break through the veil of the phenomenal to the noumenal hidden behind. This, of course, is but a declaration of human finitude: reality transcends our sensible and rational attempts to comprehend it totally. But to a materialist such as Garaudy, the thing-in-itself appears as something fantastic, beyond all knowledge, and irreducible to natural law.

This being said, one can understand Garaudy's high regard for Fichte who, believing that he had found the weakness in Kant's position, declared boldly that "the 'thing-in-itself' is an arbitrary and superfluous abstraction."[11] An early forerunner of existentialism, Fichte rejected all externally imposed limits and authority in his defense of human autonomy. He made freedom the cornerstone of his philosophical system, affirming the right of free men to refuse any law other than that given by oneself. Such an affirmation, says Garaudy, was a direct consequence of his central concept of human creativity. Although idealist and metaphysical, Fichte's idea of human existence is not something *given*, but something which must be *made*. The relationship between existence and essence is dialectical: "To exist, for Fichte, is to act, to create."[12]

Fichte's free subject, the "ego," follows immediately from this idea of freedom. The ego is not a given, not a ready-made, preexistent entity, but rather an act: "the active subject who virtually carries within himself the law of reason."[13] This acting subject is continually going beyond itself, transcending itself. It is always a projection into the future: "What I have been and what I am only assumes its full meaning in the light of what I am about to be." Such a concept of the ego goes beyond the Kantian idea of practical reason. For Kant the field of practical reason was the place of interaction between the duty discovered in the depths of consciousness and external reality. For Fichte, "practical reason . . . includes all the creative activity of man." Practice is basically historical, since history is the movement of the individual toward the universally human, the raising of the finite to the infinite, the transformation of necessity into freedom.

Thus Garaudy finds in Fichte (in an abstract and metaphysical form) both the idea of the unity of theory and practice, and that of freedom as conscious necessity. Such an epistemology signifies the end of a "thing-in-itself" forming an absolute limit to the knowledge and activity of man. "The absolute which Kant posited outside the human world is now identified with the movement of history, with the march of progress, with the effort that undermines all limitations from within."

In the final analysis, praxis, for Fichte, is the involvement of the whole man in a collective effort to make history, transform nature, and construct society.

Fichte's argument spelled the doom of the Kantian *Ding an sich*, asserts Garaudy, at the same time that it opened the way for a new, materialist understanding of the "real." Marxist materialism defines reality as "what exists outside of us and whose action on us produces our sensations."[14] Thus the "thing-in-itself" is, for Garaudy, by no means metaphysical or mysterious. It is simply the representation of matter given by science at the present stage of its development, subject to revision if the current model should prove unworkable.[15] Physical properties are manifested by the relationships between individual entities, but these relationships are in no wise determinative of the properties themselves, which exist outside us and independently of us. Marxism is a call to distinguish between matter such as it is outside of all intervention by the subject, and the phenomenon elicited by the active relationship of subject and object.

By now it should be clear that Garaudy's concern for the radical autonomy of man in the face of all metaphysical and theological heteronomies hearkens back to his development of a Marxist concept of transcendence. The same criticism must be raised now that was made at that time. Why does the presence of a truly transcendent concept of God—as, for example, the power of the Absolute Future—necessarily conflict with human autonomy? Paul Tillich has suggested that, contrary to suppressing human responsibility, a truly transcendent revelation liberates man by reconciling the conflict between autonomy and heteronomy in a new "theonomy."[16] Certainly, in suggesting a third option beyond either autonomy or heteronomy, Tillich is not using these terms in the same way as Garaudy; but it is possible that the dialectical interrelationship of autonomy and heteronomy in theonomy may present a more realistic analysis of the human situation. Further comment on this particular problem will be reserved for our discussion of freedom and necessity, where the significance of Tillich's work will more easily be seen.

Interestingly enough, Garaudy himself raises several problems of consequence for any Marxist theory of human freedom: the idea (implied by Marx in the sixth thesis on Feuerbach) that man is essentially the sum of his social relations, and the whole question of human responsibility in a materialistic philosophy. It is to these problems that we now turn our attention.

### Problems

Modern anthropology emphasizes that man as an isolated individual is an abstraction and pure fiction. In reality, man is what he is only in the context of a network of social and political relations that he shares with his fellows.[17] Marx was one of the earliest to note this interrelationship:

> Feuerbach resolves the religious essence into the *human* essence. But the human essence is no abstraction inherent in each single individual. In its reality it is the ensemble of the social relations.[18]

It is not possible to conceive of a being that exists outside of this network of reciprocal interactions which bind it to all other beings. This, in fact, poses an essential problem for Marxist humanism: the problem of subjectivity and of man's relations with other men and with the world.

Garaudy, however, is quick to point out that man's social context must not be viewed in a mechanistic way, as if the individual were only a mathematical resultant or product. It would be mistaken to interpret Marx as saying that man does not really exist, that what exists is a sum of social relations. Human freedom, from the Marxist perspective, emerges from the very *contradiction* between the personal life of the individual and the socioeconomic system which tends to dehumanize him. "The individual is not only a resultant, a knot of relations; by becoming conscious of the necessary or accidental relationships which constitute him, he has access to freedom. . . ."[19]

Freedom, then, is not simply an illusory independence from man's social relations; rather, it is the knowledge that, in changing the nexus of relationships, man possesses the power to change himself. This in no way denies the reality of the subject, any more than the affirmation that we know objective reality only through our dialectical interactions with it denies the reality of the object. Freedom is neither the simple mechanical resultant of complex social relations, nor the reflection of these relations in the mind of the individual. Rather, freedom is "a 'creation' that is qualitatively different from these social relations and the consciousness we have of them. . . ."[20] A dialectical resultant is not the same as a mechanical resultant, nor is the synthesis of social relations a simple addition. The reciprocal interaction between the individual and society, far from impoverishing man, is really the source of his fulfillment. The master idea of Marx here is "that man is not a passive product of the milieu, but an active and acting force which transforms the social milieu and nature in the course of revolutionary practice. . . ."[21]

The social nature of man is not the only difficulty with the Marxist understanding of freedom. For, contrary to all idealist philosophies, Marxism begins by affirming a basic unity of man and nature. Man is a part of nature, made of the same stuff as the rest of the material universe. He must maintain a constant relationship with it or, like astronauts lost in space, he will die. To speak of man as Lord of creation is highly equivocal, since his lordship is conditioned by the very nature over which he rules.

Such a materialist position leads Garaudy to formulate a definition of man which not only appears cold and mechanical, but seems to violate any possibility of real freedom:

> From a purely phenomenological point of view, we simply state that when the central nervous system reaches a certain degree of complexity, around 14 billion cortical neurons, we are dealing with a conscious being, with "homo sapiens," with man.[22]

Perhaps the most remarkable part of this affirmation is that it bears more than a slight resemblance to the so-called Law of Complexity and Consciousness suggested by Teilhard de Chardin in his epic work *The Phenomenon of Man*. Such similarities are not really surprising, however, if we remember that Garaudy often expresses deep admiration for the Jesuit thinker, and in fact draws many of his ideas directly from him.

Building on this definition (a striking illustration of Marx's law of quantity and quality),[23] Garaudy goes on to say that "reflection presents specific forms in different bodies and at diverse stages in their development."[24] Thus the further one descends toward inferior and simpler forms of matter, the more reflection is identified with exterior and mechanical action. On the other hand, the more complex a living structure, the higher the level of internalization, giving the being more and more the appearance of arbitrary action. This process reaches its maximum with the advent of man, the creature in whom evolution becomes conscious of itself.

The similarity between this line of reasoning and the thought of Teilhard de Chardin is immediately evident from the following quotation from *The Phenomenon of Man*: "The degree of concentration of a consciousness varies in inverse ratio to the *simplicity* of the material compound lined by it."[25] Here the resemblance ends, however, for Garaudy goes on to add that such a qualitative change in nature as in the appearance of man in no way implies some sort of transcendence. Where Teilhard de Chardin sees a "spiritual energy" tangential to the physical, Garaudy sees only "the ultimate flowering of the material."[26] At the same time, though, the Marxist thinker is careful to avoid a mechanical determinism that would rob the qualitative change in man of its uniqueness. While it remains true that the appearance of man is but "a moment in the universal development of nature," at the same time "his birth marked a new stage and a rebounding of evolution on itself."[27]

It is this rebounding of evolution on itself (also a Teilhardian figure of speech) that makes it possible for Garaudy to speak of a dialectical materialism. After having acknowledged the evidence of science that inanimate matter preceded life, and life preceded consciousness, he continues by affirming the "fundamental truth" that consciousness, once it has appeared, "becomes one of the decisive forces in the transformation of the world and of man himself."[28] Thus consciousness reacts against the material conditions of its existence, producing a qualitative distinction between biological evolution and human history. The difference is summed up in the development of culture, which is nothing less than "the power conquered by man to totalize and universalize former practice."[29] The process of "culturization" is an act of self-transformation and self-transcendence; it gives rise to an ever faster rhythm of historical development which in turn accelerates the auto-creation of man. No other conclusion is possible, claims Garaudy, without a total rejection of all that science has to teach us.

Freedom, then, is not a spiritual or psychological state, but the possibility of participating in the creation of the world and, hence, in the creation of man. This is far removed from the existentialist posture that sees man as the being in which nothing comes into the world. That way leads only to agnosticism and impotence. Man has a grip on reality because he is rooted and grounded in the real. Both consciousness and volition exist prior to man and without him! "Thought and freedom are the ultimate forms or stages of that 'reflection' which already exists in things under the most limited forms of reciprocal action."[30] But with the appearance of man the rhythm of development moves at an incredibly faster pace than in nature alone. This is partly because the field of human thought brings together a vast number of relations and interactions (thus increasing the possibilities for future development), and partly because human action is intentional, cooperative, and creative. It is human praxis that is the ultimate basis of all freedom.

Thus we see that Marxist materialism is asserted to be a true awakening to responsibility. It begins with the realization that there is no Hegelian "Spirit" in matter, and that consciousness is simply a certain state of molecular complexity, a product of natural evolution. But the appearance of man marks the start of a totally new phenomenon: human consciousness, spirit, freedom. Man becomes responsible for his own continued evolution and participates in his own creation. He ceases to be simply a biological phenomenon and becomes truly historical when he takes responsibility for the future. This is more than a concept of history. Because it incorporates man's creative practice into a methodology of historical initiative, "this conception of the world is a moment in the liberation of man."[31]

### DIALECTICS: FREEDOM AND NECESSITY

The introduction of the term *dialectical* into our analysis of Garaudy's thought indeed complicates the entire discussion. For this is, in fact, the key distinction between Marxism and all former types of materialism; to say that we are dealing with a dialectical materialism is to emphasize that "every man is other than and more than the resultant of the conditions which produced him."[32] Herein lies the secret of how Marx could construct a methodology of historical initiative based on a materialist concept of reality. If the future were rigidly determined by the past, we could dispense with history and simply go about calculating what action must be performed to bring about the desired social change. But Marx's real contribution is

> that he pinpointed the coupling of historical science and historical initiative, without sacrificing either the rational to an abstract "freedom"

or human choice to the concept in which what already exists and what has already been accomplished are summed up and illuminated.[33]

Thus, the frequently repeated assertion that men make their history only within the context of conditions received from the past is the expression linking dialectically the two poles of historical development: freedom and necessity.

But the existence of such a dialectic of history is only the logical consequence of a much broader concept of the dialectic. Not only history, but human thought, even reality itself, are dialectical. The awareness of the dialectical character of reality first becomes apparent to man through the process of thought, as was demonstrated by Kant; but it is by no means a purely abstract category of the mind. Kant was one of the first to note the existence of a "dialectical reason," by which he meant the contradiction between two ideas (such as freedom and necessity), a process taking place exclusively within the subject. Dialectical reason was the specifically speculative, non-experimental, and non-scientific use of reason.

Garaudy criticizes this conception of dialectical reason, preferring to locate the dialectic not within the abstract subject, but in the relationship of subject to object. Referring to the work of Henri Wallon, he suggests that "dialectic begins with this 'splitting of the one' by which . . . thought creates a first cleavage between the world of immediate appearance and that of underlying reality. . . ."[34] This first contradiction was, in the development of human thought, conceived in the form of myth. However, it is possible to go even further than the simple assertion of a dialectical relationship of man to nature. A second stage of the dialectic arises "when thought, abandoning the transcendent illusions of myth, recognizes that it is no more than a hypothesis. . . ." The consequence of this realization is the use of praxis to verify all conceptions of reality. Models of reality which do not stand up under the test of practice must be revised or discarded. Thus we see that "contradiction and totality are . . . two inseparable moments in this dialectic of knowledge. . . ." Dialectical reason moves from one totalization to another, always testing the current provisional conception by the criterion of practice.

Garaudy then deduces certain characteristics of dialectical reason distinguishing it from more traditional forms of reason.[35] These characteristics are four in number: (1) Unlike earlier forms of logic, built on formal and immutable laws, dialectical reason is always in the process of formation, never completed. (2) Dialectical reason depends on the interaction between ever newly formulated questions and answers. (3) For dialectical logic, "reason is not a transcendent order but the continued creation of a human order." In other words, dialectical reason brings together the elements of rationality and freedom in a creative combination at the heart of human action. (4) "Dialectical reason is an element in the rational construction of reality." Man, who is part of nature, discovers a rational correspondence between thought and reality. At one and the same time he "thinks reality and realizes his thought."

This last characteristic of dialectical reason is extremely important, for it leads us to certain conclusions about the nature of reality itself. The very fact that the human brain is capable of grasping external reality, formulating laws of nature, and finally acting effectively on the basis of those laws, is evidence of a close relationship—although not an identity—"between the concept and the 'in-itself' which it has in view."[36] In other words, "how could dialectical thought allow us to grasp a being that is in no degree dialectical?" Here we have come upon one of the most difficult, yet profound, aspects of Marxist thought: the dialectic of nature. Viewed one way, dialectical reality is reality criticizing itself (to use an expression of Ernst Bloch). It is the possibility for the radically new to emerge in the midst of reality itself, the possibility of a truly open future. Viewed from another angle, however, it is the subjection of human creativity and freedom to an endless and irresistible historical movement, the subordination of the human will to an inevitable series of painful conflicts within the production process. Garaudy has clearly opted for the first interpretation of this dialectical reality, and his defense of historical initiative and creativity hinge on this interpretation.

### The Dialectic in Hegel and Marx

When Garaudy turns to consider the origins of the concept of dialectical thought, he is bound to wrestle with the complexities of Hegel. The immense contribution of the Hegelian method and system to all later philosophy makes such a study absolutely essential. But to acknowledge the originality of Hegel does not imply a non-critical acceptance of his work; quite the contrary, the difference between Marx and Hegel signals the unique contribution of dialectical materialism. Hegel is an idealist, perhaps *the* great idealist of all time, and as such his thought remains basically theological. In the last analysis the concept is the essence of reality. The system of these concepts constitutes a whole, a totality, and the dialectic is dominated by this category of totality. Dialectics is, in essence, "the study of the laws that connect each moment to the whole (the finite to the infinite, as Hegel put it)."[37] The only recourse from the dogmatic and theological idealism implicit in Hegel is to reject completely the *system* while inverting the *method*. "For Hegel contradiction is a moment in totality; for Marx totality is a moment in contradiction."[38] To understand the real significance of this inversion we must first consider the Hegelian dialectic in its fullness.

The concept of totality dominates the Hegelian dialectic. This totality —the Absolute—develops itself through contradiction. Hegel, transposing this central concept into theological terms, presents God as the totality dying in each moment, but in each moment the death of God is at the same time his eternal life. In order to create the world, "God must die as absolute unity, he must submit himself to the law of the negative, deny himself so as to diversify and determine himself."[39] The infinite, the totality, cannot appear to finite beings except in finite form. The only true infinite is the finite in the process of going beyond itself. The Absolute, or God, thus becomes immanent in the historical process itself. The immanent presence of the totality of being in each finite being is the "source of its evolution, its death, its transcendence,"[40] and manifests itself in contradiction.

A second characteristic of the Hegelian dialectic is the identity of reason and reality; this identification explains how reality can appear transparent to reason. In effect, the Hegelian method is the process of reason finding itself and recognizing itself in all things. "Thus, for Hegel, the dialectic is the law of the movement of things at the same time as the law of the movement of thought."[41] Here there is no separation of thought and being. All of being is caught up in the dialectical movement, in whose development man constitutes but a moment. However, this participation in the unfolding of reality takes on a new character with the appearance of man: "Man prolongs, under new forms, a movement which is already, under more limited forms, the very rhythm of the becoming of things."[42] But Hegel is an objective idealist; the dialectic is not only the reproduction in thought of the unfolding of organic totality. More than simple duplication of reality, thought is actually the *source* of reality. The world is even more than the work of the spirit; it *is* spirit.

With thought defined as an objective reality, the subject of that thought accedes to pure freedom. Freedom here is the very opposite of heteronomy, whether that be the exteriority of reality or the transcendence of God. "Freedom is pure immanence, the pure welling up of Being."[43] It is identified with the infinite, since finitude corresponds to positivity. In other words, the thinking subject is no less than God thinking himself, and the process of dialectical thought is the self-realization of God in his eternal essence. Freedom is thus a process of creation; it is the creation of the world itself! It is composed of three essential moments: (1) that of abstraction and detachment from the finite, necessary for the "independence and autonomy of thought; (2) that of determination, wherein thought sets a goal or law for itself, thus negating the first moment; (3) that of speculation, which is the synthesis of the first two moments, and comports within itself the "negation of the negation."

This process of contradiction, together with the concept of totality, is the central focus of the Hegelian method. Contradiction and totality are opposed to one another as finite and infinite: "totality from the viewpoint of the infinite is contradiction from the viewpoint of the finite."[44] A finite being experiences totality as contradiction. Thus we see that contradiction is the essence of the Hegelian method, while totality comprises the key to the Hegelian system. The problem here is the relative emphasis on contradiction and totality. The criticism of Marx and Garaudy centers precisely on this emphasis. The Hegelian dialectic remains theological because "contradiction is only a moment in totality." The contradiction is actually the movement of the totality, which precedes its own becoming and will one day be all in all, thus spelling the end of the process of development. In other words, "contradiction is only the small change of totality."

It is the inversion of the order of contradiction and totality that is meant by "putting Hegel back on his feet."[45] The reversal of Hegelian idealism by Marxist materialism meant subordinating totality to contradiction. Hegel saw contradiction arising from the self-limitation of the totality of being; Marx, on the other hand, saw the generation of constantly new totalities by the development of the contradiction through negation of the negation. "It is not the universal which is first and which limits itself, but the particular which supersedes itself necessarily because it does not carry in itself its conditions of existence."[46] An immediate consequence of this revision of the dialectical method is a renewed esteem for material reality. Matter is no longer an alienation of the infinite spirit, but rather, through its internal contradictions, the very source of the dialectical process. Thought is able to understand reality not because the dialectical structure of thought imposes itself on matter, but because it *conforms* itself to the dialectical nature of reality. The dialectic, then, "is the law of development for all reality, whether it be natural, historical, or logical."[47] Consideration of the dialectical nature of reality leads us directly to our next problem.

## The Dialectic of Freedom and Necessity

Freedom, as we have seen, is considered by Garaudy to be not an essentially now-oriented choice among certain givens, but rather a future-oriented *creative act*. "Freedom is born with this possibility of projecting a number of possible acts."[48] Truly human labor, i.e., the projection of specific ends and goals, is an expression of freedom to the extent that it participates in the active creation of man by himself. In this creation the initiative of man is manifested in his projects. These projects, creations, and historical initiatives are not arbitrary; they are conditioned by all previous human activity. At the same time, however, man is not simply a link in the chain connecting past and future. It is in the present that he takes responsibility for his life, conscious of the past which influences his action, but conscious also that he initiates a new beginning in every act. Garaudy would insist, in spite of all we have said, that

> there is no web of causality so strong but that it is possible for him (man) first to fray it and then to tear it apart. . . . A man's life is really "historical" (and not biological) when it is made up of free decisions.[49]

Marx was not the originator of this paradox. The dialectic of past conditions and future possibilities is a source of tension throughout the whole history of Western humanism. Greek rationalism, through its understanding of natural order and fate, lay the groundwork for one pole in this dialectic of freedom: "that of necessity and the knowledge of necessity. The highest freedom is then understood necessity."[50] There is no real understanding of creation in this Hellenic world view. The tragedy of Oedipus' struggle against his fate, and its inexorable fulfillment through his very efforts to resist, is eloquent testimony to the Greek idea of necessity. On the other hand, the Judeo-Christian tradition has, according to Garaudy, always emphasized freedom, not as the consciousness of necessity, but as participation in the creative act. The New Testament is the announcement of this "Good News": "man can at every moment begin a new future, master the laws of nature and society."[51]

Harvey Cox has also observed the tension between the Greco-Roman and Judeo-Christian traditions. "For the Greeks, man's role as creator of meaning was not very significant. In fact man, for the Greeks, is not a creator at all."[52] The biblical tradition, on the other hand, emphasizes the cooperative action of man and God in the creation of the universe. The initial acts of God in Genesis 1 include forming, separating, and naming. It is highly significant that, with the appearance of man, it is Adam who continues this activity. The ancient Hebrew tradition states that on the seventh day of creation God rested; Garaudy has suggested an "eighth day" as the domain of man's creative activity. In actual fact, however, this eighth day is exactly what is implied by the Judeo-Christian tradition: "creation is *never* really 'complete.' The Genesis stories depict something that man and God are always doing."[53]

The problem is how to reconcile these two opposing views: that of freedom as the recognition of necessity, and that of freedom as genuine historical initiative. The Marxist response is that reconciliation is impossible; but dialectical supersession is not. Man's continued creation of himself through labor is neither wholly arbitrary nor rigidly determined.

> Man is totally responsible for becoming not what he is but what he is not yet and what is nowhere set down; and at the same time he is obliged to be conscious of the historical conditions created by man's earlier creations, which obey necessary laws, to neglect or make light of which leads to fortuity and impotence.[54]

The result of this dialectical interaction is said to be the total responsibility of man for his future.

The overcoming of the tension between freedom and necessity implies a form of transcendence, to be sure, but this transcendence may
not be thought of in terms of exteriority, for that would represent an
infringement on the autonomy of man. Garaudy's interpretation of
transcendence in categories other than exteriority inevitably takes on
the appearance of dialectical supersession, immanent in the historical
process.

> Transcendence is another, but mystified name designating the emergence
> of the new by dialectical negation and supersession of the old; it is the
> future of man—not a mechanical resultant of his past, but at once inte-
> gration, negation, and supersession of that past.[55]

Any other understanding of transcendence is but a second name for
alienation.

This, however, is not all that can be said on the matter; simply to
speak of the dialectic of freedom and necessity is an oversimplification.
In reality, there are two distinct forms of necessity. When Marx, writing in *Capital*, demonstrates the inevitability of alienation arising within a capitalistic economy based on private property and exploitation of
the working class, he is discussing the *necessary* working out of the
laws of capital. On the other hand, when he asserts that the coming of
socialism is *necessary*, the word carries a different meaning. "It means
this: the contradictions of capitalism are such that there is no other
solution but socialism for their resolution."[56] To assert that the outcome of the historical process is known in advance would be to subject
men to a purely external necessity where man would, indeed, be but a
link in a chain of events, not unlike a simple physical or biological
occurrence.

This quality of being a cog in the motor of historical development
is the condition of alienated man under a capitalist regime. Man is
then subject to *external* and necessary laws which transform him into
an object. The advent of socialism, however, is an *internal* necessity in
which man plays a distinct and creative role. The transition from the
state of external necessity, in which man is alienated and reduced to a
thing, to the state of internal necessity, in which history is subordinated
to human purposes and goals, is the transition of man from an *object*
to a *subject*. The subjective factor, that of consciousness, is continually
on the increase. "In the first case he [man] has a status close to that of

things; in the second he acts according to a human plan, fully aware of the cause."[57] Thus the conception of historical necessity requires the active and creative participation of man for its accomplishment. It is based on the "subjective participation" of man in the revolutionary struggle, the party, its doctrine, organization, and militancy. In this way it is possible for Garaudy to say, in the words of Jean-Paul Sartre, that "the subjective is a necessary moment of the objective process."[58] The existence of objective premises for the solution of a historical problem requires the participation of the subjective element for its resolution. These objective premises include the totality of social relationships in any given epoch.

Here we have the nucleus of the Marxist understanding of freedom. Human initiative is conditioned by the whole of past history, but it nevertheless exercises a decisive role "when the objective conditions are realized."[59] The highest degree of freedom is attained when human beings recognize the contradictions in the political, social, and economic structures, and take effective action to overcome them. The more "necessary" the decision to rectify the injustices inherent in the structures, the higher the degree of freedom realized; "the individual is hence a center of creation without being a center of indetermination." The "project" is rooted in the existing historical conditions, but the negation of these conditions cannot occur without the conscious participation of man. Thus Garaudy thinks to overcome an artificial opposition between freedom and necessity.

The liberty which emerges from this dialectical process is by no means arbitrary. It is not a form of Sartrian freedom, surging forth from Nothing. "It is, on the contrary, grafted on to *being*, or rather, it is the creative and conscious unfolding of being."[60] Man is not simply his past: he is also his future; he is all that he is not yet. The creative overcoming of historical contradiction and alienation by constructing a new future is the basis of human freedom. This freedom is the creative participation in the dialectic of necessity. If the solutions proposed by men to historical antinomies were not necessary, asks Garaudy, how could one have any confidence in their effectiveness? Either historical initiative is totally arbitrary—in which case it will fail—or it "*will correspond to the internal law of development and will succeed as long as it continues to do so.* . . ."[61] The necessity binding together past and future is no mechanical rearrangement of preexisting elements; rather it is the surpassing of prior contradictions. This definition of necessity is dialectical, not mechanical, and it

> permits us to understand that the new *is truly* new (and not only a particular combination of old elements) while relating it *necessarily* to the old which it contradicts.[62]

### The Paradox of Freedom and Grace

Garaudy has posed an interesting solution to the problem of freedom and necessity: our historical initiative must correspond to the internal laws of social development if it is to have any assurance of success. Only when our "project" conforms with the true course of history can we speak in any real sense of human freedom. Of course, it will be immediately obvious to anyone possessed of a background in the history of Christian thought that this dialectic, or rather this paradox, is by no means the exclusive discovery of Marx. In fact, the Marxist dialectic is but the secular form of an affirmation whose roots go directly back to the New Testament, and whose growth we may trace in Augustine and Luther as well as others.[63]

St. Paul was the originator of the logical formulation of the paradox, although the idea is present in germ throughout the Bible. In essence, the idea is this: true freedom is found only in conforming my will to the will of God. When I reject that supreme Will, I am the "slave of sin," tossed about by the dark forces of chaos whose end is death. "But now you have been set free from sin and are the slaves of God; as a result your life is fully dedicated to him, and at the last you will have eternal life" (Rom. 6:22). True freedom is not found in the willful assertion of human autonomy. "Freedom" as purely arbitrary choice is as illusory for the Christian as for the Marxist; in reality, the individual is a prisoner of the irrational forces of society (the "powers and principalities"). On the other hand, authentic freedom comes from a fusing of my will with the will of him who is pure Freedom and Futurity, just as for Garaudy freedom appears in the identification of my creative initiative with the movement of the historical process. "Freedom is what we have—Christ has set us free!" (Gal. 5:1).

St. Augustine continued and developed theologically this paradoxical and dialectical understanding of the freedom of the will. In the *Enchi-*

*ridion,* in the course of a discussion on the necessity of Grace, he reiterates the Pauline assertion that he who sins is a slave to sin, unable to choose the right. True liberty is then defined as "the joy that comes in doing what is right."[64] But this freedom, analogous to the Marxist concept of freedom as creative action, is only possible for one liberated from bondage to sin, and such liberation comes only through the gracious action of God.

> We are then truly free when God ordereth our lives, that is, formeth and createth us not as men—this he hath already done—but also as good men, which he is now doing by his grace, that we may indeed be new creatures in Christ Jesus.[65]

Martin Luther's vigorous attacks on the notion of free will—particularly in the debate with Erasmus—arose, no doubt, partly out of heated polemics, and partly from the centrality of grace in his theology (*sola gratia*). If grace is to carry real assurance to men, he reasoned, then God's will to save must be absolute and irresistible. The logical consequences of such an extreme position have frequently been criticized; but Luther felt that such difficulties were small price to pay for the positive assurance this offered to the sinner. Thus Luther appears at times to reduce the role of free will to virtually nothing.[66] The paradoxical content of the Pauline and Augustinian understanding of free will is, however, well illustrated in the famous passage from the treatise on *The Freedom of a Christian,* where it is stated that "a Christian is a perfectly free lord of all, subject to none," while, at the same time, "a Christian is a perfectly dutiful servant of all, subject to all."[67] Luther explains further that the Christian, although freed from the bondage of sin through the effective action of the grace of God, finds the working out of that freedom in doing the will of his Father, by serving his fellow man. Thus the paradoxical assertion that true freedom is found in conformity with the Will of God is as true for Luther as it was for Augustine and Paul.

When we turn to contemporary theological efforts to deal with the question of freedom and necessity, we find the work of Paul Tillich extremely enlightening. As we have already suggested, Tillich's concept of "theonomy" is an attempt to reconcile the tension between autonomy and heteronomy. Here autonomy does not mean the freedom of an individual to be a law unto himself; rather it is "the obedience of the individual to the law of reason, which he finds in himself as a rational being."[68] Autonomy is the law of subjective-objective reason. In other words, it. is the law implied in the common structure of thought and reality; it is basically a structural quality of the human mind. Heteronomy is always in conflict with autonomy, for it represents the effort to impose an external authority on autonomy. It must not be taken as a totally external phenomenon, however, since it also represents the "depth" of reason: "The basis of a genuine heteronomy is the claim to speak in the name of the ground of being and therefore in an unconditional and ultimate way." The tragedy of the struggle between autonomy and heteronomy is that it represents a battle between the structure and depth of reason, that is, a conflict within reason itself. Finally, both autonomy and heteronomy are grounded in theonomy. Theonomy is not meant in the sense of an external, divine law imposed on reason; this would simply be another form of heteronomy. Rather, theonomy means "autonomous reason united with its own depth." Here the structural laws of reason are reconciled with the power of its inexhaustible ground in the unity of God. Of course, there is no perfect theonomy under the conditions of existence, and the struggle between autonomy and heteronomy results in the quest for reunion; "this quest is the quest for revelation."

A number of salient features in Tillich's theology should be noted. First of all, the entire construction, although built on a static, "logos" concept of reason, lends itself to a dialectical and historical interpretation. Following the logic of Garaudy, we can refer autonomy, or historical initiative, to the common dialectical structure of thought and reality. For Tillich, the mind is able to grasp reality because both share the same "logos" structure; for Garaudy, it is the dialectical nature of both thought and reality that makes this possible. Thus for Garaudy, as for Tillich, autonomy refers to the structural character of mind. Heteronomy, which for Tillich is identified with the "depth" of reason, could be reinterpreted in Garaudy's terms as the irresistible dialectical movement of history, welling up from the depths of reality. Attempts to assert the autonomy of man's historical initiative in an arbitrary and willful manner would necessarily conflict with the movement of history. This historical process would then impose itself on man as an external and heteronomic force. On the other hand, the dialectical overcoming of the opposition of historical initiative and historical process would represent a Marxist equivalent to the Tillichian concept of theonomy. This would occur only when the "project" of my historical initiative (autonomy) is in conformity with the movement of the dialectic of history (heteronomy).

The problem with this approach to Garaudy's methodology is that it does not really produce a synthesis of the two poles. The thesis is indeed present in the form of human autonomy, or historical initiative; the antithesis of historical heteronomy, or the dialectic of history, is also evident. But unlike a true dialectic, Garaudy's solution offers no real synthesis, no final "negation of the negation." On the one hand, Garaudy sometimes appears to call for total conformity of the individual historical initiative to the objective laws of history. This would, in effect, collapse the dialectic into an identity, and it is difficult to see how human autonomy is preserved in such a case. It is simply a return to the Greek concept of freedom as the acceptance of destiny. On the other hand, if we accept Garaudy's assurances of a genuine dialectic, this interaction of autonomy and heteronomy continues indefinitely into the future with no hope for a final synthesis.[69] The open-ended nature of the dialectic is necessary, asserts Garaudy, to preserve true human autonomy. That may be true for his particular form of humanism, but it is not necessarily so for Tillich's theology. Synthesis of autonomy and heteronomy into theonomy does not sacrifice autonomy, but rather gives it its true depth and meaning. Autonomy and heteronomy represent two poles of an essential unity which is actualized only through the final revelation of Jesus Christ.

Tillich suggests that Jesus, as the manifestation of the divine "abyss," not only supplies depth to the autonomy of reason, but as the self-sacrifice of the finite medium of revelation, keeps heteronomous forces from overcoming rational autonomy. To use Garaudy's terminology, we might say that Jesus, having de-fatalized history, calls forth and authenticates the human historical initiative; on the other hand, the anticipation of a final consummation of the historical process, made proleptically manifest in the resurrection of Jesus, is prevented from suppressing all human initiative because of the self-sacrifice of the medium of revelation. "He who believes in me does not believe in *me*," says Jesus in the Fourth Gospel (John 12:44), thus quashing any heteronomous interpretation of his authority. Hence the theonomous overcoming of the dialectic of autonomy and heteronomy as presented in Tillich offers a theological option to Garaudy's dialectic of freedom and necessity.

It must be admitted, however, that this sketch of an alternative solution to the problem of creative freedom vis-à-vis historical necessity suffers from a certain clumsiness. This is in part due to the essentially static ontological categories chosen by Tillich for his system, which make application to a dynamic situation difficult. One way out of this impasse may be in the work now being done by certain theologians in the "school of hope." A rephrasing of the concept of final revelation in the language of the Absolute Future might provide the necessary dynamics for a truly Christian understanding of freedom and necessity. It is to this possibility that we now turn our attention.

### Christian Freedom and Futurity

Garaudy's resistance to any form of extra-human transcendence is abundantly clear from our discussion in Chapter Two. The problem arises from what appears to be a basic misunderstanding of the nature of God. As long as transcendence is felt to be a static category over against man, it cannot help but have overtones of heteronomy. Tillich himself, while using essentially "synchronic" existential-ontological categories, has perceived the problem.

> Modern secularism is rooted largely in the fact that the unconditional element in the structure of reason and reality was no longer seen and that therefore the idea of God was imposed on the mind as a "strange reality."[70]

What Tillich failed to see, of course, is that any such "unconditional element," so long as it is viewed as static, eternal, and changeless, will also be resisted by modern man as a violation of human autonomy. Garaudy rejects any idea of a "supernatural reality" which, in some way, waits for man as the *telos* of his life and history; such a God, he claims, would constitute an infringement on human freedom. Even the Christian assertion that man is "co-creator" with God is incapable of providing an exit from this impasse, "Because it would be vain to say that he had been created creator by God; if this freedom, this power of creation were given to him, they would be no more than a mutilated freedom and power."[71] A God who waits for us and judges us implies that our path is already traced, our future closed.

The problem here is that Garaudy approaches the question of God from the wrong direction. God cannot be reduced to some remote and absolute Being looking down on us puny, insect-like creatures from an infinite distance. Rather, the question of God for religious man since the dawn of history has always been the question of the possibility of hope. As American theologian Sam Keen explains, "The affirmation of faith in God is the acknowledgment that there is a deathless source of power and meaning that can be trusted to nurture and preserve all created good."[72] The denial of God is tantamount to the denial of any ground for hope. And here we return to the problem in Garaudy's presentation of the dialectic of freedom and necessity. As long as this dialectic continues indefinitely into an empty and meaningless future, there is no assurance that the final end of that dialectic (if any exists) will be good. The denial of God is the assertion that the future is empty of meaning, and the Marxist response that man creates his own meaning through the historical process is feeble indeed; what source of value shall man use in constructing the future? Once again we return to the circular argument that the purpose in the making of history is the makability of history. This kind of argument leads to an infinite regress from which there is no escape.[73]

The Christian hopes in a radically new future for the whole creation, in which all creatures will be freed from their bondage to sin and death. In this hope, personal freedom is intertwined with political, economic, and social freedom. Admittedly, this freedom exists only in partial and limited manifestations; the very limitedness of freedom is the basis for the distinction made by Moltmann between the "realm of freedom" and "freedom in faith."[74] There is a dialectical tension between the eschatological fulfillment of freedom, and its beginnings here and now. Those who expect the coming Kingdom of freedom work for its realization in history today. This distinction shatters Garaudy's dilemma that one must choose between God and freedom, but cannot have both. It is a mythical, Promethean view of religion that insists on measuring God and man with the same yardstick. Carl Braaten has suggested that a better way of thinking of God is as "the power of the future which ceaselessly opens up new possibilities."[75] The essence of God can then be described as pure freedom. The freedom sought by man comes to him from outside himself in the coming future of God. Braaten modifies the term *ecstasy*, already reinterpreted by Tillich, and affirms that "the salvation man seeks . . . is an ecstasy of life—*ek-stasis*—a vital movement beyond every stasis."[76] The Resurrection is the supreme symbol of this ecstasy, pointing as it does to an overcoming of the "stasis" of death. In God all limits are vanquished, even the ultimate limit of death.

Here we are driven back to the suggestion of Pannenberg that

> perhaps being (*Sein*) is in truth to be understood as the power of the future. As the power of the future the God of the Bible has always been and still is beyond any conception of God.[77]

Such a way of speaking about God does not limit man's freedom to surpass his present existence and historical situation. Pannenberg admits that "a being (*Wesen*) which is present (*vorhanden*) and endowed with omnipotence would destroy such freedom by virtue of its excessive power."[78] The obvious advantage in picturing God as the power of the future is that man is then liberated from the present for a new and open future in freedom. Hence man is free to the extent that he can go beyond the present toward the future. Futurity conditions or, rather, is the condition for the freedom of man. But this future which frees man to be himself is not something under his control. As we have already seen, a truly transcendent future comes to man from beyond himself; it is not simply one more human creation among many. And here is the point of divergence between Garaudy's Promethean conception of freedom, centered in man's creativity alone, and the Christian conception of freedom as assent to the new future which comes to man through the graciousness of God.

> For a Christian, transcendence is the act of God who comes toward him and summons him. For a Marxist, it is a dimension of man's activity which goes out beyond itself toward its far-off being.[79]

The shortcomings and internal contradictions of Marxism should not, however, prevent us from seeing the close relationship between Christianity and Marxism in their common regard for human freedom. Both Christians and Marxists suffer under the misery of man, and this suffering is but the negative side of their hope for the future. Marxists, with their economic point of view, see the misery of man centered in his economic and political bondage. Freedom is then the abolition of the exploitation of man by man and the glorification of a united humanity in which man will be the master of his own history. Christians have a deeper perspective, and view the misery of man not as a result of his unrealized possibilities, but rather as a consequence of his real im-possibilities. Carl Braaten has described man as "possibility limited by finitude."[80] There is a drive within man toward infinite freedom, but this drive is restricted and even frustrated by his slavery to sin. A victim of death, transitoriness, and nothingness, a Christian sees freedom as liberation from fear and death through the gracious act of God. This freedom is anticipated in hope and actualized in faith.

Christian freedom, it should be added, is not a private matter, but is always freedom *for others*; Christians share the common hope of mankind for the universal liberation of men from all forms of slavery —even those of finitude and death. While we wait with anticipation for the final revealing of the Kingdom of freedom promised in Scripture and assured by the Resurrection of Christ, we are driven to demonstrate this new freedom by participating in the struggle for the real liberation of man *in* history. This struggle cannot be identified with any political or ideological system, for no such system can contain the fullness of the future for which we hope. Neither can this hope be contained in any narrow religious superstition. We are called to work for the liberation of man from all such limited and limiting views of reality. When true to their calling, and until they find their final rest in the realm of God's freedom, Christians must remain troublemakers and revolutionaries in every society which remains closed and self-contented.

## NOTES

1. MTC, p. 150.
2. Marx and Engels, *The German Ideology,* in Feuer, p. 294. See also Engels, *Anti-Dühring,* in Selsam and Martel, p. 266: "Freedom of the will therefore means nothing but the capacity to make decisions with real knowledge of the subject. Therefore the freer a man's judgment is in relation to a definite question, with so much the greater *necessity* is the content of this judgment determined. . . ."
3. MTC, p. 131.
4. MTC, p. 132.

5. For Kant, of course, autonomy is applied in the first instance to the free use of reason in every man. This law is auto-nomos, within man as his true being. Paul Tillich points out that this kind of autonomy is the opposite of arbitrariness or willfulness: "Autonomy is not lawless subjectivity" (Paul Tillich, *Perspectives*, p. 25). It is opposed to heteronomy, i.e., submission to external authority; but it should be noted that for Tillich, "Man's autonomy does not stand against the word or will of God—as if God's will were something opposed to man's created goodness and its fulfillment" (ibid). Moreover, autonomy is only truly free when it is subsumed under *theonomy*, the awareness of the divine ground of reason. See also Tillich, *Systematic Theology*, vol. 1, pp. 83–86.

6. QMM, p. 96.

7. QMM, p. 97.

8. Compare this judgment with the following comment by Tillich: "It is unfortunate that Kant often is interpreted only as an epistemological idealist and an ethical formalist—and consequently rejected. Kant is more than this. His doctrine of the categories is a doctrine of human finitude. His doctrine of the categorical imperative is a doctrine of the unconditional element in the depth of practical reason. His doctrine of the teleological principle in art and nature enlarges the concept of reason beyond its cognitive-technical sense toward what we have called "ontological reason." (Tillich, *Systematic Theology*, vol. 1, note, p. 82.)

9. HM, p. 128.

10. Friedrich Engels, *On Historical Materialism,* in Feuer, p. 93.

11. HM, p. 129.

12. KM, p. 37.

13. The quotations in this paragraph are taken from KM, pp. 38–40.

14. HM, p. 130.

15. Cf. Engels, *On Historical Materialism,* in Feuer, p. 93. Referring to Hegel, he states: "If you know all the qualities of a thing, you know the thing itself; nothing remains but the fact that the said thing exists without us, and when your senses have taught you that fact you have grasped the last remnant of the thing-in-itself, Kant's celebrated, and unknowable *Ding an sich.*"

16. See esp. *Systematic Theology*, vol. 1, pp. 83–86, 147–150. See also *supra*, n. 5.

17. Cf. e.g., Berger, *The Social Reality of Religion,* esp. p. 3: "Society is a product of man. It has no other being except that which is bestowed upon it by human activity and consciousness. There can be no social reality apart from man. Yet it may also be stated that man is a product of society. . . . Man cannot exist apart from society. The two statements, that society is the product of man and that man is the product of society, are not contradictory. They rather reflect the inherently dialectic character of the societal phenomenon."

18. Marx's sixth thesis on Feuerbach, in Feuer, p. 285.

19. HM, p. 195.

20. HM, pp. 196–197.

21. QMM, p. 214.

22. QMM, p. 99.

23. This "law" is derived directly from Hegel's *Logic*. In the realm of the natural sciences, Engels explains it in this manner: "We could express this by saying that, in nature, in a manner exactly fixed for each individual case, qualitative changes can only occur by the quantitative addition or subtraction of matter or motion (so-called energy)." Engels, *Dialectics of Nature,* in Selsam and Martel, pp. 123–124.

24. HM, p. 139.

25. Pierre Teilhard de Chardin, *Phenomenon of Man,* p. 60.

26. QMM, p. 102.

27. QMM, pp. 100–102.

28. HCHM, p. 24.

29. Ibid.

30. HM, p. 163.

31. MTC, p. 195.

32. MTC, p. 200.

33. Ibid.

34. The quotations in this paragraph are taken from MTC, p. 55.

35. This material is taken from MTC, pp. 62–63.

36. This and the following quote are from MTC, p. 60.

37. KM, p. 90.

38. KM, p. 96.

39. DEM, p. 196.

40. KM, p. 91.

41. HM, p. 145. The essentially Platonic notion of the identity of thought and reality is also taken up by Paul Tillich in his concept of "universal reason." Referring to the *logos* idea of reason—the principle of order and structure in all reality—he can say that "reality and mind have a logos structure" (*Perspectives,* p. 30). Roger Garaudy himself has remarked that dialectical thought is capable of grasping reality because reality itself is dialectical (cf. MTC, p. 60).

42. HM, p. 147.

43. DEM, p. 182.

44. Quotations in this paragraph are taken from KM, pp. 93–94.

45. HM, p. 122.

46. KM, p. 95.

47. HM, p. 118.

48. MTC, p. 98.

49. MTC, pp. 194–195.

50. PMFS, p. 372.

51. PMFS, p. 373.

52. Harvey Cox, *The Secular City* (New York: Macmillan, 1965), p. 75.

53. Ibid., p. 76. The similarity between Harvey Cox and Roger Garaudy may

not be wholly accidental. In fact, Garaudy seems to have been influenced by a number of Cox's ideas. Cf. Chapter Five, note 58.

54. MTC, p. 77.

55. QMM, p. 165.

56. MEE, p. 92.

57. QMM, p. 159.

58. Quoted in HM, p. 180.

59. Quotations in this paragraph are from HM, p. 199.

60. QMM, p. 164.

61. HM, p. 200 (italics mine).

62. HM, p. 202.

63. Cf. Chapter Two, the section entitled "A Marxist Interpretation," p. 68–71.

64. Augustine of Hippo, *Enchiridion,* chap. IX, par. 30, Library of Christian Classics, vol. 7 (London: SCM Press, 1955), p. 357.

65. Ibid., par. 31.

66. Cf. Martin Luther, *On the Bondage of the Will* (WA 18, 753–756), Luther's Works, vol. 33 (Philadelphia: Fortress Press, 1972), pp. 241–245 where he attacks the concept of free choice in salvation. But as Gyula Nagy points out ("Man as Responsible Co-worker with God"), while the sinner is justified *sine nobis,* the process of sanctification takes place *non sine nobis:* not without us. The foundation of salvation, then, is carefully protected from synergistic overtones, while the working out of grace in daily life remains open as the realm of cooperation between man and God. Thus we have the mystery of a cooperation "in which God does everything and nonetheless still does not break the back of the creature's freedom and responsibility but rather restores to the creature his joy and freedom through that very cooperation . . ." in Vajta, ed., *The Gospel and Human Destiny* (Minneapolis: Augsburg, 1971), p. 186.

67. *The Freedom of a Christian,* trans. W. A. Lambert, in Luther's Works, vol. 31 (Philadelphia: Muhlenberg Press, 1958), p. 344 (cf. WA 7, 49–73).

68. Quotations taken from Tillich, *Systematic Theology,* vol. 1, pp. 84–85.

69. Cf. ATD, p. 91. "Authentically human history will begin with Communism. It will be a history which is no longer made up of class struggles and war. . . . *Contradictions will not be abolished,* but they will no longer be bloody contradictions among human beings. Then, starting with questions which will no longer seek in alienated answers a coward's response, *the endless dialectic* of freedom made one with creation will flower" (italics mine).

70. Tillich, *Systematic Theology,* vol. 1, p. 208.

71. QMM, p. 59.

72. Sam Keen, "Hope in a Posthuman Era," in *New Theology Number 5,* ed. Martin Marty and Dean Peerman (New York: Macmillan, 1968), pp. 86–87.

73. Cf. Chapter Three, note 28.

74. Jürgen Moltmann, "The Revolution of Freedom: The Christian and Marxist Struggle," in *Motive,* vol. 39, no. 3 (December 1968), pp. 42 ff.

75. Carl Braaten, "The Gospel of the Kingdom of God and the Church" in *The Gospel and the Ambiguity of the Church*, ed. Vilmos Vajta (Philadelphia: Fortress Press, 1974).

76. Ibid.

77. Pannenberg, "The God of Hope," p. 34.

78. Ibid.

79. ATD, p. 92.

80. Braaten, "The Gospel of the Kingdom" in Vajta, ed. *The Gospel and the Ambiguity of the Church*.

# FIVE

# Transcendence and Social Change

## CHRISTIANITY AND SOCIAL CHANGE: A MARXIST CRITIQUE

In the preceding chapter, we pointed to the two demands of humanism which have characterized the Western philosophical tradition: from Greek and Roman antiquity came the search for a rational mastery of the world, while the Judeo-Christian heritage contributed the drive for an authentically human historical initiative. The Greco-Roman mind understood man in relation to a totality of which he was a fragment or part, whether that be the *kosmos* or the *polis*, the order of nature or the *logos* of the conceptual order.

> In this philosophy of *being,* man is greater the more he is *what is,* through his consciousness of this being, through his participation in this order, the order of the cosmos and of the city.[1]

According to Garaudy, the appearance of Christianity signaled a radical break with this closed ontology. No longer is freedom seen as mere consciousness of necessity; rather, it is interpreted as participation in the creative act. Christianity gave civilization the sense that man is fully responsible for his own future, and that he is free from any predetermined and inevitable destiny.[2]

Garaudy willingly admits that authentic history became possible only with the advent of Christianity. Instead of contemplating timeless and eternal laws of the cosmic order, man finds himself immersed in the unfolding of life in time,

133

where the past is the *locus* of sin, where the future which lies always before us is the *locus* of grace, and where the present is the time for decision, the time for rejection or acceptance of the divine call.[3]

Christianity, following the Jewish tradition, substitutes a philosophy of *act* for the Hellenic philosophy of *being*. The central concept is then no longer the *logos*, but creation. Man is no longer seen as striving for consciousness of what he is and must be, but *of what he is not*, of what he lacks and yet may become. Thus we are witness to the birth of a new conception of man, one whose highest goal is no longer identification with the eternal order of *kosmos* and *polis*, but whose infinite value

> is that he in turn is, in the image of God, creator with the capacity for gift and love, facing an absolute future which is not a logical extension of the past or a phase in a given totality, but the possibility of beginning a new life. . . .[4]

God, in such a world view, is no longer the totality of being, nor a concept, nor the absolute and harmonious reflection of the human order, but personal and hidden, accessible only to the eye of faith. It is then easy to understand why the description of God as Absolute Future is so attractive to Garaudy; such a God conforms perfectly to Garaudy's understanding of the unique nature of Christianity. In fact, only if God is conceived of in terms of *act,* rather than as some sort of supreme *being*, does real history become possible.[5]

This radically new understanding of man and history, marking what J. B. Metz refers to as "that transposition from an a-historical, transcendental orientation to a historically engaged future orientation,"[6] finds its root in the prophets of the Old Testament. Garaudy points to recent biblical research, and particularly the discovery of the Dead Sea Scrolls, as proofs of his contention that God, for the prophets, "was not to be discovered in present reality (whether in nature or in history), but in the future. God is the God who is always coming."[7] The transcendence of God is then described "as a permanent future, an appeal, an exigency." Jesus himself is seen as standing within this prophetic tradition; but even more, he incorporates and sums up within himself the whole of the tradition. The proclamation of Jesus is that the times are accomplished, and the present is the time of decision.

"Henceforth, to believe will mean being wholly open to the future."
At the same time, obedience to God is concretely bound up in militant
love and concern for one's neighbor. The new and open future implies
social responsibility, since the historical initiative cannot be fully exercised except on a communal level.

It should be clear from this short introduction that Garaudy's Marxist interpretation of Christianity finds remarkably strong echoes in
Jürgen Moltmann's *Theology of Hope*. Moltmann contrasts the uniqueness of Israel's eschatological "religion of promise" with the "epiphany
religions" as they were universally practiced in the ancient world.[8]
Epiphanic religion is centered on certain "appearings" or "revealings"
of the divine, by means of which men have access to eternal being. The
presence of the eternal provides an aura of stability and reality in the
midst of the forces of chaos and annihilation that surround man.[9] Thus
the "epiphany religion forms the presupposition and the abiding foundation of the natural theology of Greek philosophy of religion, and
the oriental philosophies of religion."[10] In sharp contrast to the prevailing epiphanic religions, based on participation in eternal being,
YHWH is worshiped as the God "with future as his essential nature,
a God of promise and of leaving the present to face the future, a God
whose freedom is the source of new things that are to come."[11]

The striking convergence of thought and even of terminology between Garaudy and Moltmann is further developed in Moltmann's
discussion of prophetic eschatology. Moltmann, like Garaudy, believes
that the prophetic message and tradition are a kind of watershed, in-
fluencing the ensuing development of Jewish thought right on down to
the time of Christ. If God's promises are eschatological to the extent
to which they are directed toward the ultimate horizon of the historic
future, then the prophets can be said to have contributed in at least
two ways to the eschatologization of the Jewish faith: in the univer-
salizing of promise to include YHWH's lordship over all nations, and
in the intensification of promise by the expectation of the negation of
death. Moltmann is thus able to say that "the prophetic message in its
breadth and in its existential depth does reach the utmost bounds of
reality and thereby become eschatological."[12]

Finally, the fulfillment of the biblical promise in Christ, and its
universalization in the Resurrection event, is seen as "the motive power,
the mainspring, the driving force, and the torture of history."[13] And

here the thought of Garaudy has undergone a truly amazing evolution under the influence of Moltmann's "theology of hope." In his very latest work, as yet unpublished, Garaudy identifies himself almost unreservedly with the thought of Moltmann. The latter sees the openness of human existence to the future as "grounded, manifested, and kept alive by that openness of the revelation of God which is announced in the event of the Resurrection of Christ."[14] Garaudy sees the Resurrection as an "act": "the act of participating in limitless creation, for the Resurrection is the revelation of this new and radical freedom that the Greek and Roman world ignored."[15] This does not mean, however, that Garaudy views the Resurrection as a purely symbolic event; like Moltmann, he realizes the essential character of the Resurrection for faith, to the extent that "Christianity stands or falls with the reality of the raising of Jesus from the dead by God."[16] The Resurrection, for Garaudy, is not a historical "fact," in the positivist sense of the word, but it remains a "possibility." The simple fact of the reanimation of a corpse would have no meaning whatsoever for faith. To believe in the Resurrection is "not to insert the Resurrection into the perspective of history; it is to perceive history in the perspective of the Resurrection."[17] The convergence of the thought of Moltmann and Garaudy on this crucial point is remarkable indeed!

### Constantinian and Apocalyptic Traditions

From the very beginning, says Garaudy, Christianity was characterized by an extremely complex syncretism, composed of a variety of interrelated elements.[18] The most significant and radically new element, labeled the "Judeo-Christian current," was heavily influenced by messianic prophetism, particularly as it was manifested in the Jewish religious movements of the first century B.C. There was a strong social orientation in this prophetism, directed not only against the political and religious domination of Rome, but also against corruption in the ruling Jewish classes, the priesthood, etc. Tactics used in these prophetic movements were generally those of nonviolence, exemplary purity, and preaching, such as those found in the Essene community. Alongside these peaceful movements was, of course, the more violent activity of the Zealots. The combination of these various prophetic strains gave a certain revolutionary significance to early Christianity, "in the hostility to the cult of the emperor, in the refusal to be associated with it, and, still more, in the forbidding of Christians to serve in the imperial army. . . ."[19]

This semi-revolutionary, sociopolitical current was, we are told, soon absorbed and overwhelmed by a "Helleno-Christian current." Garaudy traces threads of at least four Hellenistic ideologies which overlaid the Christian proclamation of a new and open future:[20] *Stoicism*, emphasizing detachment from the vicissitudes of life; the *astral religions*, with their teaching of inescapable destiny; the *mystery religions*, offering salvation through the intervention of superhuman powers; *Gnosis*, with its basic dualism and subordination of the physical world. These various strains found Christian expression in "a desire to escape from the world, and to secure individual salvation guaranteed by faith in Christ, the Pauline 'Master.' "[21] Garaudy finds this Hellenistic syncretism ideally suited to the conditions prevailing in the first century, with the disintegration of the Greek "guardian deity" religions which had assured man's salvation within the framework of the city state, the *polis*. The collapse of the *polis* and the subsequent isolation of the individual led to the adoption of the Helleno-Christian current of individual salvation through escape to the hereafter.[22]

The distinction between Judeo-Christian and Helleno-Christian currents in the early Church did not, according to Garaudy, disappear with the final domination of Hellenic thought. There is an ongoing tension in the dialectic of Constantinian and apocalyptic trends throughout the history of Christianity. In other words, Garaudy sees the Church caught in a relentless battle between two Christianities: one of apocalyptic protest, the other of reactionary institutionalism.

> Since Constantine, the teaching of the Church, in its official form and during the major part of its history, has curbed or combatted the struggles of the oppressed by locating in another world the conquest of justice, freedom, and happiness, by bestowing a legitimacy as of divine right on the established order, and by teaching resignation in the face of exploitation and oppression.[23]

The apocalyptic current which found expression in various chiliastic and millenarian sects provided a continuous counterbalance to this institutional oppression. While the Constantinian trend has consecrated class dominations of all kinds, from slavery through feudalism to the salary system, "the apocalyptic tradition gave life to the rebellions of

John Huss as well as the more recent colonial heresies."[24] Garaudy views the Constantinian state to be a direct result of the doctrine of original sin, which legitimized the state as necessary to restrain men incapable of freedom. Men are told they must carry the cross in this world in order to win freedom in the next. In this sense Christianity is viewed as a true "opium of the people." But when the so-called apocalyptic current takes precedence, as in the revolts of John Huss and Thomas Münzer, Christianity, "far from being an opium, plays the role of a leaven in the people's struggle."[25]

This Pelagian reading of history is typically Marxist and is well documented in Engels's favorite illustration of militant apocalypticism: the peasant revolt of Thomas Münzer. In the sixteenth century, with the emergence of new social forces, a number of peasant uprisings disturbed Europe. The earliest of these insurrections, cited by Engels, occurred in the bishopric of Würzburg in 1476, led by a colorful prophet named Hans the Piper. By the time Münzer appeared on the scene, there had been a series of revolts, all of them quickly suppressed by the nobility. The outbreak of the Reformation, however, gave an opportunity for certain of the politically minded to link together religious and social reform.

> The common denominator of these pioneers of Christian revolution, of a revolutionary Christianity, is perhaps to have taken seriously the prayer to God that his will "be done on *earth* as in *heaven*.[26]

Münzer's understanding of the primitive Christianity that he wanted to recapture is highly attractive to the Marxist. The insurgents wanted the early Christian egalitarianism adopted as the norm for civil society. There was a kind of primitive communism implicit in Münzer's demand for civil equality and, to a certain extent, the sharing of property. Engels is enthusiastic in his description of the proposed society:

> By the kingdom of God, Münzer understood a society without class differences, private property, and a state authority independent of, and foreign to, the members of society . . . all work and all property shared in common, and complete equality introduced.[27]

He concludes by reflecting that the outbreak of the Revolution of 1848 saw many communists less well prepared theoretically than Münzer's sect in the sixteenth century.

The trouble with all the manifestations of apocalyptic and revolutionary Christianity up to now, says Garaudy, is that they lack the organization and planning found in "scientific socialism." While it can be said of movements such as the Münzerians that "spontaneous protest against a world without justice is a constituent part of their faith,"[28] this very spontaneity betrays any true revolutionary effectiveness. The revolutionary attitude rightly understood is not a spontaneous attitude at all. It arises, rather, from the interaction of scientific socialism and proletarian experience. On the other hand, the apocalyptic orientation of Christianity, because of its spontaneous character, "even when subjectively revolutionary, can easily alternate between reformism and anarchical revolt."[29]

It would indeed be difficult to assert that Christian apocalyptic leads to effective social revolution; rather, if one reflects on the origins of the apocalyptic literary genre, it is clear that this kind of discourse, despite its inflammatory language, developed precisely out of an inability to change the real world situation. The Apocalypse of St. John was written to a small band of Christians struggling for survival in the face of the gigantic and irresistible Roman Empire. No one could possibly think that St. John was inciting the early Church to a rebellion that would only mean mass suicide. The injunctions to the seven churches in the first part of the book repeatedly commend the early Christians for their patience in tribulation (Rev. 2:2, 3, 10, 13, 19; 3:10). On the other hand, it is a simplistic distortion to continually identify the institutional Church with reaction and repression. Garaudy himself states that revolutionary fervor must be subject to discipline. In the case of the Church, one might say that the apocalyptic fires need to be controlled and directed by more conservative forces in order to be effective in social change. This kind of discipline alone makes possible what Maurice Thorez, former secretary of the French Communist party, singled out over thirty years ago as the "progressive role it [the Church] has played in its fight to make human relationships more just and more peaceful."[30]

## Christianity as Reflection and as Protest

The center of the Marxist critique of Christianity rests on a dialectic that is clearly spelled out in Marx's *Introduction to the Critique of Hegel's Philosophy of Right* (1844): "Religious distress is at the same time the expression of real distress and the protest against real distress."[31] It is the "sigh of the oppressed creature," thus signaling a rejection of the status quo, if only in imagination and hope. It is only insofar as the protest remains mythological and ineffectual that Marx characterized it as "opium." This formulation provides Garaudy with the critical tools for an analysis of the religious phenomenon, allowing him to distinguish between "the faith and the ideology, the Constantinian and the apocalyptic, the existential exigency and the alienation from it."[32] There is a double movement within the religious attitude: a refusal of reality such as it appears and the exigency of a truly human community which is, in essence, the radical demand for love. This double movement can, according to the historical situation, reflect the real misery and suffering of man, or protest against it. It remains on the level of reflection,

> when there exists no historical force to permit the overcoming of objective contradictions, and religion then adds a spiritual alienation to the economic and political alienations in justifying and consecrating an oppressive order.[33]

It becomes protest when religion leads to an authentic, revolutionary struggle against the established order.

The aspect of protest is linked with the Christian emphasis on the subjective moment as exemplified in the apocalyptic pole of Christianity. When this moment of the dialectic is dominant, religion, "far from being an opium, plays the role of a leaven in the people's struggle."[34] Garaudy asserts that throughout most of history, the reflective moment has held sway, and the Constantinian pole has subordinated the apocalyptic through the power of institutional state and institutional Church. But today there is a change occurring in the traditionally conservative attitude of the Church, which reflects a significant reversal of emphasis. "The dominant trait of the present ongoing mutation is that the moment of religious *protest* against the distress of man is tending to move ahead of the moment of *reflection*."[35]

Thus Garaudy locates the whole of the religious question in historical, political, and economic events. What is suggested here is a method for analyzing the human nucleus which is mystified under the form of religion. "Religions are born, live, and die in determined historical conditions."[36] These conditions are reflected in the "human core" of Christianity: "this consciousness of a lack and this protest against it." Thus, the "core" of Christianity is in the first place a "lack," a "deficiency" in the individual who is alienated from his truly human existence, his species-life. To the extent that protest against this alienation remains a purely subjective protest, it is in the long run ineffectual. Early Christianity, it must be recalled, was not a slave revolt, but a slave religion. Religion thus remains for Garaudy what it has been for every Marxist since Marx: a form of alienation. True, there is an element of legitimate protest, as witness the apocalyptic spirit which breaks out in Christianity from time to time; but the protest is blunted by the search for a truly human community of love in another world beyond the grave.

Garaudy's Marxist methodology has succeeded in laying bare at least one important element in the development of Christian thought: the material and historical conditions underlying the history of Christianity. There is a certain idealist tendency in the Church that wants to see faith in isolation from its context. The long struggles, even armed struggles, that have accompanied every major theological development in the history of Christian thought should long ago have set that illusion straight. Nevertheless, the false notion that one can somehow isolate Christianity from history continues to exist. Ideas may not be the products of socioeconomic conditions, as Marx believed, but they are by no means independent of them!

But while Garaudy's dialectical critique of Christianity offers a much needed demythologization of the faith by pointing out the socio-economic factors underlying its history, he has not sufficiently recognized the radical dimensions of the Christian proclamation. As Jürgen Moltmann has pointed out, Christianity incorporates the "character of protest" in its very essence.[37] The freedom in faith offered through the Gospel carries with it a categorical imperative to liberate the suffering creation from its affliction. The real criterion for the criticism of the Christian Myth is even more profound than the sociopolitical context: it is the Cross and Resurrection of Christ. When the Cross of Christ is understood as "an expression of *real* human affliction, then the Resurrection of Christ achieves the significance of the true 'protest' against human affliction."[38]

The proclamation of the Cross and Resurrection is far from being an opiate; rather it calls for the "power of the Resurrection" to break the chains of oppression that bind men everywhere. Moltmann reminds us that our "horizon of concern" (Pannenberg) must widen to merge with the horizon of the Christ event on the one hand and the future of Christ in the Kingdom of freedom on the other. The Bible offers a horizon of concern which reaches out to include "the whole affliction of the present and indicates for it the new possibilities of a future open to God."[39] A true understanding of the biblical kerygma must lead to political struggle for the liberation of mankind. This kerygma is not dialectically opposed to the Church as institution, but is mediated *through* the institution.

## METHODS OF SOCIAL CHANGE

Traditionally, the debate between Christians and Marxists over the issue of social change has centered on the question of what methods may be employed to bring about the change. In essence, this argument has boiled down to whether or not the "ends justify the means"; in practical terms, is violence a legitimate technique for changing unjust social structures, provided the goal is sufficiently worthy? In the past the answer from Christians has usually been a firm and resounding "no." Use of coercion and violence was out of the question, no matter how praiseworthy the ends might appear, since employment of violent tactics invariably impugned and demeaned the goal toward which one was struggling. The evils of Stalinist Russia were frequently invoked as an illustration of a regime founded by violence and sustained by violence. The only legitimate Christian option for social change was reform of the existing system through nonviolent action.

In recent years new events have demanded a reconsideration of this problem, since real-life situations are by no means as neat and clean-cut as we might like. The struggle for liberation of the American black people, the awakening of the consciousness of the Third World, and a reexamination of the nature of violence itself have been subjects of a number of ecumenical studies. A conference held by the World Council of Churches in Geneva in 1966 offered one of the first clear evaluations of violent versus nonviolent means of social action.[40] After expressing a distinct preference for nonviolent tactics, the conference added that violence is very much a reality in our world, both the overt use of force to oppress and the invisible violence perpetuated on people who by their millions have been or still are the victims of repression and unjust social systems.

Thus,

it cannot be said that the only possible position for the Christian is one of absolute nonviolence. Wherever it [violence] is used, however, it must be seen as an "ultimate recourse" which is justified only in extreme situations.

Two years later, a meeting of theologians and social ethicists at Zagorsk expressed even less doubt as to the validity of violence in certain cases.

. . . we must realize that some Christians find themselves in situations where they must, in all responsibility, participate fully in the revolution with all its inevitable violence.[41]

The recent decision by the World Council of Churches to fund a number of organizations involved in the struggle against racism, including certain revolutionary groups engaged in violent resistance, lends the weight of action to these pronouncements. And, although the Catholic Church has been more cautious in this area, *Gaudium et Spes* and *Populorum Progressio* at least constitute the beginnings of an attempt to deal with the theme.

In view of these new developments on the ecumenical scene, the possibility of a common understanding between Christians and Marxists on the issue of violence as a method of social change is not so remote as it once appeared. Thus an examination of the point of view of Garaudy constitutes a necessary step in our search for intersections of his Marxist philosophy with new developments in Christian theology.

Garaudy begins by the affirmation that it is impossible to approach the problem of methods, or more specifically, of violence, in an abstract way. We are involved in the struggles of our world whether we like it or not, "and we never have a choice other than between two kinds of violence, our abstention automatically giving the game to the strongest."[42] Garaudy echoes the thought of Jules Girardi, who points out that, historically, we are never faced with a simple choice between violence and nonviolence, but between the violence of the oppressor and the violence of the oppressed. "Violence is already in things."[43] Garaudy would be the first to admit that "if the choice were between violence and nonviolence, there would be, for the Christian or anyone else, no possible hesitation."[44] Such a choice is, however, not in the nature of things; by our very presence in the world we are already committed, and both our action and our inaction play a role in the worldwide confrontation of forces. The old argument still appears valid: To condemn the violence of the slave who revolts is to condone the violence of the enslaver. To use a more contemporary illustration, "How is it possible to forbid participation in a revolution or a guerrilla band, without approving *the ends* of the colonizers, rather than those of the colonized?"[45]

The situation is much more complex than a simplistic distinction between "love" and "violence" would lead us to believe. Certainly, the Christian is called to love his fellow men. . . but not *all* of them in precisely the same way: "The oppressed is loved by defending and liberating him, the oppressor by accusing and fighting him."[46] Once again, Garaudy seems to echo the same theme. He insists that authentic revolutionaries have a great respect for love; it is, in fact, the goal of the Marxist struggle, incarnated in a world without exploitation and oppression where every man is a brother to every other.

> But when, instead of teaching us that the concrete historical conditions for the blooming of this love of man . . . are a work to be realized in fighting to transform all the human relationships which contradict and flout it, this love is invoked as if it existed already in reality in order to condemn the just violence of the struggle against a world which is the opposite of love, then this great dream of human unity serves as an alibi working to maintain the very institutions which are the worst obstacles to the coming of that unity and that love.[47]

It is a sad fact but true that the high ideal of Christian love has often been used by the dominant class and its clergy as a means of "defusing" the righteous anger of the oppressed masses. If the promise of our future unity in Christ is used as an excuse to avoid action on behalf of the humiliated and mistreated of the world, we have indeed become an accomplice of the oppressor by condemning, in the name of love, the revolt of the oppressed.

Frequently the ideal of Christian love is linked with the idea of nonviolence. Garaudy does not look down on nonviolence as a tactic, and, in fact, sees it as somewhat of a necessity in the highly industrialized, Western nations. "In this research oriented toward the future, one . . . illusion is to be dissipated: the myth of revolution at the end of a gun."[48] But this reservation is tactical; the method used to introduce social change must fit the context. To make nonviolence into a rigid and abstract law would be to paralyze the struggle of the oppressed peoples of the Third World, where no other recourse is available. We are never faced with a clear choice between violence and nonviolence,

> but always between two kinds of violence; and nothing can save us from the concrete responsibility of determining in each case where the least violence is, the violence most conducive to human development.[49]

At this point a digression is necessary. The use of the terms *violence* and *nonviolence* has been so widespread in recent times that a great deal of confusion reigns regarding the exact meaning of both words. For example, violence is frequently used today as a blanket condemnation of any situation regarded as unjust by the user; on the other hand, it is difficult to deny the legitimacy of terms such as "violence of the status quo" or "institutional violence," which point to the hidden mental and physical suffering arising from unjust social structures. Girardi distinguishes among three types of violence.[50] (1) Physical violence,

> when it is made physically necessary or, on the contrary, physically impossible for a person to accomplish an action; this violence is then defined as the antithesis of physical liberty.

Under this category we can list those forms of violence leading to the shedding of blood, physical oppression, and torture.

(2) Moral violence,

> when, under the influence of different forms of conditioning, it is made necessary or, on the contrary, psychologically impossible, for a person to accomplish certain actions or to think in a certain way.

Under this heading are found restrictions on free speech and the press, as well as the creation of a climate of terror.

(3) Legal violence,

> when it is made either juridically necessary or impossible for a person to accomplish determined actions or to follow certain objectives.

Here we could list the revocation of civil rights, refusal of entry to the university, or denial of certain careers.

We see immediately that Girardi makes two vital distinctions. First of all, he distinguishes between a violent act and a state of violence. It is possible for someone to be perfectly free from any particular violent *action*, while knowing that an attempt to exercise freedom of movement will bring about a violent *re*-action. This constitutes a state of violence. Secondly, Girardi always defines violence in opposition to freedom. In other words, violence is equivalent to external constraint of any kind on the free exercise of human rights.

> The state of violence is thus a condition which makes it impossible for the great majority of men to exercise their fundamental rights and duties, and which prevents their flowering as men; it is a situation in which it is impossible to love one another.[51]

Violent acts are distinct from a state of violence, just as physical violence is not the same as institutional violence, and yet the fundamental problem is identical: the loss of freedom.

This definition of violence raises an interesting question for Garaudy. If the end held in view by the Marxist is the liberation of man from exploitation and oppression—that is, from institutional violence—how is it possible to accomplish this liberation from violence through the use of violence? It places one rather in the position of the Allies who in 1916 fought "the war to end all wars," and found themselves at the end in a worse situation than when they started. And so we arrive full circle at our original question: Doesn't the indiscriminate use of the very evil you wish to stop compromise the goal toward which you strive?

Garaudy's response to this question is to attack the basis upon which it is asked. "It is remarkable," he observes, "that bourgeois morality more and more avoids considering as the central problem *the ends*. It claims, on the contrary, that this moral judgment concerns *the means*."[52] The reason for this prejudice, according to Garaudy, is that the bourgeoisie resists the clear explication of its true ends, since it is based on the exploitation and dehumanization of man. If one simply ignores the problem of institutional violence, then it is much easier for the exploiting class to concern itself with the morality of the means employed by Marxists. In reality, however, the ends sought after and the means employed to attain them are tightly bound together. For Garaudy, the real crime is not in the means used, but in the selection of ends which conflict with reality or go against the current of history. Since such ends do violence to both reality and history, the means used to pursue those ends are of necessity criminal. "These criminal means spring ineluctably from the choice of an end condemned by history and resisted by entire peoples."[53]

The ends pursued by the proletariat, unlike those of the exploiting classes, include the liberation of mankind, the creation of a new social order, and the harmonious development of the human personality. Since these goals are attractive in themselves, Marxists foresee a natural and peaceful transition to socialism. No violence is necessary to bring about these changes; rather, violence arises—is in fact necessary—when the attempt is made to brake or reverse the course of history. Thus it is that Garaudy can claim that "violence, for socialism, is but a riposte of prior violence, that of the dying regime made furious in its agony."[54] This resistance of the present system to social change constitutes a real force; it cannot be successfully countered except through the use of real force, whether that be a simple strike or more violent forms of proletarian resistance. Thus, to speak of "absolute" nonviolence is an absurdity, since one is never confronted by such an abstraction in real history. To reinforce his point, Garaudy refers to the saying of Charles Péguy: "The idealists would have clean hands . . . if they had hands."[55]

In his latest book, *Reconquête de l'espoir*, Garaudy states his conviction that Christians and Marxists are not divided by the spirit behind the means used, but by its perversion. Rejected are both the Marxist perversion which would change man by changing the economic and social structures and the Christian perversion which would solve historical problems simply by moral preaching or personal charity. "Historical effectiveness demands that structures and consciousness be attacked together."[56] Marxist thought has traditionally emphasized the first option, Christian theology the second.[57] It is much more likely that the two are tied together dialectically. The results of a false dichotomy have been clearly seen on the Marxist side in the Stalinist heresy; on the Christian side the heresy consisted of an unbalanced stress on personal piety and salvation.

What Garaudy is pointing to is nothing less than a restatement in terms of social ethics of the Lutheran dictum: "*simul iustus et pecca-*

*tor.*" Since the days of Pontius Pilate, men have tried to find some way of "washing their hands" of ethically difficult or embarrassing questions. But such is not the fate of man in this life. As Reinhold Niebuhr demonstrated forty years ago, even the most conscientious use of nonviolence may have totally unpredictable consequences in the long run. Coercion allows for no distinctions between the innocent and the guilty.

> Once we have made the fateful concession of ethics to politics, and accepted coercion as a necessary instrument of social cohesion, we can make no absolute distinctions between nonviolent and violent types of coercion or between coercion used by governments and that which is used by revolutionaries. If such distinctions are made they must be justified in terms of the consequences in which they result.[58]

At the same time it should be remembered that nonviolence—so close to the heart of the Gospel—can, through active, non-retaliatory, and suffering love, often break the chain reactions of human hatred, thus raising the humanity of both oppressor and oppressed. Sadly, it must be admitted that nonviolence is not always valid in all situations; but the step of moving from nonviolence to violence should be considered with deepest gravity. Above all, the Christian insight implied in Garaudy's observation that one cannot avoid involving himself in ambiguous situations also serves to de-romanticize every revolutionary movement, including Marxism. Sin does not restrict itself to certain classes, races, or ideologies. Moreover, the Gospel presupposes a human solidarity which transcends all human conflicts and relativizes all merely human loyalties. This is turn poses serious questions for the Christian who would commit himself to the use of violence in the revolutionary cause. But when all of these insights have been duly considered, there still remains the need for action. Those who choose to straddle the fence will be left behind by history, and will have made a decision anyway, if only a negative one. The words of the angel to the church at Laeodicea are as true today as they were in the first century:

> I know what you have done; I know that you are neither cold nor hot. How I wish you were either one or the other! But because you are barely warm, neither hot nor cold, I am about to spit you out of my mouth. (Rev. 3:15–16.)

*Christianity and Eschatology*

The ethical dilemma is rooted in the very nature of Christianity. Garaudy himself observes that Christians "live their faith across a history,"[59] and asks if this fact does not indeed constitute the essence of the biblical message. He points out that the book of Exodus documents the first case on record of civil disobedience to a "legitimately constituted" government. "For the first time political authority was desacralized."[60] Not only did God urge his people to resist the authority of Pharaoh; the prophesy about Cyrus suggests that God is equally capable of working through secular persons and communities. Further, the implication of the whole biblical testimony is that "God does not reveal himself in natural phenomena, but in history."[61] This constitutes a complete reversal of the prevailing religious conceptions in biblical times. In view of this inversion of the priority of "natural" and "historical," is it not possible, asks Garaudy, that God reveals himself as much in revolution and social change as in order and stability? The problem for Christianity, as for Marxism, is to remain open to the infinite horizon of the future as it impinges upon and leavens the present.

But we must go further. How does the Christian or the Marxist open himself to this infinite horizon of the future in concrete sociopolitical and economic terms? What drives men to commit themselves to revolution and social change? Garaudy's response is typically Marxist, and appears to raise more questions than it answers. Being a materialist, he needs to affirm that ideas emerge from socioeconomic realities. That is to say, changes in the historical situation inevitably produce corresponding changes in consciousness.[62] The Christian, on the other hand, while admitting the crucial importance of material factors, still places the emphasis on the spiritual side of man. George Cottier has criticized Garaudy for just this reason, pointing out that human society is a society of persons, each possessing a spiritual nature. Great historical changes always begin with a change in consciousness. "Christianity was historically efficacious because it was Christianity that made slavery intolerable; what is perceived as intolerable sooner or later ends up being suppressed."[63] Even the Marxist revolutionary struggle has formed its goals around certain Christian ideals at work in the subconscious of every European man, ideals which have become ingrained in the historical existence of the West. Ernst Bloch is living testimony of this fact. His "principle of hope" is an active historical ferment impelling us to recognize ever new ethical demands. That hope (a quality of the spiritual life of man) is the real driving force behind the revolutions of history.

Rahner echoes this sentiment when he describes the need to engage the creative intelligence of man in the struggle for human freedom as "a task written in the very nature of man such as God willed him."[64] The religious attitude is then nothing less than "human freedom opening itself in faith and hope to the Absolute Future."[65] The individual person here receives a meaning and significance much deeper than is possible for the Marxist, since man's faith in this Absolute Future constitutes the ground of his absolute value as a human being. More, this faith lends conviction to the efforts of men to establish the best possible social order on a profoundly solid foundation: hope in the Absolute Future of God.

Rahner's stress on hope and the future is but one example of a renewed appreciation of the importance of eschatology. In a certain sense, though, there can be no "eschato-logie," since the very idea of *logos* assumes that reality can be grasped in its totality and essence by human reason. We have already pointed out the limitations of this Greek ontology, and the innovation in historical thinking with which Christianity supplanted it. Carl Braaten makes specific, however, the idea that "if we operate with a Greek *logos* concept, we can have no eschatology, for the future of Christian hope is not an extension of the past, or recurrence of the present."[66] Reality as it is perceived in nature is basically circular and repetitive; reality as history is open-ended and unfinished. It is the promise of a radically new and open future that creates and reinforces the Christian hope which, in turn, drives the "motor of history."

This Absolute Future which is the real source of the Christian social ethic "does not signify a purely contemplative relation to the future," according to J. B. Metz, but rather "a productive and fighting relation which liberates man and invests him with the task of transforming the world through the exercise of his free activity."[67] A number of contemporary Christian thinkers echo the idea of an eschatology in active relation to the present. Rahner, for example, believes that one must express "the eschatological hope across the structures of the 'worldly life' itself. . . ."[68] Braaten affirms that Christ's lordship over church and world is a direct consequence of its "eschatological finality with respect to the totality of the created world."[69] The Christian understanding of the "last things" is an eschatology of struggle, aiding in the birth of a new world and straining toward the future of God. It is an eschatological hope which Ernst Bloch has described as not simply giving us something to drink, but a meal to prepare.

The "realized eschatology" which has held sway in theological circles since Karl Barth is now being replaced by an eschatology which stresses the futural dimension of the Kingdom of God, a dimension which cannot be divorced from its present impact. A dialectical tension exists between that Absolute Future continuously breaking in on us, and our present struggles continuously reaching out toward the not-yet. The Kingdom is never fully realized, never an accomplished fact; but neither is the aspect of realization to be totally surrendered. It is the power of God *as* future that calls us to change the present. Speaking at the Salzburg colloquium, Johannes Metz expressed this dialectic in terms of a "collaboration" of man and God in the ultimate realization of the divine promise of universal peace and justice. "Eschatological faith and earthly commitment are not mutually exclusive."[70] The quintessence of this dialectic is found in the Resurrection of Christ. Faith in Christ is more than an "I-thou relationship"; it is intimately bound up in the belief that the future of the world *will participate* in the victory of Christ's Resurrection over death.

Marxism shares many elements of this messianic eschatology, although it represents an anthropocentric and terrestrial kind of messianism. Once again, it is Cottier who pinpoints the error in an idolatrous overemphasis on the problems of this world. In what could easily be a quotation from Garaudy, he explains that, for the Marxist, "the final end of man is, in a manner of speaking, immediately present in earthly tasks, and that is why they take on an absolute value."[71] Seeing as he does the tremendous power of human reason, the Marxist makes reason a weapon with which to dominate history, and in the process he thinks to forget his own happiness. This messianic conception of human reason is viewed from an eschatological perspective. Reason is militant; it is allied with the struggle of the masses for freedom. Thus, far from being irrational, "violence itself is conceived as a positive element."[72] By this rationalist myth, violence finds a rational justification. Since the eschatological attainment of human freedom is the highest goal envisaged by reason, any means to that end is justifiable. This may easily lead to what has been termed "the sacrifice of the present generation to the Moloch of the future." Whether Garaudy can escape this criticism remains to be seen.

### Toward a Theology of Revolution

Up to this point we have talked only about social change; but mere social change—even *rapid* change—does not constitute revolution. Real revolution, to make a clear distinction, has to do with

> a sharp, sudden change in the social location of political power, express-ing itself in the radical transformation of the process of government, of the official foundations of sovereignty or legitimacy and of the concep-tion of the social order.[73]

The various theologies of revolution or revolutionary theologies that one finds in contemporary literature do not, in general, take seriously the radical implications of this definition. The movement from perma-nence to change in theology, however, implies revolution, and revolu-tion is, by definition, anti-establishment. Walter Capps has clearly seen that "the *novum* is a revolutionary principle. It is designed to change the world and not to interpret it."[74] To use Braaten's terminology, the Spirit must be seen as a "revolutionizing presence." Braaten refers to the Greek definition of *parakaleo*, i.e., "called to the side of."[75] This in turn suggests the warning of Rev. 3:15–16. The Spirit does not preside over a lukewarm middle point; rather, He could be called the "principle of one-sidedness." He calls us to take a stand, to make up our minds. That may easily mean going against the will of the estab-lishment, and perhaps even changing the establishment. If the Chris-tian is en route toward the future—if the people of God are truly the "Exodus Church"—this means being in tension and conflict with those who accept the status quo as the ultimate form of society. This is not necessarily the same thing as *aggiornamento*, which means something more like a combination of renewal and reform. Linking the new future with *aggiornamento* implies that change can be internalized and, ultimately, controlled. Revolution, on the other hand, is considerably more than a simple refurbishing of what already exists. To return to Braaten once again, we are reminded that "talk about changing the world implies that we assume responsibility for the future. Revolutionary change is the responsibility of eschatological hope."[76]

Garaudy is not convinced that it is possible for the Church as Church to foment and inspire real revolution. Rather, following the ideas of Harvey Cox, he feels that Christians must search for the revolutionary activity of God *outside* the Church. "The problem is to decipher in the event the Word of God which reveals itself only in historical events."[77] There is some confusion here on Garaudy's part, since Cox talks less about revolution than about rapid social change.[78] There are nevertheless certain useful ideas in Cox, particularly his fourfold analysis of the essential elements in any revolutionary theory.[79] Such a theory (or theology) must include (1) an explanation of why a revolution is necessary, (2) a rationale for the refusal of people to act on this necessity, (3) a way of encouraging people to take action, (4) an understanding of catastrophe. Cox calls these elements (alliteratively) the catalytic, cataleptic, cathartic, and catastrophic, respectively, and believes that they provide an adequate basis for analysis of any revolution. Marxism has for some time offered a strategy of revolution which takes all four of these factors into account. Christian theology has yet to wrestle seriously with the problem.

The traditional Marxist analysis views the *catalytic* agent as a "gap" or "lag" between the form of society demanded by the pressures of economic development and the actual, capitalistic and exploitative system.[80] As Cox points out, this theory is now outdated, since the Marxist critique of the economic substructure outrunning the political superstructure does not take into account the vastly increased complexity of modern society. Marshall McLuhan and Herbert Marcuse now offer a more realistic analysis of the hitherto unknown pressures bearing down upon modern man. Not only is our technology rebounding on our very consciousness, altering the way we perceive reality in a thousand subtle ways but, if Marcuse is correct, the oppressive nature of industrial society is so pleasant that no one feels the necessity to change it. Thus, to quote Cox once again, "we are now choking on a serious imbalance between the technical and the political components of technopolis."[81] In this situation the catalytic gap described by Cox is that tension between the present and the always arriving Kingdom of God. Cox sees this gap in terms of secularization. Perhaps it would be better, however, to choose the concept of transcendence as futurity, since what Cox calls the "Kingdom" is nothing other than Rahner's Absolute Future. Braaten reinforces this interpretation, identifying God with the ultimate future and equating that future with pure freedom.[82] Thus the catalytic gap is really the tension between the promised freedom of God and the actual situation of bondage—bondage to our technology, to our automated and controlled environment. This is not really so very far from Garaudy in the long run for, as Braaten points out, "Marxism calls for liberation from the alienating forms of life which man has created on top of the world of nature."[83]

Cox's second factor is really a question. Why are people so *cataleptically* bound to the existing structures that they do not rise up and throw off the yoke that binds them? The Marxist response would be in terms of "false consciousness." People are bound to the material conditions of their society—to the means of production—and consequently their awareness of reality is truncated. The classic answer to the situation (somewhat simply put) is to "liberate" men by freeing them from their property. The Bible paints a different picture. It, too, describes men as suffering under a false consciousness, but it gives this warped awareness the name "sin." There are enough biblical metaphors associating sin with a failure to perceive the world clearly to illustrate the parallel between Marxism and Christianity at this point. The appearance of Jesus, for example, is announced by declaring that the blind see and the deaf hear.

The biblical word for *catharsis* is conversion. Marxists would see cathartic action in the liberation of man from private property. In either case, the change is radical and traumatic, which is why Cox feels it cannot occur without some form of *catastrophe*. From the Marxist point of view, the catastrophe is the revolution, which is nothing less than bringing the political superstructure in line with the existing reality of the economic substructure. It is at this point that Cox's analysis breaks down, for he fails to demonstrate that the coming of the new order of the Kingdom constitutes a true catastrophe. Rather than revolution in the Marxist sense, Cox sees the birth of a renewed secular city. His talk of recurring catastrophe and permanent change is not a call to revolution, but a demand for political pragmatism. When he is forced to be specific, he implies that existing structures and institutions are to be experimented with and extended. It is hard to see how a simple renewal process can cope with problems of the magnitude indicated by Marx, Marcuse, and McLuhan. At this point we must humbly admit that the inbreaking of the *novum* may well call us to a revolutionary action far beyond the suggestions of Cox; but what form of action, and under what circumstances, are questions that can be answered only in the context of real, concrete situations.

## GOALS OF SOCIAL CHANGE

There is a thin line between eschatology and utopianism, and it is often difficult to determine on which side of the line Garaudy falls. Of course, Garaudy would deny that his Marxist philosophy is utopic, since utopia literally means "no place," and the Marxist is quite adamant in the belief that his goals are achievable. Marxist social aims are neither fantastic nor unhistorical; rather, "authentically human history will begin with Communism."[84] That is to say, communism is not the utopic conclusion of the dialectical process, since that process has no end—it is inherent in the very nature of reality. Contradictions cannot be abolished; they can only be rendered bloodless and constructive. This Garaudy refers to as the flowering of "the endless dialectic of freedom made one with creation. . . ."[85] The Marxist does not hope for a world of perfection, but a world in which both individual and community can develop and exercise their talents freely. This is more than the simple augmentation of industrial production; it is, above all, the creation of fully developed human beings. Since men have a responsibility to make this world come about, the hope of the Marxist is an endless driving force to reconstruct the future.

This endless dialectic, ever pushing men to create their own future, plays an essential role in the socialist revolution, not unlike that of the ever-arriving and never-attained Kingdom of God in Christian theology. Robert Havemann, speaking at the Salzburg colloquium in 1965, pointed out that revolution is always in danger of being discredited when it begins to achieve its aims and goals. The gap between utopia and reality can *never* be overcome; "it would be a pernicious error to believe that utopia and the new reality created by revolution can be brought into agreement."[86] The tension is inevitable first of all because the utopia, as it is conceived of before the revolution, is really the negative reflection of the old social order, and must be abandoned with that old order. Moreover, as the new social structure grows, it is influenced by the remnants of the former, unreal utopic conception.

The old utopia loses its revolutionary force because "man, for his effort toward progress and freedom, needs a utopia which is formed around the demands of his *own present*, and at the same time points already to the future."[87] In other words, the conceptualization of the future which informs our present struggle must be continually reappraised and reformed. The present-conditioned future must constantly be called into question by an "absolute" and forever receding future which forms the horizon of all our limited expectations.

Christian faith has long held to such a transcendent utopia, in the sense of a "beyond," an openness toward the future which, in spite of fantastic and mythological representations, resists all false claims of its ultimate realization in the present. The Marxist utopia has the same potential, although it remains a theoretically obtainable goal *in* history, while the Christian utopia forms the ultimate horizon *of* history. Such a utopia can never be totally assimilated into existent reality, and when a society claims to have achieved such an integration, it destroys all faith in its own future. This was the basic error in Hegel's glorification of the Prussian state. Garaudy realizes the truth in this argument, as evidenced by his insistence on the necessity of an ongoing and never ending dialectic. Moltmann has expressed it in this way: "What disappoints in truth is the experienced or foreboded human existence itself as it emerges or will emerge out of the industrial society."[88] To the extent that socialism is actually achieved, it loses its magical aura of transcendence. There is nothing more detrimental to our essential humanity than the total disappearance of future possibility.

This is but another way of expressing what Moltmann calls the tension between "hoping and planning."[89] That is, if there is no true hope, planning finds no source of inspiration; but if there are not definite goals for hope, if there is no planning, hope remains unrealistic. Karl Rahner maintains that Christian hope in the Absolute Future deters man from blindly sacrificing the present generation to the future, thus making the future "a Moloch to which really existing man is immolated for the advantage of a man who will never exist in this life, a man who will always remain beyond human possibility."[90] Secondly, the Absolute Future serves to protect the dignity and worth of each individual, even when he is unable to contribute tangibly to the creation of a better future. Finally, it invests the struggle to build a new future with supreme and radical importance. Thus the Christian hope protects man's concrete humanity because it resists the "gigantomachy" (Moltmann) of a violently brought about change in society. This function is an integral part of the Church's task of witnessing to the ultimate values and goals of life, giving the individual a sense of personal worth that can never be exhausted by his social, economic, or political functions. The future of the individual must not be sacrificed to the social well-being of present or future generations.

## Utopia and the Absolute Future

While the concept of Absolute Future protects against the very real possibility of ethical abuse of the present generation for the sake of dubious future generations, the question may legitimately be asked if such an eschatologically grounded ethic, relegating the new humanity to the end of history, does not in fact vitiate real historical action here and now. The Absolute Future serves well its critical function, pointing to the limited nature of all planned and projected futures; can it also serve as a source of historical change and social reform?

Such an Absolute Future presents real problems for the Christian, since it remains always final and incomprehensible. Thus the Christian turns out to be "the one who knows the least what to take hold of, since he has not penetrated to the depths of himself until he has come directly up against his true depth, the unfathomable God."[91] The question then poses itself: What is the future? Is it not greater than the extrapolation of our plans and projects? Is not such a "dotted-line" future really no more than the logical extension of the present? A truly "future" future must transcend all images and schemes that seek to give it content, somewhat along the lines of Ernst Bloch's metaphor of a "vacuum," an unfilled area which exerts a forward pull on man and the world. Rahner has warned of the danger of confusing the real future with either an evolutionary or technological future which could be said to exist already in germ, "to identify 'future' with an ensemble of plans, to which is added a formal and empty chronological time, and hence to misunderstand the true relation of man to the real future. . . ."[92]

Garaudy is prepared to accept such an open future, since "it is not a matter of seeing into the future, but of inventing it."[93] He is dismayed by the new pseudosciences collectively lumped under the heading of "futurology," which attempt to foresee the future, and end up forestalling it.[94] These future-oriented researches are carried out on the basis of an unspoken presupposition that such conceptions of the prospective are indicative of some sort of destiny which we can decipher. The consequences of these attempts at prevision are disastrous. "Decisions taken as a result of such 'previsions' and of such calculations really engage the future in such a way that it resembles as much as possible the past."[95] We then find ourselves in the midst of a kind of preemptive war against the future designed to turn it into a "colony" of the present. Rather than extrapolating the present trends, says Garaudy, a truly legitimate prospective must reflect the development of every level in the life of society. Moreover, it cannot be undertaken in a positivist manner. The present must be analyzed dialectically in its contradictions, and the future seen as the result of revolution as much as evolution. Finally, the development of a truly human prospective cannot be left in the hands of a few "experts"; rather, the invention of the future "is first of all an invention of the future ends of man, and this invention cannot be the work of a few, but of all."[96] This is the only way to insure the possibility of the emergence of the truly new into the present.

This being said, it still remains unclear how Garaudy can protect himself against the historical relativization of the Absolute Future. He has stated that we must avoid transforming the future into a "colony of the present," and yet it is we who must invent this future. How can one be sure that what is emerging from the struggles of the present is the truly new, and not simply an altered version of the past? Where are we to find the absolute by which to judge our plans and projects? This remains a problem as long as the future is invented or created by the present generation. Garaudy has affirmed that, for the Marxist, the future is "a dimension of man's activity which goes out beyond himself toward its far-off being," and not an "act of God who comes toward him and summons him."[97]

For the Christian, according to Rahner, the very opposite is true. "The future is not that toward which we are going ourselves, but that which, by itself, comes to us. . . ."[98] The truly "future" future is that which transcends all our plans, surprising us with the new and the unexpected. It does not rest forever beyond man, the final limit to life, but it *comes toward us*, all the while remaining the eternal and nameless mystery. God calls men to construct the new future while simultaneously criticizing and judging all our efforts as insufficient. The relationship between the plannable future and the Absolute Future is an unending dialectic between the now and the not-yet, between the old and the new, between the present and the future.

## NOTES

1. MTC, p. 130. Leslie Dewart supports this interpretation, characterizing Western Christianity by the word *charity* (i.e., action) and the Greek tradition by the word *fate*. Cf. e.g., *The Foundations of Belief* (London: Burns and Oates, 1969), p. 50: "The most fundamental concept at work in Greco-Roman culture was the idea that whatever happens, happens necessarily. The course of events is essentially inexorable; the problem of man is how to cope with a world of reality, and with a human situation, the outcome of which is (at least in principle) set beforehand." A. T. van Leeuwen points out that Stoic philosophy "located true freedom in the discovery by the individual man, within himself and with the aid of his logos, of the cosmic law. The Hellenistic conception was that this law, which man discovers in himself and in the cosmos, was embodied in the person of the divine king, who also represented the law of the state. The *polis* came to be identified with the cosmos—the Greek citizen was cosmopolitan." *Christianity in World History* (London: Edinburgh House Press, 1966), p. 138.

2. Cf. e.g., Moltmann, *Theology of Hope,* pp. 40–41. "The real language of Christian eschatology, however, is not the Greek *logos,* but the *promise* which has stamped the language, the hope, and the experience of Israel. . . . That is why history was here experienced in an entirely different and entirely open form."

3. ATD, pp. 57–58.

4. MTC, p. 131.

5. The idea of Christianity as centered on the act of God in history is a strongly Barthian notion. It is strange that Roger Garaudy rarely refers to Barth, and never on this particular theme. The explanation may simply be that Barth's extreme theocentrism is incompatible with Garaudy's anthropocentrism, or it may be that since he is writing in Catholic France, Garaudy does not view Barth as a significant support for his case. Nevertheless, Garaudy must be acquainted with Barth, for while a student at Strasbourg in 1935–36, he lived among theologians of the "evangelical circle," where there was great enthusiasm for the theology of Barth and Kierkegaard.

6. Metz, "God Before Us," p. 42.

7. This and the following quotations are taken from ATD, p. 103.

8. See Moltmann, *Theology of Hope,* pp. 95–101.

9. Sociologist Peter Berger elaborates on the implications of this eternal presence for human existence. "The sacred cosmos emerges out of chaos and

continues to confront the latter as its terrible contrary. . . . The sacred cosmos, which transcends and includes man in its ordering of reality, thus provides man's ultimate shield against the terror of anomy. To be in a 'right' relationship with the sacred cosmos is to be protected against the nightmare threats of chaos. To fall out of such a 'right' relationship is to be abandoned on the edge of the abyss of meaninglessness." Berger, *The Social Reality of Religion,* p. 27.

10. Moltmann, *Theology of Hope,* p. 99.

11. Ibid., p. 30.

12. Ibid., p. 133.

13. Ibid., p. 165.

14. Ibid., p. 196.

15. Roger Garaudy, private communication.

16. Moltmann, *Theology of Hope,* p. 165.

17. Roger Garaudy, private communication.

18. Cf. MTC, pp. 111–112.

19. MTC, p. 111.

20. See ATD, p. 101.

21. MTC, p. 112.

22. Cf. e.g., L. Mumford, *The Condition of Man,* pp. 74–75. "The Christian is one who escapes from time: eternity lies before him. . . . Within the Church, then, the Christian worked out a new drama: preparation for death as the essential way of life. . . . The Christian is a person who rejects the usages of a dying society, and finds a new life for himself in the Church."

23. ATD, p. 97.

24. ATD, p. 56.

25. ATD, p. 113.

26. PMFS, p. 371.

27. Friedrich Engels, *The Peasant War in Germany,* in Feuer, p. 465.

28. ATD, p. 116.

29. ATD, p. 117.

30. MTC, p. 114.

31. Feuer, p. 304.

32. ATD, p. 100.

33. MR, p. 18.

34. ATD, p. 113.

35. PMFS, p. 359. Roger Garaudy, in a private conversation, stated that he has been impressed with the change in attitude on the part of the church since Vatican II.

36. Material in this paragraph is taken from MTC, pp. 119–120.

37. Cf. Moltmann, "Toward a Political Hermeneutic," esp. pp. 78–81.

38. Ibid., p. 79.

39. Ibid., p. 80.

40. Although Roger Garaudy frequently cites the work of Vatican II (e.g., the constitution "Gaudium et Spes"), and the socially oriented papal encyclicals (e.g., "Populorum Progressio"), he seldom refers to the World Council of Churches and other Protestant agencies. This is strange in itself since the Protestant declarations on social change have been, if anything, much more practical than their Roman Catholic counterparts. See William Lazareth, "Political Responsibility as the Obedience of Faith," in *The Gospel and Human Destiny,* ed. Vilmos Vajta (Minneapolis: Augsburg Publishing House, 1971), for a detailed comparison. Either Garaudy's Pelagian bias is showing, or there is a tactical reason for the omission.

41. Citations are from David M. Gill, "Power, Violence, Non-violence, and Social Change," in *Study Encounter,* (W.C.C.), vol. 6, no. 2 (1970), p. 67.

42. QMM, p. 166.

43. Jules Girardi, *Amour Chrétien et violence révolutionnaire* (Paris: Editions du Cerf, 1970), p. 80.

44. RE, p. 142.

45. RE, p. 144.

46. Girardi, *Amour Chrétien,* p. 62.

47. Roger Garaudy, MCES, p. 88.

48. RE, p. 73.

49. PMFS, pp. 370–371.

50. See Girardi, *Amour Chrétien,* pp. 29–30.

51. Ibid., p. 35.

52. QMM, p. 166.

53. QMM, p. 169.

54. QMM, p. 171.

55. Quoted in QMM, p. 171.

56. RE, p. 144.

57. E.g., the comment by Charles M. Savage in "Critiques Reconsidered," *Study Encounter* (W.C.C.), vol. 4, no. 1 (1968), p. 3: "Were we to caricature the traditional position of the Christians and the Marxists we might say: Christianity proclaimed a new heaven, but forgot about a new earth; while Marxism proclaimed a new earth, but forgot about a new heaven."

58. Reinhold Niebuhr, quoted in David M. Gill, "Power, Violence, Non-violence, and Social Change," p. 70.

59. GPG, p. 169.

60. Ibid. Note the close parallel to Harvey Cox, "The Exodus as the Desacralization of Politics," in *The Secular City,* pp. 25 ff. The striking resemblance is clear evidence of Garaudy's enthusiasm for Cox's "secular" interpretation of Christianity. Cox also suggests that Marxism, although possessing certain "semi-religious" qualities, participates in this process of desacralization by denying the legitimacy of any form of society not consonant with human needs.

61. GPG, p. 184.

62. Cf. e.g., HM, p. 53. "Hence, we dwell in the pure immanence of the histori-
    cal dialectic in which the thoughts, feelings, and volitions of men constitute
    one moment. But this subjectivity of man is also a product of history."

63. Cottier, *Chrétiens et marxistes*, p. 119.

64. Karl Rahner, MCES, p. 228.

65. Ibid., p. 229.

66. Braaten, "Toward a Theology of Hope," p. 100.

67. Johannes Metz, MCES, p. 124.

68. Karl Rahner, "La 'nouvelle terre,' " p. 112.

69. Braaten, "The Gospel of the Kingdom of God and the Church."

70. Johannes Metz, MCES, p. 125.

71. Cottier, *Chrétiens et marxistes*, p. 61.

72. Ibid., p. 56.

73. E. Kamenka, "The Concept of a Political Revolution," in *Nomos VIII—
    Revolution*, ed. C. J. Friedrich (New York: Atherton Press, 1966), p. 124.

74. Capps, "The Hope Tendency," p. 71.

75. Braaten, "The Gospel of the Kingdom of God and the Church."

76. Carl Braaten, *The Future of God*, p. 26.

77. PMFS, p. 362.

78. Cf. Cox, *The Secular City*, p. 107, where it is explicitly stated that "since the
    phrase *rapid social change* serves often as a euphemism for *revolution*. . . .
    We are trying to live in a period of revolution without a theology of revo-
    lution."

79. Ibid., p. 114.

80. Thus Engels declares that the revolution "presupposes that the development
    of production has reached a level at which the appropriation of means of
    production and of products, and with these, of political supremacy, the
    monopoly of education and intellectual leadership by a special class of soci-
    ety, has become not only superfluous but also economically, politically and
    intellectually a hindrance to development." (*Anti-Dühring*, in Selsam and
    Martel, p. 222.)

81. Cox, *The Secular City*, p. 115.

82. See Braaten, "The Future as the Source of Freedom," esp. p. 384, where he
    refers enthusiastically to a statement by Pannenberg which suggests "that
    God should be conceived as pure freedom."

83. Ibid., p. 390.

84. ATD, p. 91.

85. Ibid.

86. Robert Havemann, MCES, p. 270.

87. Ibid.

88. Moltmann, "Hoping and Planning," p. 59.

89. See Moltmann, "Hoping and Planning."

90. Karl Rahner, MCES, p. 231.

91. Karl Rahner, "Humanisme chrétien," p. 66.

92. Karl Rahner, "Autour du concept de l'avenir," p. 98.

93. GPG, p. 253.

94. Such attempts to plan the future rest on the presupposition of what might be termed a "surprise free" future. This is defined by sociologist Peter Berger as "a world in which present trends continue to unfold without the intrusion of totally new and unexpected factors" (*A Rumor of Angels*, p. 30). Roger Garaudy is highly critical of such an approach to the future, which is really an effort to suppress futurity; he prefers to speak of the "prospective" of the future, and in fact, teaches a course under that title at the University of Poitiers.

95. GPG, p. 255.

96. GPG, p. 257.

97. ATD, p. 92.

98. Karl Rahner, "Autour du concept de l'avenir," p. 98.

# SIX

# *Transcendence and Subjectivity*

## THE SUBJECTIVE ELEMENT

Garaudy clearly adopts and adapts the Marxist understanding of transcendence from the Christian concept of transcendence. Similarly, Garaudy's attempt to integrate human subjectivity into a Marxist humanism owes a great debt to Christianity, a debt which he in no way denies: "Christianity in fact raised the problem of transcendence, and with it, moreover, that of subjectivity; indeed; even the way of approaching the problem of subjectivity is specific to Christianity."[1] Christian emphasis on the subjective depth of the human person found its contemporary philosophical expression in existentialism. Prior to the rediscovery of this subjective mode of thinking, the deep existential insights of Christian thinkers from Paul and Augustine to Luther had been largely overlaid by a dogmatic rationalism which found its fullest and richest expression in the Hegelian system. The merit of post-Kierkegaardian existentialist philosophy consisted in demonstrating that such a rationalistic approach robbed consciousness of an essential dimension: that of subjectivity.

### The Fichtean Origins of Existentialism

Garaudy traces the origins of existentialism back much further than Kierkegaard, all the way to Johann Gottlieb Fichte. He finds Fichte's work situated at a junction point in history, a time of the collapse of traditional, feudal values. Because of this historical dislocation, questions arose concerning the existing political order's lack of internal logic, the failure of religious faith, and the increasing conflict of conscience and obedience. "This situation explains the exaltation of the importance of the individual, of his radical autonomy, of the supreme value accorded to freedom as the mother of all values, and to responsibility."[2]

Garaudy asserts that Fichte's first and basic thesis was the affirmation of the ego, postulating itself by itself. This represented a marked departure from traditional philosophy, since it overthrew the venerable axiom of the primacy of essence over existence. Man is not defined by some a priori essence; "he is nothing other than what his own free activity makes him; every man makes himself what he is."[3] This line of argumentation also carries echoes of Sartre's "first principle of existentialism," that man is what he makes of himself. Secondly, Fichte is reputed to have asserted the "ambiguity of subject and object, of constituent and constituted, of facticity and freedom."[4] Third, he described the ego as absolute freedom, conditioned only by the necessity of choice. Fourth, and most important for the future development of existentialism, Fichte described the ego as "project," i.e., as continually moving beyond itself, propelled by the need to find its own fulfillment.[5] Thus Fichte is found to possess all the elements of an existentialist philosophy, but within a rationalist framework. This rational dimension is not seen as unfortunate in Garaudy's eyes; quite the contrary, the Marxist is urged to integrate Fichte's existential subjectivity into the wider context of both rational and social dimensions.

It is this movement from the subjective and personal to the objective and social that poses the greatest problem for the existentialist. Existentialism, according to Garaudy, suffers from two essential failings: (1) Although it is based on the radical autonomy of the ego, "this concept of freedom is nontemporal and extra-historical; to put it briefly, it is metaphysical and speculative."[6] Such a concept introduces a split between the ego and concrete, historical practice. (2) Such an a-historical understanding of human autonomy of necessity leads to moral formalism. The individual person is called to freedom and responsibility, but there are no concrete ends and goals toward which to strive. To put it simply, the existentialist finds himself trapped in his own subjectivity with no means of relating practically to other, similarly isolated subjectivities.[7] This problem does not arise if one begins from a Kantian, transcendental ego; it is, however, unavoidable if we start from an existential ego.

This inability to escape the limits of my own consciousness leads to a form of solipsism. As long as the other person remains beyond any real, objective knowledge, "I cannot escape from myself, since I cannot say what others feel."[8] Neither does it do any good to try to inject some sort of idealist intersubjectivity at this point, since then there are really only two possibilities: either the other person is "entirely transparent" to my ego (which would lead right back to solipsism, since the other would then be nothing more than a part of my own ego), or he has some kind of existence "in himself." The only way to avoid the first option is to admit that "each 'subject' is an 'object' to the other, and I am then obliged to analyze the reciprocal action of the one on the other."[9] Thus we are led back to the original problem of the subject-object relationship. The conclusion is clear: I am "me" for myself and "you" for the other; I am at one and the same time both subject *and* object.

Fichte's solution to the problem is somewhat different; it rests on the postulate of an existential self that is *already* inhabited by others. That is to say, the existence of others is a precondition for any kind of consciousness whatever. This arises out of the ego's experience of limitedness. Fichte asserts that a free activity (ego) cannot be limited except by another free activity (ego). Thus, "my autonomy has as the condition of its freedom the freedom of the other."[10] Fichte is able to arrive at this conclusion because he did not begin from "an insular, solipsist cogito." Thus the basic condition at the root of all individuality is the relationship one has with other individual beings. "In Fichte the pure 'I' is opposed to the empirical 'I' in the same way as the 'we' is opposed to the 'I.' " The conclusion of Fichte, i.e., that all those around us represent "ends" but no one is his own "end," is based on the presupposition of a "point of view from which the consciousness of all rational beings is united, an object, into One: hence the point of view of God."[11] Finally, therefore, the Fichtean solution to the existentialist dilemma depends on the existence of a God who sees each rational being as a unique and final end. Our mutual interaction is effected through the mediation of a divine Being. Such a solution is clearly unacceptable to a Marxist, and Garaudy must look elsewhere for the means of bringing together, within a rational framework, both social and subjective dimensions.

*Act, Being, and Subjectivity*

Garaudy seeks to steer a middle way between the excesses of dogmatic materialism and idealism.

> The principal failing of materialism was in ignoring the activity of the subject. But conversely, idealism, in rightly analyzing this activity, finished by forgetting what was the starting point of it all, i.e., the external world . . .[12]

Following the trail blazed by Fichte, Garaudy warns against both a closed, solipsistic subjectivism and against an empiricism which would conceive experience as immediate perception of reality, claiming to know once and for all the inner nature of being. Experience, he insists, is of the nature of a question, and consequently the answer one receives is a function of the kind of question one asks. In other words, our knowledge of reality is always conditioned by the relative state of the sciences at the time the question is asked.[13] All of this is a roundabout way of saying that Marxism is not a philosophy of *being*, but a philosophy of *act,*

> that is, one which makes of consciousness and the human practice which engenders it and constantly enriches it a true reality, rooted in earlier activity and in the real, and reflecting them, but constantly going beyond the given and continually adding to reality by a creative act, which is not yet given at the level of pre-human nature and the success of which nothing can guarantee in advance.[14]

The connection between such a theory of knowledge and the concept of subjectivity is found in the affirmation that it is impossible for consciousness to be equated with itself. Consciousness may at times be equated with being, as we saw in Chapter Four, where reason and reality were found to share a similar dialectical structure; however, even if consciousness can at times make being transparent to itself, "it cannot be equated with its own *act* by which it necessarily transcends and creates itself."[15] Garaudy concludes that subjectivity, like Marxism itself, is of the order of act, rather than being. Hence it is possible for him to assert that Marxism not only can be approached existentially; it must be approached that way.

The ultimate reconciliation of subjectivity and society, of the one and the many, is effected through a Fichtean reading of Marx. Garaudy begins by asserting that our earliest and most basic experience is *not* that of solitude.[16] Rather, human beings develop self-consciousness only in relationship to others. This, of course, is the most elementary psychology. Since Freud, it has been commonly accepted that infants develop their personalities in the context of a web of interpersonal relationships, without which the child would wither and die. This is simply an affirmation of the fact that man is not an isolated, ethereal "self," but a human being, possessed of a physical body in contact with other physical bodies. Just as the self-concept of an infant develops within the context of a vigorous interaction of parent and child, so Garaudy can say that "subjectivity is born of communication."[17] From the very beginning I understand myself as individual only within a communal nexus. Thus there is no such thing as the "rugged individualist." We cannot exist without the active presence of others. Robinson Crusoe is a myth. I am conscious of myself only through the presence of others *in* me, a presence demonstrated both by the language I use and the labor I perform. Subjectivity therefore always carries within itself a social dimension.

In contrast to "existentialism" as it is commonly conceived, this social dimension, made tangible in labor and language, exists outside us and before us. This is because the historical initiatives of earlier generations have become crystallized into the products and institutions making up the given historical conditions under which we live. This does not mean, of course, that human subjectivity, in the form of historical initiative, is essentially subordinated to these preconditions. This we have already seen. The question of how man creates his own history by an act that is both necessary and free is really the question of the transcendence of human subjectivity. If Garaudy's handling of this question often seems vague or contradictory, it is undoubtedly because of the basic ambiguity in his position. His entire purpose is to "hold onto both ends of the chain," to bring together freedom and necessity, subjectivity and materialism, historical initiative and rational understanding. The paradox of this purpose is clear from the words of Garaudy himself:

> The study of the laws of social development, the possibility even of plotting, at least in its essentials, the trajectory of a more or less probable immediate or distant future, does not at any time excuse us from making ourselves conscious of our own responsibility as *subjects* who act and create our own history, and not as *objects* of a history in a con-

cept that would reduce us to no more than the resultant or sum of the conditions of our existence. [18]

The question is simply whether the method Garaudy suggests permits us to accomplish this goal. What room remains for "our responsibility as subjects who act and create our own history" when it becomes possible for us to plot "at least in its essentials" the future course of historical events? What value has individual subjectivity when the meaning of history is reduced to man's work rather than man himself? These are questions that have not yet been answered.

### Distortions of Marxism: Sartre and Althusser

The attempt to couple subjectivity with historical materialism leads Garaudy to walk a tightrope between the two extremes of anti-historical existentialism and anti-humanist structuralism. In order to clarify his own position, he takes to task the two best known proponents of these symmetrically opposed "distortions" of Marxism: "Sartre, neglecting the essential element in scientific socialism by overemphasizing subjectivity, and Althusser, on the contrary, eliminating subjectivity and retaining only the conceptual aspect."[19] Beginning with Sartre, we find that Garaudy's critique rests on two basic issues: the problem of freedom, or negativity, and the problem of social ethics, of the "other" and of history. Accordingly, we will examine Garaudy's arguments in that order.

### Negativity and Freedom

Sartrian freedom, we are told, is intimately related to negation; it is the act by which consciousness refuses what is in favor of what is not. "Freedom is first of all autonomous choice and negation."[20] Thus the first characteristic of freedom for Sartre is that man is not what he *is*, but what he *does*. This negation of the given situation necessitates a choice, and in order for man to be more than a simple fact of nature, that choice must comport intentionality. The first difficulty with this understanding of freedom, says Garaudy, is that it can in no way explain the origin of such a negation or of such an intentionality. Man is defined as the being by whom Nothing comes into the world. Consciousness is essentially negation; but "its breaking into the world becomes a real mystery, since nothing occurs within being, and nothingness cannot exist except as a function of being."[21] This means that there is no way to explain the sudden appearance of Nothing at the heart of being. It is absolutely contingent. Therefore the freedom which is the result of this negation is nontemporal, extra-historical and metaphysical; it is a mystery. "What he [Sartre] is trying to do," says Garaudy, "is in some way to construct a society from metaphysically defined individuals, to construct history from the nontemporal, an historical materialism without matter."[22]

Thus what contradiction exists is not a conflict within reality itself, within being, but rather a contradiction between matter and mind, between being and nothingness. Garaudy thus criticizes Sartre's definition of man as a return to a form of idealism because of its insistence on the notion that "the spirit alone is the negative, i.e., denying the dialectic of nature."[23] There can never be a true dialectic, since the opposition of being and nothingness is non-dynamic. Nonbeing, says Garaudy, is more than just the opposite of being: it is its contradiction. For Sartre, "there is contradiction at the heart of being, but no dialectic, no supersession."[24] This eternal contradiction between being and consciousness is the source of *Angst*, since no resolution is possible the way the problem is stated.

Sartre's concept of negation is, as we have seen, the foundation of his understanding of human freedom. Herein lies Garaudy's second principal criticism. The welling up of nothingness at the core of being is a totally contingent and individual event. It is not tied in any way to historically determined, prior conditions. "Freedom is the power to say no . . . to the being constituted by our personal history and by the world around us."[25] Garaudy would be the last to criticize Sartre for affirming that human decisions are not mechanical results of a priori conditions, but he opposes vehemently the attempt to uproot man from history and reduce freedom to abstract choice. In making freedom simple autonomy of choice, Sartre has robbed it of any real social content. Since freedom is ontological, rather than historical, it falls victim to the same errors as the "bourgeois theories of liberty." In this warped perspective, "freedom is a formal attribute of the abstract individual . . . it is without content; it does not imply the understanding of any objective law. . . ."[26] Such a freedom is identified with the most radical individualism; there is no interaction with others, and no interest in power or effectiveness. It is therefore atemporal, absolute, and irrational. And herein lies its essential failure, since "freedom cannot be divorced from the content of action: and Sartre's initial individualism bars him from the passage from one to the other."[27]

The Problem of the "Other"

The nature of Sartrian "freedom" undoubtedly poses grave problems for the Marxist; however, when we approach the question of the "other" person, the difficulties become well nigh insurmountable. Sartre has simply reduced all human relationships to a one-to-one basis: "At the origin of the problem of the existence of others, there is a fundamental presupposition: Others are *the Other,* that is the self which *is not* myself."[28] To avoid the pitfall of solipsism, the relationship is ontological rather than epistemological; i.e., it is a relation of being with being. The supreme example, given by Sartre in *Being and Nothingness,* is that of the "regard," the "look." This look has a certain symbolic value, recognized by Garaudy; but its drawback is that it transforms me into a thing alongside other things, thus alienating my freedom and creating a situation similar to that of master and slave. At the same time, however, it is the look of the other which reveals my being to me, which allows me to grasp myself as I really am. So powerful is this process of transformation "that I always end up more or less resembling what is expected of me."[29]

Garaudy sees the essential stumbling block in the kind of relationship Sartre has chosen for consideration; the objectifying consequences of the "look" actually illustrate the form of relations within an individualist and bourgeois capitalist society, "with its social relations that make man an object, a thing, with its relationships of domination and slavery."[30] Thus Sartre has mistakenly taken a certain limited socioeconomic reality—that of capitalism—and given it ontological status. It is interesting to note that this is essentially the same criticism Garaudy made of Heidegger: "From what was the situation of men in a certain nation and a certain class of that nation, Heidegger made the human condition the tragic characteristic of all existence."[31] Thus Sartre's ultra-individualism fits in perfectly with a form of society that fragments and isolates men by the law of the jungle, the law of "every man for himself."

When Sartre attempts to describe the nature of concrete relations with others, his examples are almost exclusively drawn from the world of one-to-one encounters: love, hate, masochism, and sadism. In the whole of *Being and Nothingness*, he devotes only twenty or so pages to " 'Being with' (*Mitsein*) and the 'we.' "[32] Even here social collectivities are reduced to little more than aggregates of individual relationships: " 'We' can be subject and in this form it is identical with the plural of the 'I.' "[33] Such an attitude is the direct result of an ontology that begins from the individual ego in order to rediscover, within its depths, the "other." As long as Sartre remains on this metaphysical level, it is impossible to recognize the "specificity" of the social and historical realms. "Such relations boil down to a multiplication of personal relations, and their character is not historical, but metaphysical."[34] On this basis no movement is possible from the one to the many. Even when Sartre attempts to deal with social and political questions, e.g., in his novels and plays, the problems posed remain on the metaphysical plane. The sheer individualism of his ontology, coupled with the irrationality of his understanding of freedom, leads to "an inability to distinguish at every moment between the real forces from which a human future can be secured, and speculations which are the fruit of impatience and impulse."[35] The problem, simply stated, is that individual subjectivities are incapable of providing the structure with which to distinguish genuine, objective historical forces on the sociopolitical level. For the Marxist, Sartrian existentialism fails to take seriously the demands of history and society. As long as one clings to this kind of metaphysical ontology, "history is not engaged, and the struggles of men will never be anything but the allegory or the parable of a metaphysical drama."[36]

While Sartre has so magnified the subjective element that the objectivity of the concept is all but eliminated, Louis Althusser's "theoretical anti-humanism" has gone to the opposite extreme in creating "the illusion of being able to entrench oneself in the concept and so treat structures and social relationships without reference to human options."[37] Essentially, what Althusser has done is to break the basic unity of theory and praxis so critical to Marxist thought, and this in such a way as to make it appear the intention of Marx. Such a reinterpretation clearly requires a stringent overhaul of traditional Marxist thinking on the subject; indeed, it necessitates a radical break with the usual interpretation of Marx, and even the postulate of a break within Marx's own thought. Thus Garaudy can with some justification state that "Althusser thinks everything in terms of 'rupture' or of 'break.' "[38]

The Epistemological Break

Althusser's rereading of *Capital* begins with an epistemological break, a mutation in the thought of Marx dating from the years 1845-1850. This break signifies the movement from a humanist and anthropological kind of thinking to a scientific thinking expressed in terms of objects, abstract concepts, forms, and structures. This "scientific" thinking is the only basis of a true Marxist science. It must be strongly emphasized that this change does not constitute some sort of Hegelian evolution in Marx's conceptualization, dialectic or otherwise. Jean Conilh, in an article dealing with Althusser's work, makes clear that there is no overlapping, no gradual development leading from the humanist Marx to the scientific Marx. "The epistemological break is a true rupture."[39] By this rereading of Marx, Althusser proposes to eleminate from "scientific" Marxism all traces of the "pre-scientific" and "pseudo-philosophic" Marx as he appears in his early writings. Hence Althusser must constantly delete from *Capital* various anachronistic references to ideas such as alienation, dialectic, and the unity of theory and practice. Garaudy vigorously attacks this reading of *Capital*, and accuses Althusser of imposing on Marx a metaphysics of radical break which is precisely the opposite of Marx's true thought, since "he does not think metaphysically in terms of radical rupture, but dialectically in terms of supersession and inversion."[40] The idea of an unconscious development of Marx's thought serves, in reality, to strip his philosophy of both man and the dialectic of history, substituting in their place an abstract structuralism.

Such an epistemological break makes a unified vision of reality, a traditional philosophy, impossible for Marxist thought, since it disqualifies the "ideological discourse" as "negative or simply indicative," and not "the place of Marxist truth."[41] On the other hand, while attacking an ideological Marxism, Althusser recognizes the necessity for ideological praxis. In this case, ideology (as a way of representing the masses) is indispensable for the formation and transformation of men into a state in which they are capable of responding to the demands of life. The question is then how Althusser proposes to ground such an ideological practice after having eliminated any philosophical overtones from "scientific" Marxism, and the answer appears to be that he views scientific theory itself as a form of philosophy.

Garaudy responds that in attempting to rid Marxist "science" of all anthropological and humanist elements, Althusser has grossly misunderstood the nature of Marx's humanism. For Marx, says Garaudy, it is not a question of some abstract, individualist, and metaphysical conception of men: "he gives them a new meaning: materialist, dialectical, and historical."[42] Thus Garaudy returns to his classic three-point definition of man as (1) labor anticipated by a future project, (2) labor performed by a social being, and (3) labor done by a historical being, transforming both nature and himself in the process. This Marxist humanism is hence both militant, in the sense that it calls on men to battle for the creation of truly human social and historical conditions, and it is scientific, in the sense that it is built on practice. Garaudy speaks frequently of Marx's sixth thesis on Feuerbach as demonstrating the Marxist ties with structuralism, but he condemns the Althusser school for going too far when it declares: "The subject is only the support of production relations constitutive of economic objectivity."[43] Garaudy points out that Marx always distinguished between man as he is dehumanized by the structures of capitalism (and to which abstract structuralism tends to reduce him) and man as subject of history. Thus, to eliminate humanism from Marx is to rob Marxism of the essential element distinguishing it from positivistic political economy, which deals only with alienated labor. Finally it must be recognized that, for Marx, "the subject is no longer . . . either the isolated individual or the absolute spirit, but historical man. . . ."[44]

## "Scientific" Marxism

Althusser's desire to eliminate all anthropological humanism from Marx is only the first part of the problem; the second concerns the "science" with which he would replace traditional Marxism. From Althusser's point of view, theoretical practice serves as its own criteria of validation without reference to external facts.

> It is not any different in the real practice of the sciences: once they are truly constituted and developed, they have no need for verification from external practice. . . .[45]

Althusser then proceeds to draw an illustration from the science of mathematics, for which truth is not dependent on external experimental support, e.g., from physics. This understanding of science is not only naïve, as Garaudy points out, but it leads to a false mathematization of the inexact, or "human," sciences. The naïveté of a sharp dichotomy between theory and practice, even in mathematics, is demonstrated by Garaudy in the example of Galileo and other scientists, who discovered various mathematical principles through the development of technology and the exigencies of economics. Thus the science of hydraulics received a great impulse through the necessity to control the mountain streams of Italy in the sixteenth and seventeenth centuries.[46] Moreover, the extension of the special case of theoretical mathematics to political economy disregards the distinct nature of pure mathematics as a self-contained, formal construct, a kind of intellectual game far removed from the human sciences.

In effect, such a "scientization" of Marxism leads to a complete rejection of Marx's insistence on the unity of theory and practice. Since the unity of theory and praxis is a constant theme in *Capital,* Althusser must find some way to separate the theoretical "wheat" from the humanistic "chaff." For this process he employs what is termed a "symptomal reading." It is assumed in this reading that "Marx did not think through theoretically, in an adequate and developed form, the concept and the theoretical implications of his theoretically revolutionary approach."[47] Thus one must uncover at certain symptomatic locations in *Capital* the silences, lapses, and theoretical lacunae which point to the true meaning of the text. Garaudy finds, to the contrary, that "this 'symptomal' reading of Marx is in reality a long polemic against Marx."[48] This is not to say that Garaudy feels the Marxist texts are sacred or untouchable, but simply that Althusser's alterations in the obvious intent of the text are so gross as to be untenable. The unity of theory and practice is so engrained in *Capital* (not to mention the earlier writings) that any attempt to remove it destroys the very fabric of Marxism. To remove the active subject and its praxis "thereby eliminates dialectic, history, and practice; it gets rid of all that is fundamental in Marxism."[49]

Thus Althusser and his disciples are accused by Garaudy of having followed a false path, stripping *Capital* of everything that is not pure structural and conceptual theory, to the point of emptying history of all subjectivity and of making unintelligible the transformation of the structure itself. But this is not what an open reading of Marx himself reveals. For Garaudy, as for Marx,

> the specificity of man must be considered: he is the animal who, in the act of labor, gives his present action the law of the goal pursued: with man—and this is the reason he transcends nature and every other animal species—the future exercises its action on the present.[50]

Man is not to be totally identified with structures, nor is he to be reduced to an object; rather he is free to struggle against exploitation, he is capable of personal responsibility, and he is not a prisoner of fatalistic economic laws: "the dialectic of history moves through the minds of men. . . ."[51]

## TOTALITY AND INDIVIDUALITY

The preceding polemic against the structuralist distortion of personal subjectivity in history reflects the interplay of the individual and society in Marxist philosophy, especially as it is viewed by Garaudy. It is clear from the entire thrust of this chapter that, for Garaudy, individuality develops itself most fully within the context of community. This dialectic between the individual subject and the total collectivity means that a careful line must be drawn between individuality and individualism. The former is a vital element in the "limitless transformation of nature, of society, and even of man. . ."[52] whereas the latter leads only to isolation and despair. The burst of human creativity in which man is transformed in the very process of transforming the world is made possible only by the harmonization of social goals with individual goals. This harmonization leads to, or rather constitutes what Garaudy calls *"l'homme total,"* "total man." The definition is straightforward: "This total man is essentially the man who will be born from a society which has overcome alienation: unalienated man."[53]

At the Salzburg colloquium Garaudy referred to "total man" as the anchor point for all Marxist humanism. Total man will overcome the alienation of work, and in so doing he will put an end to all the other forms of the splitting and doubling of man. To bring about this totalization, two things are necessary: first, "to create the social conditions enabling each man to carry within himself all mankind," through having assimilated the totality of past culture and participating in the future of all men; second, "to confer on mankind, i.e., on the unity of humankind as race, its concrete sense in a world without war, in a society without classes. . . ."[54] This clearly means the end of all alienation. Garaudy asserts that communism, and communism alone, possesses the means for overcoming the basic contradictions in human existence, because only in Marxism does science become a moral force for change. Moral consciousness, i.e., the drive to overcome the divisions between and within men, is both a product of historical development and one of its contributing factors. The end and goal of this moral and scientific struggle is the creation of total man.

"This man is 'total' both in time and in space,"[55] says Garaudy. By this he means that the struggle for the communist society will include and crown the collective efforts of mankind's total history. Total man, fully human man, is he who consciously carries within himself the totality of human development. "Communism alone places this total culture at the disposition of all men."[56] Moreover, communist man is total because his life is planetary. Overcoming narrow parochialism and petty rivalries, total man will achieve a planetary organization of needs and resources. "Human unity can from then on cease to be an ideal and become an objective reality."[57]

It is interesting that Garaudy credits Christianity for having introduced the idea of "a limitless human community," i.e., the consciousness of the self-realization of humanity. But caution is needed at this point for, as Cottier is quick to point out, Garaudy's conception of total man is strongly reminiscent of Feuerbach's pantheism of the collective humanity.[58] The true relation of Christianity to Marxism is one of contrast: on the one hand, humanity is seen as the society of God's sons, each possessing the capability of creation, initiative, and love; on the other, humanity is seen as the "hypostasis of the collective, a kind of immanent 'Super Being' to which individuals are subordinated."[59] It would appear that, if Cottier is correct in his analysis, Garaudy's total man is more Feuerbachian than Christian. The consequence of endowing the species with all the attributes of the infinite (as Pannenberg has rightly shown) is a neglect of the individual and his particular existence and fate. For Garaudy, as for Feuerbach, the real human situation, with its daily struggle against intolerable odds, gives way to the vision of "a human species which, untouched by the suffering of individuals, nonetheless is still supposed to be distinguished by every good quality imaginable."[60]

Garaudy responds, of course, that Marxism deprives man of none of his essential dimensions; in fact, it offers the only real chance of personal fulfillment through the struggle to transform the earth. The perspective of an infinite future open before man evokes "the feeling of a personal responsibility of each for the realization of this program for a total humanity."[61]

But once again Cottier warns of two incompatible conceptions of man. Garaudy calls for a human community without limit but, in point of fact, this community makes of totalized humanity the source of meaning and action for individual man. "In other words, this man, who lives and is fulfilled within the limits of an exclusively earthly horizon, is a collective, social being."[62] The collectivity is what gives the individual his *raison d'être*. Such a theory is foreign to Christian anthropology since, while the social dimension is essential to man, it does not constitute his essence. The earthly salvation preached by Marxism is the salvation of man as collectivity. Social man is the true agent and goal of history, and the dimension of personal transcendence over all temporal societies is negated. The city of God disappears and the city of man becomes all in all. The consequences for ethics are formidable. If man is not individual, but some sort of fraternal collectivity viewed from the horizon of the future, then there are no longer any criteria for defending the individual against the excesses perpetuated by the collectivity in its efforts to construct an as yet nonexistent world. "In the name of Man, the existence of real men is relativized."[63]

Here is where Christianity must forcefully state the case for the importance, nay, the *absolute value* of each individual person over against all social collectivities. As Rahner points out, the Christian doctrines of God, Christ, freedom, responsibility, and judgment are neither arbitrary theological constructs nor ideological opiates, "but the supreme radicalization of the dignity of man."[64] This individual dignity is different for Garaudy, who views the value of each person not as something intrinsic to human existence, but rather as resting on the active and creative capacities of man. Thus the ultimate goal of Marxism is "to make *every* man a man, that is to say, a creator, a center of historical initiative. . . ."[65] But active and creative man is conceivable only within the context of a network of reciprocal relations upon which he depends. In spite of his rejection of the idea that man can be reduced to the sum of his social relations, that "there is no center, no subjects who create meaning, no men who make history. . ."[66] Garaudy cannot escape the conclusion that, for him, the individual is enclosed within the horizon of his social relations. Nor does it change the situation to assert that these relations are inexhaustible because of their infinite complexity. The Christian must affirm, in opposition to any reductive view, that each person is endowed with a spiritual autonomy and transcendence which is both the source and the meaning of all social life.

Thus Braaten, for example, interprets the Gospel as pointing to an ultimate horizon of fulfillment that goes beyond all objectifiable goals of the social-political order.

> The Gospel affirms the infinite value of the individual person, in such a clear way that it withstands every effort to exhaust the definition of an individual's worth in terms of his role in society or his contribution to the state.[67]

The Christian is hence obligated to work for the highest possible self-definition of man at any given moment.

On the other hand, while the Christian perspective views each human being as personal, with value in and for himself, value growing out of his spiritual capacity to enter into dialogue with others and with God, this in no way denies that man is also a social being, with obligations and needs that relate him to other men. Man is *one,* says Rahner, to the extent that

> every dimension is found in reciprocal interaction with every other, that none fulfills itself in a manner fully independent of another, thus that none can be *entirely* healthy without the other being so.[68]

It is thus the dignity of the individual that is the driving force for social justice, since the mutual interaction of individuals requires that I treat every man with the respect due to a child of God. "This point is, in effect, capital," says Cottier, since "if man is a person, he has absolute value: each human being ought consequently to be treated personally."[69] The meaning of "person" given to us by Christian theology impels us to struggle for the defense of the rights of every man *precisely because he is a person.*

CHARACTERISTICS OF SUBJECTIVITY

*Love*

Garaudy is not unaware of the apparent conflict between Christian theology and Marxist humanism vis-à-vis individuality and totality; indeed, he asserts this to be the specific contribution of Marxism to religion: "to remind religion that its birthplace is the earth. That is where we start from in order to grasp, in a different way, the personal relationship of man to the totality."[70] It is the future that confers meaning for the Marxist, a future already here as the "leaven of our action in the present." This future is directly tied to the realization of "total man." To be human, according to Garaudy, is to reflect by one's daily life a personal relation with this future or, what is evidently the same thing, with this totality. "This is the demand of the future which—if I may say—is a *demand of love* giving a sense to our life and to our death."[71]

Of course, Garaudy uses the term *love* as he does *future,* in an altogether immanent and human manner. Nevertheless, he acknowledges the fundamental contribution of Christianity to this Marxist concept of love. His criticism is simply that love, as it is conceived by Christians, is lived in an alienated way, in terms of exteriority. To put it simply, human love has been projected on a divine being outside this world, "into another world, into a hereafter," in a "love which is this iron world's 'other.' "[72] This is not to say that Garaudy's critique is wholly negative; he does credit the vision of the "infinite love of Christ" with a certain tragic beauty, witnessing not to the greatness of God, but to the greatness of man. "It is this act of faith that proves that man never considers himself wholly defeated."[73] But the communist task is to work and struggle lest this "dream," this "hope," remain eternally distant and illusory. Moreover, the Marxist is duty bound to remind the originators of the dream that the easy use of words such as charity and love has often served as an excuse for perpetuating an unjust and unloving social system which denies the very content of the words. Here the Christian can only, with Job, place his hand across his mouth and acknowledge his guilt and responsibility.

But humility should not deter us from questioning the totally anthropocentric character of Garaudy's understanding of love: "Love displays the specifically human dimension of history; poetry and love disclose man's transcendence in relation to each of his provisional realizations."[74] As we have already seen, this kind of transcendence remains entirely within the human historical horizon.

> The closest image, then, we can form of this transcendence is perhaps that of the love, of the strictly human love, through which we learn to see, or rather to postulate in the loved being, a quality which shares no common measure with the contents of his acts.[75]

Love, for Garaudy, points to the impossibility of living in isolation. It is the cry of every being to find the key to its own inner meaning in the "other." Religious mystification of this basic human drive begins, says Garaudy, with the belief that it has been impressed on man's nature by God, whereas the Marxist would maintain that the meaning of love—even physical love—is a cultural phenomenon that comes only with the emergence of man *per se*. "For us, specifically human love is man's creation, not a gift of God."[76] Thus love is not a fact of nature, but of culture. Nature precedes meaning, admits Garaudy, but human initiative is capable of conferring meaning even on nature. Love witnesses to the genesis of mind *through* matter rather than outside it; "mind is not the opposite of nature but the information of nature."[77]

Although Garaudy views love as an entirely human phenomenon, transcendent only in the sense of man's capacity to transcend himself, he still shows high esteem for the Christian conception of love. Specifically, he contrasts the Christian understanding with the docetic, Platonic notion. To the Christian, love is grounded in the Incarnation, which "means treating every being, no matter who, as though he were Christ, as though he were the living God, standing before us."[78] The Platonic concept of "erotic" love, on the other hand, falls far short of the lofty heights of Christian *agape*. Platonic love, says Garaudy, "takes us outside this world, outside other men, outside time."[79] The *Symposium* or the *Phaedrus* characterizes *eros* as a movement from the mundane world to the Supreme Being. This dialectical progression begins with love of the body, moves to love of the mind, and finally achieves that which epitomizes both body and mind: beauty itself. "The other being, accordingly, is loved not for what it is but for that which it evokes of another reality."[80] There can be no Christian understanding of "neighbor" in such a Platonic kind of love, since other beings are but stepping stones toward the true reality which lies above and beyond every physical realization. What is loved is not the other, but love itself.

Garaudy correctly interprets the radical contribution of Christianity vis-à-vis this kind of erotic love: "It was its transition, through the central experience of the Incarnation, of the God-man and the man-God, from the love of love to the love of the other."[81] Thus "this world" received from Christianity an absolute value in its own right, not simply as a means to an end, but as good in itself. Referring to Cardinal Bellarmine in the sixteenth century and Teilhard de Chardin in the twentieth, Garaudy affirms the Christian principle that "to turn to God in no way implies turning away from the world,"[82] since God is to be found in everything.

This celebration of the intrinsic worth of every man (which is, incidently, difficult to reconcile with Garaudy's understanding of totalization) finds strong echoes in contemporary theology, but in terms that affirm both the immanence *and* transcendence of love. Rahner, for instance, suggested at Salzburg that the Absolute Future cannot be divorced from a fundamental responsibility for the concrete future of mankind. This is, in effect, the meaning behind the twin commandments joining love of God and love of neighbor: "Man cannot live his true relationship with God as his Absolute Future, his salvation, except through the relationship with the neighbor, measured by the love we have for one another."[83] Moltmann agrees that the other side of man's hope for the future is a suffering and a dissatisfaction with the present, and that this suffering presupposes love. Obviously one can avoid suffering by avoiding the commitment of love, but that option leads to emptiness and futility. Hope, on the other hand, tends to reinforce love, "for it gives love the freedom to renounce itself completely and to take upon itself pain and suffering. . . ."[84] Love recognizes the suffering arising from material want and unfreedom; it struggles for happiness for the poor and freedom for the oppressed. Thus love, for Moltmann, is not to be divorced either from the future of God or from a sense of solidarity with the suffering of humanity.

The reason behind this merging of transcendence and immanence, of Absolute and finite future, is, according to Rahner, man's inability to "understand himself except as projected in a future which belongs *to this world.*"[85] A real relationship with God, as portrayed in the twenty-fifth chapter of Matthew, cannot be conceived of apart from a positive and responsible relationship with the world of men. But the radicality of our love for the neighbor is such that it can be understood only as grounded in an Absolute, beyond and greater than ourselves. Thus "there would be, either expressly or in an unreflective way, a supreme and original unity of love of God and love of neighbor. . . ."[86] Love of God is inseparable from love of neighbor and love of neighbor springs from the love of God.

### Faith

It might at first seem strange that Garaudy would affirm the significance of faith for both Christian and Marxist, but it is his definition of the term that makes such a claim possible. For the Christian, states Garaudy, faith is an assent, a saying "yes" to God; for the Marxist this assent takes the form of creation. Yet for both "this consists in openness to the future and supersedure."[87] Certainly, there is a difference in the direction or orientation of faith: for the Marxist, assurance is found at the terminus of his effort, while for the Christian it is the driving force at the beginning. "But what remains is that we are both experiencing the same tension."[88]

Garaudy refuses simply to pigeonhole faith as "ideology" and so dismiss it. Faith, he says, is not a rigid system of thought: it is a "life-style." This life-style in principle "leaves man his full freedom in the true sense of the word: a full responsibility for his history. . . ."[89] Faith, then, does not constitute a metaphysical concept of the world; it is not on the order of understanding, but of act, of question, of exigency. Referring to Bonhoeffer, Garaudy describes faith in Christ as a call to full responsibility within human existence: "Christ is the opposite of fatality and the opposite of alienation."[90] Faith in that kind of God cannot be an escape from reality; it is a call to new life which affirms man's autonomy over all natural or social "fatalities." It is a commitment of our total being to responsibility for man's future. This commitment is in essence dialectical: "It is at once knowledge and action, being and act; it is both assurance and uncertainty, commitment and awareness of risk, dependence on the past and a breakaway which creates the future. . . ."[91]

Christian faith, says Garaudy, is prior to both institution and ideology, and therefore falls outside the pale of Engels's critique of religion. Faith is not a representational system for understanding the world, for that would constitute an ideology; rather, it is "a particular way of *standing up* before the world, of behaving in it, of living in it. . . ."[92]

Prior to ideological "contamination," faith in Christ, his death and Resurrection, was the source of certainty that man, "redeemed from sin, had 'emerged' from the cosmos into which Greek humanism had plunged him, and that everything had become possible." Drawing on this definition and understanding of faith, Garaudy is able to conclude that whether our faith is in God or the human task, it imposes on us the responsibility of drawing out the creative transcendence of each individual, making him a "poet" and a "man"—"what Christians call his transcendence and we call his authentic humanity."[93]

In this way it is possible for Garaudy to talk about a kind of Marxist "faith," although such a faith does not necessarily imply any belief in God. It is a strictly human, strictly immanent faith in man and his destiny. Such a faith certainly entails risk, for there is no guarantee of success at the end of the trail—for that matter, there is no guarantee of an end. But Garaudy would reply that nothing permits Christians to assert the existence of a guarantee. Therefore, considerable caution should be exercised when reading statements by Garaudy such as: "For the atheist, the depth of his humanity depends on the strength of the believer in him."[94] Obviously the object of this Marxist faith is man himself, his history, and his future.

This humanist definition of faith as a life-style centered on man's responsibility for the future allows Garaudy to declare that the demands Marxists make on their Christian counterparts "are in no degree philosophical exigencies incompatible with their beliefs."[95] These demands include a faith "freed from class ideologies," which recognizes the autonomy of human values in science and action, which welcomes the Promethean creation by man of himself and his world, and which accepts socialism as a real possibility for the flowering of mankind. From the very nature of these demands it is easy to see that Christian faith, if not simply an illusion, is at best relegated to an attitude on the order of sentiment, deprived of any objective foundation. It is a "life-style," but a life-style based on trust in One who does not exist; thus adoption of such a perspective would amount to a surrender of the faith, since faith *begins* with the certitude of God's reality.

What Garaudy has overlooked is that while Christian faith, like hope, does drive toward the achievement of certain historical tasks, neither faith nor hope can be *reduced* to the accomplishment of such objectives. Cottier points out that "faith is adherence to the Word of

God who reveals himself; hope is leaning on the Almighty."[96] Expressed in such traditional terms, the sharp contrast between this understanding of faith and Garaudy's Marxist faith is instantly clear. For Garaudy, the norm of faith is a particular concept of man, metaphysically liberated from transcendence, creating himself through his own labor, and constituting the ultimate goal of history. In short, man is for Garaudy the supreme being. Such a "de-transcendentalization" of religion has a familiar ring to it. The nonspecificity of faith, the reliance on practical criteria, the supreme glorification of the human collectivity: all point to a restatement of Feuerbach's concept of religion, somewhat updated by reference to Marx, Bonhoeffer, and Barth.

Garaudy, in fact, refers specifically to Barth as the first theologian since Luther to have affirmed the radical transcendence of God: "God intervenes in the life of men by a sudden breakthrough and not by the extension of our thoughts or actions."[97] It was Barth, he believes, who first took seriously the Kantian critique that all I can say about God is tempered by the fact that it is a man who is saying it.[98] This attempt to strip religion of "non-verifiable," metaphysical discourse is reflected in some school-of-hope theologians as well. Of course, no theologian (with the possible exception of certain of the so-called God-is-dead people) will restrict theology entirely to language about man, which seems to be what Garaudy is demanding. Rather, as in the case of Pannenberg and Moltmann, the unfulfilled nature of the future of God requires that we exercise caution in our "God-talk," not eliminate it altogether. Even Feuerbach's idea that God is a projection can be accepted, provided one is very clear in what way this is meant. As Pannenberg has pointed out, simply to state that religion is a projection does not explain it away. Instead our attention is directed to the future, the moving screen upon which this projection is cast.

In effect, what Pannenberg is saying is that the God-projection is an illusion only if one agrees to adopt the standards of verification used in the natural sciences. Helmut Gollwitzer has written convincingly on this theme, asserting forcefully that Christianity cannot defend itself in an effective way against the accusation of illusion, for to do so would be to submit to empirical criteria of reality.[99] Garaudy's error (together with Feuerbach's and Marx's) is in assuming that God, like faith, is a means to an end, even if this means is alienated and ultimately unsuccessful. This understanding of God as a means invested with value by man is utterly incompatible with the biblical witness, which sees God as absolutely prior to all human value statements. In the words of Gollwitzer,

> Prior to all else, God is Subject; and He is important as Subject because He is himself, and only secondarily because of his 'attributes,' i.e., the values which we have associated with the idea of God.[100]

There is thus a hermeneutical gap between Garaudy and Christian faith: what faith affirms is not what Garaudy denies. The whole of Garaudy's critique, like that of Feuerbach before him, shows that he sees God as an "assumption," his existence a "hypothesis" for Christian faith; but Bonhoeffer has already dealt with this approach to religion when he stated: *"Einen Gott, den 'es gibt,' gibt es nicht."*[101] Barth was right, then, when he said that Marxist atheism could not hurt the living God, but only a "conceptual idol"; the important task for Christian theology is to demonstrate to Marxists that this conceptual idol is *not* the God of Christian faith.

The *living* God, who transcends all objective criteria of verification, is the One to whom Metz referred at Salzburg as the "God before us." Pointing to Rom. 15:13 and Exod. 3:14, Metz described God "as the always greater future of our historical existence, the future always beyond the projects of that existence."[102] Christian faith, then, means to have confidence in the future as the coming mystery of God. The future remains always greater than the sum of our descriptions and projections of it, beyond any *logos* which might attempt to capture and reify it. Faith in the Absolute Future, the future of God, is indeed a "life-style," a way of "standing up before the world," but it is a lifestyle rooted and grounded in the reality of God's future, a future breaking in upon our present, judging our limited and finite projects and calling us to ever new and greater efforts to build the world of man.

### Death

The problems presented by Garaudy's discussion of death are complex and difficult since here it is not a matter of a simplistic polemic against Christian dogma, but an earnest attempt to wrestle with what is, for all of us, the ultimate question mark of human existence. As might be expected, Garaudy approaches death from a social perspective.

In an extension of the ancient idea that a man lives on after death through his sons, Garaudy sees the survival of the individual taking place in the class or community in struggle. That is to say, the conscious participation of a man in the struggle for earthly happiness for all, putting the well-being of others above even his own life, gives meaning to both death and life. It can then be said that "this man achieves immortality in his own lifetime, since he has permanently put his mark on the world and given something personal to the construction of the future of all. . . ."[103] A life sacrificed for others participates in the destiny of man not only in human memory, but in the concrete lives of future generations. Human responsibility does not cease with the physical extinction of the individual since, as James Klugmann has stated, "man is mortal, mankind immortal."[104]

The self-transcendence of man through his realization in the collectivity finds its noblest expression in martyrdom: "this splendid death of the man who feels himself responsible for the destiny of all and who gives his life its meaning and beauty in sacrificing it in the service of all mankind."[105] The presence of the future is found in these modern martyrs in embryonic form; for them the future is not an abstraction "but the lived presence of all other men,"[106] each with his individual uniqueness and depth. The presence of the totality in the individual and the individual's sense of responsibility for the totality is what Garaudy calls the certitude of immortality, or what Paul Eluard once referred to as "moving from one man's horizon to the horizon of all men." Such obviously sincere and moving words testify to the courage and integrity of the Marxist commitment; they also leave us with several serious unanswered questions.

The first is the question of *theodicy*. Originally coined by Leibnitz, the term is a construction from the Greek words *theos* and *dike,* and means literally "justification of God."[107] The word was first applied to theories that sought to explain how an omnipotent God could permit suffering and evil in the world. Max Weber expanded the meaning in a social dimension to refer to any theoretical explanation of suffering and evil. In this sense there are, of course, secular theodicies, and Marxism is one of them. But as Peter Berger has pointed out, Marxism's theodicy fails to interpret the extremes of human existence— particularly death—in a way that makes them easier to bear.[108] Garaudy's understanding of death does indeed offer a kind of theodicy: if we participate in the building up of socialism here and now, we will participate vicariously in the new communist society that is being born. Certainly, this theodicy offers comfort to an individual facing death on the barricades. Such a death takes on meaning in terms of the theory. But what comfort can Garaudy's theory offer to someone confronted by death from cancer or famine or natural disaster? Such a death is entirely meaningless in terms of a theodicy oriented toward this world. Few indeed are stoic enough to embrace this Marxist version of ultimate "truth."

The question is by no means simple, and theological opinion seems divided on the answer. Carl Braaten, for example, is quite firm in his assertion that any hope for man's personal fulfillment means that "in some sense he must hope for life beyond death, for he knows that such fulfillment cannot occur within the finite limits of his earthly existence."[109] Man is so constructed that he desires to transcend all limitations, even his own death. This striving has received two classical symbols from the Christian tradition: immortality and resurrection of the dead. Both are relevant for modern man—even Marxist man—since the question of hope "cannot ultimately disregard whether there is something to hope for that transcends death, the last hindrance to hope." Thus Braaten stands squarely on the essentially individual character of death.

Karl Rahner, on the other hand, is not altogether convinced by this argument, and even suggests that "the Christian as Christian should not take *too* seriously the death of the individual."[110] Death is a universal fact of life to which God cannot be entirely opposed, since he continues to allow it free reign in his creation. Rahner feels that Western humanism has become too sensitive about death, a sensitivity which may indeed represent a noble human instinct, but is not necessarily "a clear exigency of Christianity."[111] This does not imply, of course, that Christians must accept without protest the cold-blooded sacrifice of men and women to some speculative future utopia. Nevertheless, says Rahner, it is necessary to determine the Christian attitude toward death in the development of a true humanism. And death is, first of all, "simply and coldly, the place made biologically for a later life, for other beings."[112] In other words, if living beings did not die, there would be no room for new beings, and the process of generation being considered a constant, the world would soon be overwhelmed.

Thus death, even in its most primitive, biological form, already carries certain social implications; it is "political" in the broadest sense of the word. Moreover, it can become a radical act of love, all the more as one gives place not to a specific man, but to the abstract "future" man. Death frees and opens the future for others, but this open and indeterminate future is given only in the Absolute Future that is called God. Whoever gives his life up voluntarily for others "affirms both God, as Absolute Future which man does not control or create, *and* the right of others to their own future," and even without knowing it, "he therefore loves God and men in a radical act of accepting death."[113] If an individual offers himself freely for the good of those who follow him, if he gives himself openly and without reserve to that unknown future, even without the assurance of a personal continuity after death, it is impossible to believe that God would wholly reject such an act of loving self-sacrifice. That, at least, is the Christian hope.

## NOTES

1. MTC, p. 133.
2. MTC, p. 86.
3. Ibid.
4. Ibid. Cf. also Jean-Paul Sartre, *Being and Nothingness,* trans. Hazel E. Barnes (New York: Philosophical Library, 1956), p. 485: "If, therefore, freedom is defined as the escape from the given, from fact, then there is a *fact* of escape from fact. This is the facticity of freedom."
5. In Sartrian terminology this would represent the impossible attempt of consciousness to be both "in-self" and "for-self."
6. MTC, pp. 88–89.
7. Sartre's failure to provide a social ethic in spite of his long-standing promise to do so is a classic and eloquent example of this inherent block in the existentialist posture.
8. HM, p. 135.
9. HM, p. 136.
10. Quotations are from MTC, p. 94.
11. Johann Gottlieb Fichte, *The Science of Ethics,* trans. A. E. Kroger (London: 1897), p. 234. Cited in MTC, p. 95.
12. HM, p. 138.
13. N.B., the slip from a discussion of subjectivity to a discussion of knowledge, betraying a certain intellectual bias in Garaudy's understanding of the "subjective moment."

14. MTC, p. 84.

15. MTC, p. 85.

16. Here we are following the argument of MTC, pp. 96 ff.

17. MTC, p. 96.

18. MTC, p. 78.

19. MTC, p. 203.

20. PH, p. 88.

21. PH, p. 83.

22. MTC, p. 92.

23. HM, p. 194.

24. PH, p. 85.

25. PH, p. 88.

26. HM, p. 210.

27. MTC, p. 91.

28. Sartre, *Being and Nothingness,* p. 230.

29. PH, p. 97.

30. Ibid.

31. PH, p. 53.

32. Sartre, *Being and Nothingness,* pp. 413–432.

33. Ibid., p. 484.

34. PH, p. 98.

35. MTC, p. 204.

36. PH, p. 110.

37. MTC, p. 205.

38. PH, p. 332.

39. Jean Conilh, "Lecture de Marx (Louis Althusser)," in *Esprit,* no. 360 (May 1967), p. 884.

40. PH, p. 355.

41. Jean Conilh, "Lecture de Marx," p. 887.

42. PH, p. 347.

43. Jean Rancière, "Le concept de critique et la critique de l'économie politique des manuscripts de 1844 au Capital," in *Lire le Capital,* vol. 1, ed. Louis Althusser (Paris: François Maspero, 1965), p. 163. Cf. PH, p. 352.

44. PH, p. 360.

45. Louis Althusser, "Préface: Du Capital à la philosophie de Marx," in *Lire le Capital,* vol. 1, p. 75.

46. See Engels, "Letter to Heinz Starkenburg (1894)," in Selsam and Martel, p. 202. Cf. also PH, pp. 328–329.

47. Louis Althusser, "L'objet du Capital," in *Lire le Capital,* vol. 2, p. 75.

48. PH, p. 333.

49. MTC, p. 206.

50. PH, p. 363.

51. PH, p. 365.

52. QMM, p. 216.

53. QMM, p. 217.

54. Roger Garaudy, MCES, p. 347.

55. QMM, p. 223.

56. Ibid.

57. Ibid.

58. In all fairness it should be pointed out that Roger Garaudy condemns the dogmatic anthropology of Feuerbach: "The reconciliation of man with other men, in love, is humanism realized. Feuerbach has thus replaced one religion with another, deifying love, the dialogue between 'me' and 'you' " (KM, p. 27). Cf. also Cottier, *Chrétiens et marxistes,* p. 95.

59. Cottier, *Chrétiens et marxistes,* p. 95.

60. Pannenberg, "The God of Hope," p. 33.

61. Roger Garaudy, MCES, p. 347.

62. Cottier, *Chrétiens et marxistes,* p. 117.

63. Ibid., p. 122.

64. Rahner, "Humanisme chrétien," p. 52.

65. MTC, p. 146.

66. MTC, p. 149.

67. Braaten, "The Gospel of the Kingdom of God and the Church."

68. Rahner, "Théologie pratique et tâches sociales," p. 86.

69. Cottier, *Chrétiens et marxistes,* p. 122.

70. Roger Garaudy, MCES, p. 346.

71. Ibid., p. 347.

72. MTC, p. 135.

73. ATD, p. 86.

74. MTC, p. 143.

75. MTC, p. 104.

76. MTC, p. 140.

77. MTC, p. 143.

78. MTC, p. 137.

79. MTC, p. 138.

80. Ibid.

81. Ibid.

82. Ibid.

83. Karl Rahner, MCES, p. 236.

84. Moltmann, "Hoping and Planning," p. 61.

85. Karl Rahner, MCES, p. 236.

86. Karl Rahner, "Humanisme chrétien," p. 50.

87. ATD, p. 111.

88. Ibid.

89. GPG, p. 172.

90. RE, p. 115.

91. MTC, p. 210. Cf. *supra*, Chapter Two, note 11. Roger Garaudy emphasizes this understanding of faith in his latest work: "Faith therefore cannot be a justification of history, but an opening of history. It is that question that holds history in suspense" (private communication).

92. This and the following quotation are taken from ATD, pp. 115–116.

93. ATD, p. 123.

94. MTC, p. 162.

95. PMFS, p. 377.

96. Cottier, *Chrétiens et marxistes,* p. 173.

97. PMFS, p. 360.

98. This neo-orthodox position must seem particularly attractive to a Marxist since it removes God completely from our realm of experience. It is strange, therefore, that Roger Garaudy generally ignores Barth and the entire neo-orthodox school in his treatment of Christian theology. If God, for Barth, can only be known as he reveals himself in the Christ-event, and if this event can be appropriated only through some kind of "God-man encounter," then Christianity is reduced to pure subjectivity and can be handily ignored by the practically minded materialist.

99. On the other hand, Helmut Gollwitzer points out that theology's rejection of dogmatic assertions is equally devastating as a critique of those who casually try to dismiss religion as simply "metaphysics masquerading as physics" (Péguy). Cf. Gollwitzer, "The Marxist Critique of Religion," p. 17.

100. Gollwitzer, "The Marxist Critique," p. 17.

101. Ibid., p. 18: "A God of whom you can say *'there is a god'* is not God."

102. Johannes Metz, MCES, p. 246.

103. Roger Garaudy, MCES, p. 88.

104. Klugmann, "The Marxist Hope," p. 65.

105. An unidentified quotation from Roger Garaudy's article "Notre combat comme marxistes est un combat pour l'homme," *Témoignage Chrétien,* no. 1080, 18 March 1965. Cited by George Cottier, *Chrétiens et marxistes,* p. 132.

106. MTC, p. 153.

107. Cf. Tillich, *Perspectives,* p. 55.

108. Berger, *A Rumor of Angels,* p. 41.

109. Quotations are from Braaten, "Toward a Theology of Hope," p. 103.

110. Rahner, "Humanisme chrétien," p. 61.

111. Ibid.

112. Ibid., p. 62.

113. Ibid., p. 63.

# Postscript

In casting an eye back over the distance we have come, we can now distinguish certain unifying themes. In general, as might be surmised from the title of our book, these key motifs revolve around the problem of transcendence and the various ways Christians and Marxists have attempted to come to grips with this question in recent years. These efforts were seen to boil down to a single, wide-ranging search for a means of describing transcendence in terms of the power of the future. Moving out from the dominant motif, we touched upon questions surrounding the creativity, responsibility, and freedom of man as active subject in history.

In fact, it is Roger Garaudy's concern for human freedom and initiative that leads to his rejection of traditional religious formulations. He rightly points out that Marxism, in its mistrust of any ideology or religion that might strip man of his essential humanity, has played a prophetic role in world history. It reminds Christianity of the centrality of the Incarnation, while at the same time attacking any idolatrous absolutizing of culturally conditioned "religious objects." On the other hand, it is clear that Garaudy's vigorous defense of human autonomy stems from a misunderstanding of the nature of transcendence; the *truly* transcendent cannot serve as a restraint on the freedom of man, but is that from which man derives his real freedom and responsibility.

Thus, while Garaudy's understanding of transcendence as a new and open future bears some similarity to Karl Rahner's transcendence of the Absolute Future, it was seen to be both immanent in the historical process and empty of any real content. These deficiencies are the consequence of Garaudy's refusal to see the future as a *real* transcendent which *comes* to man, judging him and calling him as his own Absolute Future. For the Marxist, the future remains a creation of man, as he reaches beyond himself toward his own far-off being.

Transcendence is clearly tied to both creativity and historical initiative. But without the frame of reference provided by the notion of the Absolute Future, Garaudy's understanding of human creativeness becomes enmeshed in an endless dialectical process, in which the makability of history becomes itself the goal of the making of history. Simply to define historical initiative as the interplay between the historically given and the free creative activity of man is not enough, for it overlooks the fact that it is God's future which calls forth and authenticates man's creativity. On the other hand, we ought to admit that Garaudy's critique is a healthy corrective to that form of Christian "quietism" which views history as outside the provenance of its responsibility. Christianity, like Marxism, must be a method of historical initiatives.

The essential problem, in any discussion of transcendence, is the question of freedom. Garaudy's chief concern is to protect human autonomy from the crushing pressure of traditional forms of transcendence. But it is questionable whether this goal is achievable within the framework of a materialistic humanism. Garaudy seeks to ground freedom in the sheer inexhaustibility and indeterminacy of matter; however, this technique, far from guaranteeing freedom, easily leads to its very opposite, reducing freedom to fortuity and subordinating man to the relentless grinding of history.

But while a simplistic materialism compromises the very freedom Garaudy wishes to protect, it does offer a valuable corrective to gnostic tendencies in Christian theology, forcing the Church to take seriously the material factors associated with its development, factors often ignored or underestimated. Garaudy's analysis is, in one sense, a call to meditate on the implications of the Incarnation: the Church is *in* the world. Moreover, it becomes clear that traditional approaches to the problems of social change, violence, and revolution are simply not adequate. We have not yet taken seriously the need for a political theology, much less a theology of revolution. Here Christians might well learn from their Marxist counterparts. Conversely, Christian theology may offer Marxism a sharper delineation between the "now" and the "not-yet," between present realized reality and future realizable possibilities.

The Absolute Future stands over against our tendency to absolutize our own limited plans and projects. The future cannot be made into a colony of the present. It is that which *comes* to man, and cannot be reduced to a projection of our creative historical initiative.

Finally, we are forced to ask if Garaudy does not forfeit all his efforts to preserve individual initiative by subordinating individuality to the collective totality. The question of the inviolability of the individual vis-à-vis the needs of future society leads back to the question of "Moloch," the false god to which this generation is sacrificed for the sake of speculative unborn future generations. It is not clear whether Garaudy has sufficiently guarded himself against this danger.

In summary, then, we must conclude that Garaudy's understanding of transcendence as futurity, while it represents a significant narrowing of the distance between Christians and Marxists, fails to overcome several substantial difficulties. This failure stems from the altogether immanent and empty nature of such a transcendence. Lacking a true absolute, man is trapped in the vicious circle of making history for the sake of making history. His true autonomy is jeopardized in the process, since freedom is reduced to conformity with historical necessity. Moreover, since there is no absolute beyond man himself, there is no way to protect human individuality and dignity from the excesses of our utopic imagination. In the end, individual worth is subordinated to the supposed well-being of the species.

This is not, of course, the whole story. The object of our study was not simply to criticize or polemicize; it was to enter into a dialogue. Dialogue is a risky undertaking. To be honest, it must be approached openly and in good faith. If one begins with covert dogmatic assumptions which can never be questioned, the spirit of dialogue is broken. All of us, of course, carry certain presuppositions, and we must probe these as deeply and as honestly as we are able. For a genuine dialogue means not only that we share our point of view, but that we listen with open ears to what the other is saying. This means that there exists a very real possibility of change and growth *on both sides*. We may find ourselves actually altering our own opinions and views, changing what we previously thought inviolable. Garaudy is a case in point. He has been involved in this dialogue for a long time—more than forty years. And he has truly entered into the encounter with openness and honesty.

The results are clear for all to see. Thus it seems appropriate to conclude with the words of Roger Garaudy himself, taken from his forthcoming book: *Alternative to Chaos;* they are the most eloquent witness to the possibilities of dialogue.

> All my life I have asked myself if I were Christian. For forty years I answered no. Because the problem was badly stated—as if faith were incompatible with the militant life. I am now convinced that the two are the same, and that my militant hope would have no foundation without that faith.

> Now, if I hesitate to answer yes, it is for altogether different reasons. Such a faith seems to me such an explosive force, that it would be presumptuous to lay claim to it before having proven it in radical action. And this proof can only come at the end of a life, not in its midst, before having fully realized our part in creation.

*Bibliography*
*and*
*Index*

# Bibliography

Althusser, Louis. "L'objet du Capital." In *Lire le Capital,* edited by Louis Althusser. Vol. 2. Paris: François Maspero, 1965.

————. "Preface: Du Capital à la philosophie de Marx." In *Lire le Capital,* edited by Louis Althusser. Vol. 1. Paris: François Maspero, 1965.

Altizer, Thomas J. J., and Hamilton, William. *Radical Theology and the Death of God.* New York: Pelican, 1968.

Augustine of Hippo. *Enchiridion.* Translated by A. C. Outler. Library of Christian Classics, Vol. 3, Philadelphia: Westminster Press, 1955.

van der Bent, A. J. "Le dialogue entre chrétiens et marxistes." In IDOC International, no. 18, 15 February 1970, pp. 339–371.

Berger, Peter. *A Rumor of Angels.* New York: Doubleday & Co. 1969.

————. *The Social Reality of Religion.* London: Faber & Faber, 1969.

Bloch, Ernst. "Man as Possibility." In *Crosscurrents,* vol. 18, no. 3, summer 1968. Also in *The Future of Hope,* edited by Walter H. Capps. Philadelphia: Fortress Press, 1970.

Braaten, Carl. *The Future of God.* New York: Harper & Row, 1969.

————. "The Future of the Source of Freedom." In *Theology Today,* vol. 27, no. 4, January 1971, pp. 382–393.

————. "The Gospel of the Kingdom of God and the Church." In *The Gospel and the Ambiguity of the Church,* edited by Vilmos Vajta. Philadelphia: Fortress Press, 1974.

————. "Toward a Theology of Hope." In *New Theology Number 5,* edited by Martin Marty and Dean Peerman, pp. 90–111. New York: Macmillan, 1968.

Capps, Walter H. "The Hope Tendency." In *Crosscurrents,* vol. 18, no. 3, summer 1968.

————. "Mapping the Hope Movement." In *The Future of Hope,* edited by Walter H. Capps. Philadelphia: Fortress Press, 1970.

Conilh, Jean. "Lecture de Marx (Louis Althusser)." In *Esprit,* vol. 35, no. 360, May 1967, pp. 882–901.

Cottier, George. *Chrétiens et marxistes—dialogue avec Roger Garaudy.* Paris: Maison Mame, 1967.

Cox, Harvey. "Discussion: Communist-Christian Dialogue." In *Union Seminary Quarterly Review,* vol. 22, no. 3, March 1967, pp. 223–227.

————. *The Feast of Fools.* Cambridge: Harvard University Press, 1969.

————. *The Secular City.* New York: Macmillan, 1965.

Dantine, Wilhelm. "The Dialogical Character of Human Existence." In *The Gospel and Human Destiny,* edited by Vilmos Vajta, pp. 139–177. Minneapolis: Augsburg Publishing House, 1971.

Dewart, Leslie. *The Foundations of Belief.* London: Burns and Oates, 1969.

Duprés, Louis. "Marx and Religion: An Impossible Marriage." In *New Theology Number 6,* edited by Martin Marty and Dean Peerman, pp. 151–164. New York: Macmillan, 1969.

Eliade, Mircea. *The Sacred and the Profane.* Translated by Willard R. Trask. New York: Harcourt, Brace & World, 1959.

Ellul, Jacques, *The Technological Society.* Translated by John Wilkerson. London: Jonathan Cape, 1965.

Feuer, Lewis S. ed. *Marx and Engels: Basic Writings on Politics and Philosophy.* New York: Doubleday & Co. 1959.

Fichte, Johann Gottlieb. *The Science of Ethics.* Translated by A. E. Kroger. London: 1897.

Garaudy, Roger. "As Marxists We Are Struggling on Behalf of Man." In *Background Information* (WCC), no. 34, December 1965. (Translation of "Notre combat comme marxistes est un combat pour l'homme," in *Témoignage Chrétien,* no. 1080, 18 March 1965).

————. "Des éléments nouveaux dans le dialogue chrétiens-marxistes" (with Gilbert Mury), in *Témoignage Chrétien,* no. 1167, 17 November 1966, pp. 12–13.

————. *Dieu est mort (Etude sur Hegel).* Paris: Presses Universitaires de France, 1962.

————. *D'un réalisme sans rivages.* Paris: Plon, 1963.

————. *L'Eglise, le communisme et les chrétiens.* Paris: Editions Sociales, 1949.

————. *From Anathema to Dialogue.* Translated by Luke O'Neill. New York: Herder & Herder, 1966.

————. *Garaudy par Garaudy.* Edited by Claude Glayman. Paris: La Table Ronde, 1970.

————. "L'homme révelé." In *Réforme,* no. 1395, 4 December 1971, pp. 10–11.

————. *Humanisme marxiste.* Paris: Editions sociales, 1957.

————. *Initiative in History: A Christian-Marxist Exchange* (with others). Cambridge, Mass.: The Church Society for College Work, 1967.

————. *Karl Marx.* Translated by Nan Aptheker. New York: International Publishers, 1967.

————. *Marxism in the Twentieth Century*. Translated by René Hague. New York: Charles Scribner's Sons, 1970.

————. *Marxisme et existentialisme* (with others). Paris: Plon, 1962.

————. *Marxisme et religion*. (Text of the conference organized at the Catholic University of Louvain, 7 April 1965, by the society *Ad Lucem*.) Brussels: Cercle d'éducation populaire, cahier 17, 1965.

————. *Perspectives de l'homme*. 4th ed. Paris: Presses Universitaires de France, 1969.

————. *Pour un modèle français du socialisme*. Paris: Gallimard, 1968.

————. *Qu'est-ce que la morale marxiste?* Paris: Editions sociales, 1963.

————. *Reconquête de l'espoir*. Paris: Editions Bernard Grasset, 1971.

Gill, David M. "Power, Violence, Non-violence, and Social Change." In *Study Encounter* (WCC), vol. 6, no.2, 1970, pp. 66–72.

Girardi, Jules. *Amour Chrétien et violence révolutionnaire*. Paris: Editions du Cerf, 1970.

Gollwitzer, Helmut. "The Marxist Critique of Religion and the Christian Faith." In *Study Encounter* (WCC), vol. 4, no. 1, 1968, pp. 6–19.

Kamenka, E. "The Concept of a Political Revolution." In *Nomos VIII—Revolution*. New York: Atherton Press, 1966.

Kaufman, Gordon. "On the Meaning of 'God': Transcendence Without Mythology." In *New Theology Number 4*. Edited by Martin Marty and Dean Peerman, pp. 69–98. New York: Macmillan, 1967.

Keen, Sam. "Hope in a Posthuman Era." In *New Theology Number 5*. Edited by Martin Marty and Dean Peerman, pp. 79–89. New York: Macmillan, 1968.

Klugmann, Jack. "The Marxist Hope." In *The Christian Hope*, pp. 49–68. London: S.P.C.K. Theological Collections 13, 1970.

Lazareth, William. "Political Responsibility as the Obedience of Faith." In *The Gospel and Human Destiny*, edited by Vilmos Vajta, pp. 218–270. Minneapolis: Augsburg Publishing House, 1971.

van Leeuwen, A. T. *Christianity in World History*. London: Edinburgh House Press, 1966.

Lehmann, Paul. "Discussion: Communist-Christian Dialogue." In *Union Seminary Quarterly Review*, vol. 22, no. 3, March 1967, pp. 218–223.

Luther, Martin. *Bondage of the Will*. Translated by Philip S. Watson in collaboration with Benjamin Drewery. Vol. 33. Luther's Works. Philadelphia: Fortress Press, 1972.

————. *The Freedom of a Christian*. Translated by W. A. Lambert. Vol. 31. Luther's Works. Philadelphia: Fortress Press, 1958.

Marcel, Gabriel. *Being and Having*. Translated by A. and C. Black. London: Collins, The Fontana Library, 1965.

Marcuse, Herbert. *One Dimensional Man*. Boston: Beacon Press, 1968.

*Marxistes et chrétiens—Entretiens de Salzbourg*. Paris: Maison Mame, 1968.

McLuhan, Marshall. *Understanding Media*. New York: McGraw-Hill, 1964.

Mehl, Roger. "La Crise actuelle de la théologie." In *Etudes théologiques et religieuses,* vol. 45, no. 4, 1970, pp. 355–366.

————. "La Crise de la transcendance." In *Revue d'histoire et de philosophie religieuses,* vol. 49, no. 4, 1969, pp. 341–354.

Metz, Johann Baptist, "God Before Us Instead of a Theological Argument." In *Crosscurrents,* vol. 18, no. 3, summer 1968.

Moltmann, Jürgen. "The Future as a New Paradigm of Transcendence." In *Crosscurrents,* vol. 1, no. 4, fall 1969, pp. 334–345.

————. "Hoping and Planning." In *Crosscurrents,* vol. 18, no. 3, summer 1968.

————. "The Revolution of Freedom: The Christian and Marxist Struggle." In *Motive,* vol. 29, no. 3, December 1968, pp. 40–52.

————. *Theology of Hope.* New York: Harper & Row, 1967.

————. "Toward a Political Hermeneutics of the Gospel." In *New Theology Number 6,* edited by Martin Marty and Dean Peerman, pp. 66–92. New York: Macmillan, 1969.

Mumford, Lewis. *The Condition of Man.* New York: Harcourt, Brace & World, 1944.

————. *The Myth of the Machine.* New York: Harcourt, Brace & World, 1967.

Pannenberg, Wolfhart. "Appearance as the Arrival of the Future." In *New Theology Number 5,* edited by Martin Marty and Dean Peerman, pp. 112–129. New York: Macmillan, 1968.

————. "Can Christianity Do Without an Eschatology?" In *The Christian Hope,* pp. 25–34. London: S.P.C.K. Theological Collections 13, 1970.

————. *Disputation zwischen Christen und Marxisten.* Munich: Kaiser Verlag, 1966.

————. "The God of Hope." In *Crosscurrents,* vol. 18, no. 3, summer 1968.

————. "Redemptive Event and History." In *Essays on Old Testament Hermeneutics.* Edited by C. Westermann. Richmond: John Knox Press, 1964.

Perottino, Serge. *Garaudy.* Paris: Editions Seghers, 1969.

Rahner, Karl. "Autour de concept de l'avenir." In *Ecrits théologiques* 10, pp. 95–104. Paris: Desclée de Brouwer/Mame, 1970.

————. "Humanisme chrétien." In *Ecrits théologiques 10,* pp. 47–68. Paris: Desclée de Brouwer/Mame, 1970.

————. "La 'nouvelle terre.'" In *Ecrits théologiques 10,* pp. 105–120. Paris: Desclée de Brouwer/Mame, 1970.

————. "Théologie pratique et tâches sociales." *Ecrits théologiques 10,* pp. 69–94. Paris: Desclée de Brouwer/Mame, 1970.

Rancière, Jean. "Le concept de critique et la critique de l'économie politique des manuscrits de 1844 au Capital." In *Lire le Capital.* Vol. 1. Paris: François Maspero, 1965.

Ricoeur, Paul. "Approche philosophique de la liberté religieuse." In *L'hermé-neutique de la liberté religieuse*, pp. 215–252. Paris: Aubier, 1968.

————. *Freud and Philosophy: An Essay on Interpretation.* Translated by Denis Savage. New Haven: Yale University Press, 1970.

————. *History and Truth.* Translated by C. A. Kelbley. Evanston, Ill.: Northwestern University Press, 1965.

Sartre, Jean-Paul. *Critique de la raison dialectique.* Paris: Gallimard, 1960.

————. *Being and Nothingness.* Translated by H. E. Barnes. New York: Philosophical Library, 1956.

Savage, Charles M. "Critiques Re-considered." In *Study Encounter* (WCC), vol. 4, no. 1, 1968, pp. 3–6.

Selsam, Howard and Martel, Harry, eds. *Reader in Marxist Philosophy.* New York: International Publishers, 1963.

Shinn, Roger. "Discussion: Communist-Christian Dialogue." In *Union Seminary Quarterly Review*, vol. 22, no. 3, March 1967, pp. 213–217.

Siebert, Roland. "Political Theology." In *The Ecumenist* (Paulist Press), vol. 9, no. 5, July/August 1971, pp. 65–71.

Teilhard de Chardin, Pierre. *The Phenomenon of Man.* Translated by B. Wall. New York: Harper & Brothers, 1959.

Tillich, Paul. "Existentialist Aspects of Modern Art." In *Christianity and the Existentialists.* Edited by C. Michaelson. New York: Charles Scribner's Sons, 1956.

————. *Perspectives on 19th and 20th Century Protestant Theology.* Edited by Carl Braaten. New York: Harper & Row, 1967.

————. *The Protestant Era*, pp. 161–184. Chicago: University of Chicago Press, 1963.

————. *Systematic Theology.* Vols. 1, 3. Chicago: University of Chicago Press, 1951.

Vajta, Vilmos. "Theology in Dialogue." In *The Gospel and Unity.* Edited by Vilmos Vajta, pp. 25–66. Minneapolis: Augsburg Publishing House, 1971.

# Index